Unconsidered Trifles

MIKE AMOS

For Sharon,
without whom nothing would be possible
(and who nagged me into writing
the thing, anyway)

Unconsidered Trifles

First published 2020

Published by Mike Amos
8 Oakfelds, Middleton Tyas, Richmond, North Yorkshire
Email mikeamos81@aol.com
Blog www.mikeamosblog.wordpress.com

Designed and typeset by Jon Smith
using Adobe InDesign and Adobe Photoshop.
Text set in 11/12.5pt Times New Roman

Printed by County Print, 11 Collingwood Court, Riverside Park
Industrial Estate, Middlesbrough TS2 1RP
01642 225867
sales@countyprint.co.uk

ISBN:
978-1-8380404-1-3 (hardback)
978-1-8380404-0-6 (paperback)

2020 05 15

NEWSLIST

ends

The Northern Echo

evening Despatch

Inside
A special 12-page souvenir today for all Despatch readers

John North

The Northern Echo

FAST FOREWORD

FIRSTLY some housekeeping rules, as now health and safety suffusion demands whenever two or three are gathered together (and no matter that that's usually about fire escapes and flushing the toilet.)

Most urgently, it is necessary to define the borders of North-East England, a rich and joyous region around which this book almost entirely is written and supposed sometimes to be the area between Berwick-upon-Tweed and York. Others argue that the North-East ends at the north bank of the River Tees, beyond which lies Yorkshire, a sovereign and wholly owned subsidiary state populated in the main by parsimonious curmudgeons.

Many Yorkshiremen might agree with the first bit, advising their offspring that anywhere north of the Tees lies a land where it's best not to venture, lest the bogeyman get them.

The *Northern Echo*, for which I toiled for more than half a century and which long had offices as far south as York, understandably found – still finds – regional identification problematical. Sometimes it employs the phrase 'North-East and North Yorkshire' to define its patch, on other occasions simply 'North-East'. For the purposes of this book, 'North-East' must generally suffice though 'North Yorkshire' may silently, perhaps surreptitiously, be assumed. The book won't even attempt to explain, nor does it matter, what defines a Geordie.

A further dilemma lies with whether the region's name should command upper case initials – one capital or two? –

11

and whether it should be hyphenated. Throughout a serious shift in regional journalism I've always written 'North-East', though lesser regions might be 'south-west' or whatever the lower case may be. 'North-East' is a genuflection, a homage to home, but let's not get into a debate about those pesky little hyphens. We'll save that, later, for the ubiquitous aberrant apostrophe.

The *Echo*, it's fair to say, hasn't generally agreed with my version. The preferred house style was usually 'north east', sometimes 'North east'. In that respect, as in many others, they humoured – or possibly ignored – me. For the next 390 pages, 'North-East' it will be.

Perhaps it should also be explained before further proceeding that, though I spent most of the first 26 years of life in Shildon – very much in the County Palatine of Durham – I've lived for the past 40-odd in North Yorkshire, crossing the Tees each day on the way to work. The United Society for the Propagation of the Gospel has much the same mission statement. As they say in those parts, I still belong Shildon.

Two other words of warning, the first that I could digress for England and the second echoing Lewis Carroll, whose own childhood was spent in the rectory at Croft, about three yards on the southern bank of the Tees (and rather less when, familiarly, it flooded). Carroll employed Humpty Dumpty as his spokesman: "When I use a word it means exactly what I choose it to mean, nothing more nor less."

Same here. Alice's supplementary question may for these purposes be ignored.

As (of course) would be expected from a subaltern in HM Press Corps, every word of *Unconsidered Trifles* is true to the best of my knowledge. Nor have names been changed, though in a couple of cases – the story of the curate who slept in for Evensong, the tale of the unlocked lavvy – surnames have been omitted to avoid further embarrassment.

Finally, it should be explained that *Unconsidered Tri-*

fles carries none of those tediously irritating footnotes with which clever folk decorate the bottom of almost every page in order to authenticate their sources. No need: you can trust me, I'm a journalist.

Perhaps the housekeeping budget should also have pondered whether what follows is an autobiography or, as these days is more fashionable, a memoir. That doesn't matter, either, and both terms are fearful to write in Pitman's.

The life story chiefly relates to 55 years in the once-inky trade, though – and long-time readers will exhale deeply at this point – it meanders down all manner of alleys, if not blind then seriously myopic. Often they follow football, the author frequently with pint pot or hymn book in hand – once or twice simultaneously – and always with a spiral-bound notebook stuffed curvaceously into the back pocket of Marks and Sparks' best breeks. North-East naturalisation notwithstanding, there are also fairly frequent forays north of the border, seduced by the skirl of the pipes.

They've been almost entirely happy years, paid to have a good time, ever aware that people like me are greatly privileged to do what we've done and always escorted by Lady Luck. Those who quote the adage "The harder I worked, the luckier I got" – and heaven knows who coined that one – may have a point, however. Though journalism's hardly sweat-of-the-brow stuff – nine-tenths inspiration, one-tenth perspiration – I've always put in very long hours. Partly, immodestly, it was because I believed that folk enjoyed my stuff, might even have bought the paper because of it.

Though readers are everything, much the biggest stroke of luck was meeting in improbable circumstances the Welsh lass to whom this book is dedicated.

For all that fortune, it's necessary to issue what the television columns call a spoiler alert… it all ended badly, dreadfully even. After 55 years of almost daily interaction with the North-East community, a love affair readily requited, the liaison was arbitrarily annulled on November 27 2019 when an

13

official phone call pronounced my post at risk of redundancy. Despite the beer bottle glasses, I hadn't seen it coming. A week or so later I was history.

Unconsidered Trifles was already well under way, though not by that title. Always a possibility, the book had been ever-more urged by my wife during a June holiday in the Hebrides in which I was experiencing a few cardiac problems and she had a rather too vivid dream about my mortality. Suffice that the blue lights were a sort of Luciferian red. If no one else, she said, the grandchildren might quite enjoy the book.

So this is also dedicated to marvellous Maeve, brilliant Bethan, fabulous Freddie and fantastic Francis (in chrono-logical order.) No more bairns on the way, are there? Their parents – Adam and Stacey, Owen and Sam – have played blinders, too.

Not another word should be written before acknowledg-ing the huge part played in the editing and production of the book by my old friend and former colleague Jon Smith, a superb journalist whose expertise and indefatigability are im-mense and who also made *Northern Conquest*, the last of the Northern League histories, the attractive volume that it is.

At the time of writing, Jon wouldn't so much as accept a hot dinner for his efforts – and I can't afford to buy him a pint at his up-market village local.

I greatly hope that others will want not just to read the book, but to respond to it. The thread which stretched through all those 55 years was that of continuity, cohesion and com-munity, of reader reaction, the joy of feedback, of getting to know *Northern Echo* readers and sometimes even of raising a glass with them – or of they, poor things, having to listen to one of my talks. It was old school journalism, probably now impossible in the straitened circumstances which threaten to choke the life out of the provincial newspaper industry, but arguably only the job's third greatest pleasure.

Ahead of it was the endless joy of turning a phrase and,

in first place, the satisfaction of pressing the 'send' button on another column and thinking it a job well – half-decently – done.

Some readers – invidious to name just some of them – stayed in touch after my dark day defenestration and I'm truly grateful to them. Others, inevitably, have fallen by the wayside; many more have died. Newspaper buyers these days have a pretty whiskery age profile; no wonder nostalgia rules.

So while the book is chiefly intended as a celebration of North-East life and North-East people, its sub-plot is an attempt to re-start some of those conversations – these days usually by email – maybe to instigate others, to mobilise memories, to widen the embrace. Encountered or imagined, it's been a camaraderie of kindred spirits.

Whether kudos or criticism, memories or miseries, it would be wonderful to hear in turn from readers of *Unconsidered Trifles*, not least those – or their kin – whose activity is recalled in the book. Was old Rubberbones as black as he was painted or was that just the non-climbing paint from the top of the Durham jail wall? Did Madame Cyn really? Is the Demon Donkey Dropper of Eryholme still bamboozling all he meets? Did Hodgy ever find work? Does the Prince of Wales remember that unlikely morning in Bishop Auckland?

It would be great to hear on those and a million other topics – mikeamos81@aol.com – and there's also a daily blog, now my only writing outlet and decidedly non-stipendiary, on www.mikeamosblog.wordpress.com. A first cousin to all that went before it, the blog enjoys substantial feedback, but would always welcome more.

A final preliminary, much uncertainty at the time of writing surrounds the coronavirus pandemic. Goodness only knows how it might affect publication of the book, but it could well be another nail in the coffin of the provincial newspaper industry. Digital publishing will outlive it.

So it's not really been a fast foreword at all – the word

count, bless it, hovers around 1,300 – but you know what they say about journalists, don't you?

Mike Amos MBE
Middleton Tyas
North-East England
May 2020

1 : TIN TACKS RETURNS

THE Queen was greatly gracious, though she would never have been allowed to start a sentence with a conjunction in old Geoff Hill's third form English language class – or, for that matter, by readers of the *Gadfly* column.

"And are you a journalist?" the monarch began.

The question was perceptive, nonetheless. The truthful answer might have been "Of a sort, Your Majesty," but since everyone knows the relationship between journalists and the truth, the response was simply "Yes."

It was December 2006, notification of the MBE having arrived from 10 Downing Street about seven months earlier. "Services to journalism in North-east England," it said.

The four of us scrubbed up quite well, though Owen – younger son by two-and-a-half years – could find no suitably sober hosiery and wore his black football referee socks instead. It was probably quite fortunate that, unlike Timothy Hackworth Junior Mixed and Infants in Shildon, there wasn't a handkerchief inspection, either.

On such state occasions, it's said, most recipients take nearest and dearest for lunch at the Savoy, or somewhere similarly swanky. We – Sharon, Adam, Owen and I – had pie and chips in a nearby pub called the Coal Hole. It seemed somehow appropriate.

Who'd have thought it, though? Not the folk on the pre-school milk round in Shildon, nor the kids in our crazy-cobbled back street, nor the woodwork master known as Isaiah who awarded eight out of 100 for a matchbox holder and wrote in the end of term report that the eight was for spelling my name correctly on the back of the bit of wood.

I always was good at spelling.

SHILDON'S a shrinking town in south-west County Durham, once home to several smallish pits and, until 1984, to a very large railway wagon works which employed 2,500 men and went, as they say, hammer and tongs.

Hammer and tongs on day shift, anyway. Perhaps exaggerated, perhaps the stuff of dreams, tales abounded of less frantic activity after sundown.

My mate Tommy Taylor, lovely bloke and former Lib-Dem parliamentary windmill tilter, was once passing a night shift by howking the wax out of his ear with a matchstick when a passing workmate inadvertently jogged his elbow.

The match snapped, half somehow subsumed inside Tommy's cranium. He was taken to Darlington hospital, an experience which much enlivened the casualty department's own night shift and really did prompt the doctor to enquire if he'd enjoyed the match.

One of my better stories, that.

My dad, a wartime sergeant in the Queen's Own Cameron Highlanders – garrisoned on Bermuda, someone had to be at the sharp end – helped make anxious ends meet by holding down two jobs and cultivating two allotments, occasionally escaping with a pipeful of St Bruno Flake to the

OUT ON HIS EAR:
Tommy Taylor

18

doubly noxious netty down the yard. More of the netty down the yard a little later.

He was one of precious few men in Shildon who didn't work at the wagon works, and thus – a minor regret – was unable to claim concessionary rail travel. By day he'd ride round the town on his heavy-duty bicycle – sixty years later there are still folk who remember that bike – collecting Provident club money. By night he was a GPO telephonist in Bishop Auckland. Being a London lad originally, he was also an Arsenal fan, an allegiance which with mixed fortunes I inherited for life.

MY mam kept the home fires burning, made a terrific rabbit pie, enjoyed a game of bingo after the last of the old town's four cinemas was screened out in the sixties and made her own immortal contributions to the English language.

Someone of whom she wasn't very fond might be termed "as pleasant as a cow's husband", a weak cup of tea supposed "neither watter bewitched nor tea begrudged." The classic, rather vulgarly, was the frequent observation that it was "kettle calling the pan grimy a**e". We probably didn't hear that one until we were over 16.

"Jump up and give your leg a dother" wasn't one of hers, mind. That was dear old Aunty Betty.

WE were twins, me and our kidder, though by no means identical. I was the good-looking one. Dave was 20 minutes younger, altogether brighter, similarly short-sighted. Like the Arsenal, myopia also has much for which to answer as, paradoxically, will become clear.

Dave went off to read English at Lancaster University, having already learned where not to put his conjunctions, became an English teacher – inspired and inspiring – in Hartlepool. What of his brother, who when invited in an O-level history paper to write about Sir Samuel Plimsoll waxed not about the gentleman who gave his name to the Plimsoll line

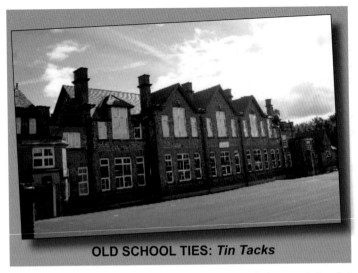

OLD SCHOOL TIES: *Tin Tacks*

but about the guy who (allegedly) invented the sandshoe? I was the one who just didn't fancy university, hadn't great A-level grades and couldn't even make a half-decent matchbox holder. The rest is mystery.

SHILDON'S most famous son – a child by adoption, anyway – was Timothy Hackworth, an early 19th century locomotive engineer from Wylam in the Tyne Valley who'd set up the first railway works in the town and helped pioneer the Stockton and Darlington Railway.

As well as our primary school – known locally as Tin Tacks – the park, a couple of streets, a pub, a business park and a care home all bear Hackworth's name. Once there was a Timothy Hackworth Museum, too, now replaced by a much more brightly burnished place called Locomotion, after the engine which inaugurated the world's first passenger railway service, from Shildon on September 27 1825.

Back in the 1980s, when newspapers enjoyed very much more profitable times than now they do, I'd booked on expenses a late-night taxi from the Timothy Hackworth back home. The beer was probably on expenses, too.

Usually Station Taxis were punctual to the minute, belying their railway location. This time no one showed. It was about 11.30pm, the landlord anxious for his bed, when I rang to ask the driver's whereabouts.

"Outside the Timothy Hackworth," said the old-hand controller, assured in turn that that was exactly where I was. The taxi, it transpired, was outside the museum.

The buildings were about a mile apart, the museum in darkness and closed for several hours, the pub a much more regular haunt. The driver didn't get a tip, save to get his finger out.

The school was built in 1910, still stands, still answers to Tin Tacks. I'd gone back for the centenary, blethered nostalgically. "Ah yes, the good old days," said Anne Dockray, the head. "Diphtheria, rickets and getting whacked around the back of the legs for not having the seams of your stockings straight."

Or, of course, a handkerchief.

FIFTY of us were in Tom Coates's class for three years; 47 of us passed the 11-plus – the scholarship, they called it. The boys went to King James I Grammar School in Bishop Auckland, founded in 1605, the girls to the more recent school across the playing field.

An invisible barrier was drawn between the two, but at that age we didn't much care – not when there was football, anyway.

Tom Coates was an outstanding teacher, if much more liberal with the stick than would have been acceptable today. He lived with his parents nearby, stalked homewards one wintry afternoon by a small gang of us daring one another to throw a snowball at him.

No guesses. To universal surprise, it hit him right behind the ear. Others would have fled; the elder Amos stayed to admire his accuracy and to await the reaction – delayed, both hands, next morning.

Margaret Wanless and I usually contested the distinction of being top of the class, which is to say that I was top once and Margaret the rest of the time. Probably self-subscribed, Tom always gave a 7/6d book token to the winner.

Margaret would buy books of what used to be termed an improving nature. I found an extra three bob from somewhere and fulfilled a childhood ambition by buying the *Ian Allan Locospotters' Annual* "combined" edition, not just listing every steam engine in the land but its mechanical specification and pretty much what the driver had in his sandwiches. It was all but impossible for a Shildon lad not to be a train spotter.

Becoming an engine driver, however – or a fire fighter, or a famous footballer or just about anything else – was tricky for someone who couldn't see what was on the blackboard, not even from the very front row.

2 : GRAMMAR RULES

FOR the first three or four years of our time there, King James I Grammar School in Bishop Auckland remained boys only. It suited us fine: girls didn't play football, or fag cards or chucks. For the first year or so the head was Edward Deans, a formidable and wholly fearsome man known as Neddy – though never, of course, to his face – most kindly described as a disciplinarian and more accurately as a sadist.

He was followed by Denis Weatherley, an altogether more enlightened head who was one of the North-East's best known singers and musicians. Twenty years later, Denis was a freelance music critic for the *Northern Echo* when I was news editor and, nominally, his boss. He lived in Darlington.

HEAD MAN:
Denis Weatherley

We got on very well and occasionally bumped into one another on the High Row. The last time it happened he was in his eighties and, truth to tell, looking his years.

"Denis, you're looking well," I lied.

He paused but briefly. "Mike," he said, "there are three ages of man – youth,

23

middle age and 'By God you do look well'." Two weeks later, singing with his son's choir in Nottingham, he died on the very note of 'Swing low sweet chariot, coming for to carry me home.' If ever there were a perfect way to go, that was it.

The boys' and girls' grammar schools, formerly separated by that football pitch and by a force field of indifference, amalgamated in 1963. In the fifth form we began to appreciate the timing.

Geoff Hill had impregnated the rules of grammar, part of what rather grandly was called 'arts', as opposed to science. With maths and science it was even trickier not being able to see the board. With football it was just possible to make out the ball, on a sunny day and a grassy pitch, though it visibly did nothing to improve my credentials as a goalkeeper. After one particularly dismal display for Kings, the house meeting was addressed the following morning by Melvin McConnell – house master, head of history and a Methodist local preacher.

Melvin, a gentle man, usually practised what he preached. On this occasion frustration overcame him. "That bloody Amos," he began. The house fell silent, inaction louder than words. He died in February 2020, the funeral at the Methodist church which for so long he'd loved and served. For some reason that story wasn't mentioned.

I'm not sure that Melvin had a nickname, other than Mac. Isaiah was so called because of the spurious claim that one eye was higher in his head than the other, Ichabod – a bald gentleman who taught maths – gained his soubriquet from the biblical Hebrew for 'There is no glory' – while Geoff Hill had a permanent limp and was forever Chester, a nod to Matt Dillon's hirpling sidekick in the early days of ITV.

CRICKET, compulsory in the first form, was different. I couldn't see the cricket ball at all, though the charm of it all led to an improbable but lifelong allegiance to Somerset County Cricket Club (and a still unachieved and fiendishly thwarted ambition to see them win the County Championship.)

Part of the problem, once explained to Jean Foster – with her husband Geoff, my greatly long-suffering opticians – was that a cricket ball is red and a cricket pitch green. "Ah," divined Jean, "so you're colour blind as well."

"As well as what, Jean?"

"As well as everything else," said Jean.

It was a real bolt from the green.

It might help explain why, reporting on sport these past 35 years, much of the content may legitimately have been supposed waffle. The funny thing is that, however monochrome, in the trade such stuff's called a colour piece.

BACK at Bishop they launched a school magazine called *Then There Was One* – with hindsight, singularly awful – on which I was advertising manager, crossword compiler and a pedestrian and wonderfully pompous contributor. Still I tried not to start a sentence with a conjunction or to end one with a preposition and never, ever, to split an infinitive.

About that time I also had a letter, for some reason about Judy Garland and every bit as pompous, published in the *Sunday Sun*. It was a first tiny footprint on the pages of provincial journalism.

Unification of boys' and girls' grammar schools also meant seeing more of the opposite sex. The first real girlfriend was the daughter of the station master at Barnard Castle though, wretchedly, Dr Beeching had got to the station shortly before I did.

She was only the station master's daughter but briefly she seemed just the ticket. We became engaged, a liaison which ended when university studies sent her to France for a year and she discovered things which – then as now, very likely – had never been heard of in Shildon, not even in the French quarter.

My A-levels – English, history, German – had been average, an indolent outcome chiefly influenced by too much football down the Rec. Others had already decided that they wanted to be doctors, or teachers, or lawyers. All I knew was that I didn't fancy university, didn't like exams, didn't want to be any of those things and, most particularly, had no intention of joining the Civil Service.

Besides, the Civil Service required a medical. Journalism didn't.

Half-blind leading the blind, I spotted an advert for a sub-editor on the *Northern Echo*. Harry Evans, the legendary editor, replied kindly, explained that a sub-editor needed to know the point of a spike, referred me to Fred Hurrell, editor of the *Durham Advertiser* series of weekly newspapers.

Fred, a charming man who looked like the elder partner in *Dr Finlay's Casebook* and wore trousers at half-mast, as if the cat had died, decided at interview that I should in turn be diverted to Arnold Hadwin, editor of the *Northern Despatch*, the *Echo*'s sister evening paper.

It was a bit like passy-the-parcel, and when the music stopped, poor Arnold was left holding the wet-eared baby.

FIRST EDITOR:
Arnold Hadwin

Arnold was a Spennymoor lad, had entered journalism at 15, became a Royal Marine commando, gained a scholarship to Ruskin College, Oxford, became president of the Guild of British Newspaper Editors, taught journalists in Africa and was deservedly appointed OBE.

In retirement in Lincolnshire he still followed

the store horse, or its equine equivalent, to gather manure for his roses, still looked forward to the fortnightly visit of the Rington's tea man, still cared passionately – as all provincial journalists should – about community.

Back in the sinning sixties he offered me a job as a junior reporter with North of England Newspapers, as the company was then called, part of the Westminster Press group. The *Despatch*, regarded much to the frustration of successive editors as a poor relation to the *Echo*, sold about 20,000 copies every evening, mainly in the Darlington and Bishop Auckland areas.

Not many years before I sneaked in, Reginald Grey, a post-war *Echo* editor, had issued a 16-page guide to young journalists which included the advice that it was black tie with dinner suit but white tie with tails and the injunction not to use a long word when a short word – "or perhaps two or three short words" – would suffice. I remembered the bit about white tie, anyway.

I stayed for 55 years, latterly clinging somewhat precariously to provincial journalism's upturned hull, until finally they threw me to the fishes.

3 : STRING'S ATTACHED

THE launch day was August 30 1965, the first year that the traditional bank holiday had been moved from first Monday to last. The weekly wage was £9 1s 6d, seven weeks later to rise to £10 2s 0d when I reached 19.

The paper was part of the Westminster Press group, the company chairman Mrs Angela Campbell-Preston who periodically paid us a visit and who seemed genuinely interested in the young 'uns. One of the Scottish dukes, the one said alone in Britain to have the right to raise a private army, was also somehow involved, though I never saw him. The National Union of Journalists might engage in a little mild sabre rattling, but His Grace's forces were never needed. They seemed, back then, to be very fair employers, often paying a Christmas bonus of up to two weeks wages and sometimes, misty memory suggests, a mid-summer bonus on top.

On that first day I bought a tanner notebook at Rufus Pedelty's paper shop in Shildon, caught the No 1 bus, reported as instructed to an amiable rogue called Dick Tarelli, the *Despatch*'s news editor. None could have been greener: I was innocent and Darlington – just ten miles from home – was abroad.

Among other *Despatch* reporters were Paul Routledge, to become the *Daily Mirror*'s political editor and a leading figure on the left, and Philip Norman, later a celebrated pop music biographer and friend of the famous. Other stars shone more briefly, and less brightly.

Dick had little idea what to do with the mewling apprentice with the sixpenny notebook. At 12.30 it was decreed that I should have some lunch in the canteen, and that's when the trouble began. Amid the cabbage lurked, almost slithered, a nine-inch piece of well-boiled string. Three hours into an unpromising career, what was a Shildon lad to do – take it back and complain or say nowt and swallow the evidence? I took the first option.

The canteen fell silent, as if Oliver had walked in and asked for more. Tables of inky tradesmen, hard-wired and heavy-metalled, turned to stare at the preposterous parvenu, simultaneously green and cabbage-looking.

It's unlikely that Mrs Dodds, the canteen manageress, suggested I keep quiet lest everyone want a bit. What she did say escapes memory but clearly there was a catalyst among the Priestgate pigeons.

Already there'd been talk of a move to the Bishop Auckland branch office; now they couldn't wait to get me northwards up the A6072. A week in Darlington was deemed quite enough – the young Scrooge facing a brief Christmas at home came to mind – and still there were four-and-a-half days to go. Just about the only regret was that Darlington was the Pork Pie Capital of the World – Snaith's, Zissler's, Prest's, Holloway's and Taylor's all in heated competition. Now only Taylor's ambrosially remains, and seems every day to feed the five thousand.

ON the second morning I was sent out with a photographer – someone had to drive – to find a story, any story, in Gainford, a village a few miles west. I found two, not including the monkey in a cage in the Queens Head. In 1965 there was nothing greatly unusual about a pub monkey in a cage (but for pub parrots, see under Barnard Castle.)

On the third day they sent me to Barton, just across the border in North Yorkshire, to gain evidence on something which on first telling sounded like a dispute among neighbours but proved altogether more newsworthy. The Burn family had a nice bungalow about a quarter of a mile from a quarry, near what is now the A1 motorway. Its blasting operations were wayward, to put it very mildly. Boulders the circumference of giant snowballs had torn holes in their garage and landed in the garden. How long, the family feared, before they hit the house and its occupants?

It was a good story, made the front page – sadly without a by-line – still hangs, framed, on the wall at home. Dick probably flogged it to the nationals.

SO the five days passed, or should have done – until doughty Dick decided that he needed someone to cover the Darlington v Carlisle rugby union match on the sixth, providing running reports not just for the *Despatch* but for Saturday sports editions in Carlisle and Middlesbrough and more considered stuff after the final whistle.

There was to be a match report for the *Sunday Sun*, that of the Judy Garland letter, a piece for the *Echo* and 500 further words for a Cumbrian weekly paper. Payment, appropriately, was to come from something called the lineage pool in which sharks like Dick swam confidently but tiddlers could easily be breakfast.

There were three reasons why that match wasn't a good idea, firstly that I'd never watched rugby in my life and didn't remotely understand the rules, secondly that a running report conjured images of a school magazine piece on the 100-yard dash and thirdly – of course – that I couldn't see the blessed ball. Dick waved protest aside, like a referee denying an obvious penalty; there'd also be overtime and a day off in lieu, he said.

Those Saturday evening *Pinks* – sometimes they might be *Green Uns*, very occasionally blue – were remarkable creations, mind. For a while in the early 60s I'd helped deliver them, patient queues outside Coulsons' paper shop awaiting the little red van which expelled a bundle of *Sports Despatches* almost without stopping. Usually it was no later than

6 15pm, a little hot metal miracle, another 2/6d pocket money and home in time for Dixon of Dock Green.

Apart from anything else, the only call box in Darlington RFC's clubhouse was out of sight of the pitch. Then, as always would prove the case, I got lucky. A Samaritan spectator himself offered to provide an account of the action while I struggled to raise the operator for yet another transfer charge call.

The 'considered' stuff – 'considered' is a journalistic term, again meaning waffle – was completed the following day on the dining room table at home on which we more customarily played table tennis. Probably it's unnecessary to add that there never was a toe in Dick's lineage pool and that after more than half a century they still owed me overtime and a day off in lieu.

No matter, Bishop again beckoned. It was to prove the most memorable three-and-a-half years of my career, articles of apprenticeship which will continue shortly.

4 : BLIND SPOT

BEING hopelessly short-sighted has never bothered me for long – partly because it's something to which you become accustomed, partly because friends and colleagues have always been greatly understanding with lifts and partly because life has provided very many compensations.

Mind, I wouldn't mind a quid for every time I've been standing in the cold and wet waiting interminably for a bus and someone a few days later has said: "I saw you as I drove past the bus stop the other morning."

Sharon, as ever, has been wonderful. Thank goodness she passed her driving test, and no matter that it was at the ninth attempt, though it was a bit unfortunate when she failed properly to set her handbrake and the car ran into the back of a police vehicle.The reality is that many have been far worse off, not least Mark Turnbull, blind from birth, who became both president of the National Union of Journalists and the first blind man in Britain to chair a magistrates' court.

Mark, who never had a guide dog, worked both for BBC Tees – an accomplished interviewer whose Sunday morning programme was particularly appreciated – and as the *Darlington & Stockton Times* man in Barnard Castle, to which garrulous garret he'd commute from his home in Redcar. At Barney he owed much to the compassion and camaraderie of Nigel Metcalfe, the *Echo*'s man, and to the supply of whisky which seemed forever to top up the filing cabinet.

For several years, yet more remarkably, Mark also covered the Embassy World Darts Championships in Redcar,

UNSIGHTED:
Mark Turnbull

providing reports to numerous media outlets. It required determination, courage and cheek, all of which he possessed abundantly. Mark would stay with the players at the competition hotel in Middlesbrough. If territory proved unfamiliar, one or other would guide him, Mark's hand on the shoulder of the darts professional in front.

On one occasion he was being guided by Dave Whitcombe, an England international who had a pub in Ipswich. No one really knows how Dave, blessed with 20-20 vision, came to break his nose after walking into a piece of street furniture while Mark, unscathed, lived joyfully to tell the tale.

Mark was indomitable, tenacious, able and very, very large. At Teesside magistrates court, he liked to recall, an aggrieved defendant had somewhat tautologically called him a big fat blind bastard. "That may be so but I'm also a magistrate," said Mark, and sent the guy to the cells to consider, with perfect hindsight, the error of his ways.

Like many more blind people, he was also a talented musician, said once to have met Frank Sinatra in the Savoy and to have enjoyed a late-night jam session with him. He'd also put himself forward for the Church of England ministry and, disappointed, converted to Roman Catholicism several years later.

He died, aged 51, in 2016. The thronged funeral was at Middlesbrough's Roman Catholic cathedral.

RON Johnston had been blind from the age of five, when a routine dental operation went wrong. Hartlepool lad originally, he moved to Bishop Auckland, gained secretarial skills – 140wpm shorthand, tell that to the National Council for the Training of Journalists – became a district councillor and community champion and from 500 applicants was appointed Oxfam's north regional organiser.

Ron and his guide dogs became greatly familiar in Bishop and throughout the north, his independence extraordinary. "He cared passionately about those less well-off than himself," wrote his daughter Linda Dodd – herself a priest – in a biography simply called *Blind Courage*. "He always said he'd rather be blind than deaf, because being deaf left you isolated."

Oxfam wanted him to accept yet greater worldwide responsibility, Ron declined and became depressed. "It was hard for us to continue to keep him safe, the darkness overcame him," wrote Linda. He died, aged just 51, in 1976.

NORMA Town and John Stancombe had guide dogs, too. Norma was a dedicated and long-serving Labour member of Darlington Borough Council and a pillar of her local church. John, who lived in Suffolk, would travel the land in search of football – a ground hopper, as they're called (and more of ground hoppers later on.)

Another big lad, like Mark Turnbull, he'd ring officials at his intended venue to ask if someone might provide a running commentary. Frequently the games were in midweek, after which he'd make his way to the nearest big town, catch an overnight coach to London, get off again at some Northern Line Underground station, travel on to Liverpool Street and then catch a main line train home.

"It's nothing," he'd say, "I'm usually back for my lunch."

Most recently I've become quite matey with Dave Thomas, a West Auckland lad originally who won seven England international football caps in a career with Burnley, Queens

Park Rangers and Everton but, approaching 70, is now registered blind and has a guide dog, Hannah. Lloyd, his father, also lost his sight. The glaucoma is hereditary.

Though completely without peripheral vision, Dave still manages a decent round of golf – with sighted help – still fly fishes in the Tees, close to his lovely home in Lartington, near Barnard Castle. Brenda, his smashing wife, is loving and invaluable.

Dave published his autobiography, *Guiding Me Home and Away*, at the end of 2019. Royalties went to Guide Dogs, adding to the £75,000 he'd already raised for the charity. "I've been very lucky," he said.

Not being able to read a number plate from 25 yards – or ten, very likely – may have narrowed horizons a bit, but it's very easy to agree with David Thomas.

5 : BENCH OF BISHOP'S

BACK in 1965 we were officially indentured juniors, articled to the company for three years and with a requirement to be good and faithful servants (as it says in the Parable of the Talents, if not in the articles of indenture.)

The firm, in turn, agreed to teach us all that was needful. In truth, junior reporters were pretty much thrown in the deep end – certainly in district offices like Bishop – with the requirement to swim or to do the opposite. We were in turn greatly lucky that it was that way.

The *Despatch*'s district chief reporter was Harry Stott, known as Harrystottle, a delightful and ever-amiable chap who'd transferred from the *Wythenshawe Recorder* – doubtless on a free – when his wife, Milly, took on a lorry drivers' B&B in Darlington. Harry liked a drink: as a man he was lovely, as a journalist hopeless.

No pre-entry or post-graduate courses in those days – there weren't all that many graduates – just two eight-week block release courses, conveniently at Darlington College of Technology, where the refectory chicken pie was the best in history.

There'd also be biannual weekend schools, residential boltholes with a happy social side. After one, at a college in Durham, most of us headed down the road to the Top Hat, a nightclub in Spennymoor known for a sort of giant gilded cage in which a little-clad young lady would dance suggestively.

One of the young ladies in question was Dot Bainbridge, whose day job was a reporter on the *Despatch*. Most of the weekend scholars knew of her saucy sideline; Maurice Wedgwood, course tutor and old school deputy editor of the *Echo*, did not. His pipe almost fell from his mouth, though we never did learn whether there was anything in the indentures against cage dancing.

The block release courses had youngsters from long-disappeared weekly papers like the *Stockton and Billingham Express*, the *Brighouse Echo* and the *Whitley Bay Guardian & Seaside Chronicle* (honest). Mostly we learned shorthand and journalistic law, of which the best-remembered lesson is that it's all but impossible to libel the dead. It makes writing an autobiography very much easier.

At the end of it all I somehow finished top of the class – mightn't have done had Margaret Wanless been in it – winning a £2 book token with which it was possible to buy 16 fashionable Penguin paperbacks like *Catcher in the Rye*. Most of them, but not J D Salinger's masterwork, remain unread to this day. Probably it would have been better sticking to the *Locospotters' Annual*.

Throughout those first three years, the only formal exam was something called the proficiency test, which I managed to pass with a distinction – rather different from the cycling proficiency test, ten years earlier, which I failed ignominiously. Compared to all that, journalism seemed as easy as falling off a bike.

BISHOP Auckland was a market town of perhaps 20,000 people, an urban district of 35,000. It was best known for the exploits of its football team in the FA Amateur Cup days of the 1950s and as the seat of the Bishops of Durham (who in the 1960s still wore gaiters.)

On the only occasion on which there was a Bishop Auckland press ball – old jokes may be inserted here – the diminutive Dr Ian Ramsey, then Durham's bishop, could be seen dancing the Gay Gordons in gaiters and episcopal frock coat. None who was there would ever forget it.

The patch also included neighbouring towns like Spennymoor, Crook, Willington, Ferryhill and Shildon and the more rural delights of Weardale. The senior reporters usually bagged the Weardale runs, however: Weardale was good on expenses. We also stretched up to Tow Law, a near-Arctic place of 2,500 souls high on a wind-blasted ridge in west Durham, which until 1974 had its own urban district council.

On a snow-capped Wednesday afternoon in December 1967, Tow Law Town FC thrashed mighty(ish) Mansfield Town 5-1 in the FA Cup first round, half the local schoolkids and a rather higher percentage of local journalists playing truant.

Some years later, while covering a match at Colchester United – goodness knows why – I fell into conversation with Hal Mason, United's long-serving and highly esteemed programme editor. For three decades, he said, he'd spent his summer holidays in the same little B&B at Tow Law and absolutely loved the place. Colchester was the glasshouse by comparison.

The *Despatch* and the *Echo* employed three reporters apiece, housed in a smoky little office above a money lender's. In the room next door, another two or three worked for the weekly *Auckland Chronicle*, which cost fourpence. The *Chronicle* office was posh, it had a proggy mat, though probably not company issue.

The Middlesbrough-based *Evening Gazette* shoe-horned another four reporters into a little box, no less carcinogenic, down the road. The district chief reporter, about the same age as Harrystottle, was Charles Verdun Browne. Even in those golden days, it seemed, the *Gazette* might have had more reporters in Bishop than it had readers.

We also had Bill Oliver, our resident photographer, a pearly-toothed and generally good natured old boy who wore a battered hat, smoked Capstan, drank the occasional rum and pep – when someone else was buying – and knew almost everyone.

Bill drove one of the firm's little red vans – number 25, it said on the side – periodically sent off to the chateau-like Bowes Museum at Barnard Castle where the Queen Mother, after whose family the building was named, would be opening something or other. They told him to park round the back.

On one occasion he was late, discovered that Her Majesty had already cut the ribbon, deferentially doffed the battered hat. "Excuse me, luv," said

CUTTING EDGE:
HM The Queen Mother

Bill, "but would you mind just doing that again?"

The Queen Mother paused but momentarily. "Why certainly, Mr Oliver," she said, held both ends of the ribbon in the same hand, scissors in the other and affected once more to do the honours. Bill got his picture. Who says that you can't believe all you see in the newspapers? Like much else, and for all sorts of reasons, it could never happen today.

OUR office above the money lender's was spartan, to say the least. For six reporters there were five desks, five chairs – some literally held together by string – three elderly typewriters, a temperamental gas fire, a kettle, a telephone, a well-thumbed pack of cards and a great deal of stuff employed in the losing battle to keep the rain out.

If all six incumbents were in temporary residence, the last in from the cold – or, more likely, the youngest – perched upon a pile of old newspapers, plaintively but oft-successfully suggesting that a game of three-card brag might be in order. You could sit on the end of the desk to play brag.

The real bane of our lives, however, was carbon paper. Everything we typed had to be double-spaced and, for some reason, in quintuplicate. The copies were known as blacks. Every few minutes the carbons had again to be interleaved and if that wasn't creating a sort of journalistic blacks-hand gang, then forever reinserting the truculent typewriter ribbon completed the effect.

Among the many blessings and wonders of the technological age, none is greater than no longer having to use carbon paper.

The *Auckland Chronicle* had two desks and another phone. Mike Deary, one of its reporters, was still officially a junior but being older and more experienced than I was – he must have been at least 20 – was regarded with reverence until the day I walked in and found him standing on a chair in terror.

Below him, probably bearing a slightly amused expression, strolled a spider. It was how I learned to spell arachnophobia, and it was as naught compared to my subsequent fear of heights (of which more anon.)

By day Harry would stumble around in a semi-daze, in the evening he might attend a council committee meeting, fail to make a note, rise early the following morning, buy the *Echo*, rewrite a couple of words from the morning paper report and phone it to the *Despatch* while the copytakers were contemplating their first coffee and their fingernails.

Courts reported in the morning, council committee meetings in the evening, we would sometimes sneak off – all of us, even sporting female reporters like Dorothy Allan and

Anne Brunskill –for a game of football on Cockton Hill Rec. Harrystottle went in goal until the day he busted his braces. You know what they say about all work and no play.

Most of us enjoyed a drink, of course – particularly on Thursdays – though even Harry was sometimes sober compared to Ken Calcutt, an *Echo* man who not long before had been a lieutenant commander with the Fleet Air Arm. He was known as Ken Halfcut, though often it was only 50 per cent accurate.

THE staple journalistic diet was those courts and councils, 21st century economies meaning that both are now rarely attended. In the late 1960s they were very rarely missed.

Not that Bishop was big on crime. Arthur Stephenson, the village bobby in nearby Coundon a few years before I arrived, still tells the story of how his superintendent ordered him to summon nine juveniles to court for playing hum-dum-dum outside Rinaldi's café.

Hum-dum-dum (finger or thumb) was an innocent game in which a queue of kids formed 'backs' against a wall – in Hartlepool they called it montakitty – and someone else vaulted on top of them.

In Coundon they were said to be obstructing the highway and fined ten bob apiece. Dum and dumber, it did little for Arthur's street cred.

A rare example of serious crime occurred at Whitworth Hall, ancestral home near Spennymoor of Bonnie Bobby Shafto, from which burglars stole a highly valuable Ming Buddha statuette belonging to Mrs Rosa Edwina Marguerita Duncombe Shafto. Why do I remember all that? I remember even better the face of Charlie Organ, the local detective inspector, when he reported that they'd recovered the treasure and locked up a gang from Leeds but best of all I remember his face when, a few weeks later, he told us one morning at the magistrates' court that the Ming Buddha had been stolen again.

Bishop Auckland magistrates sat on Mondays and Thursdays, Spennymoor's justices on Tuesdays, the courts at Stanhope and Wolsingham – up the dale – once a month. Again it was the senior men who usually went to Weardale, partly because they'd all claim expenses for one car and partly because there'd be a few beers in the Phoenix thereafter.

One of the very few occasions on which I attended Stanhope court followed the only murder in my three-and-a-half years on the patch. It was a Sunday morning, my dear old dad finishing an all-nighter at Bishop telephone exchange when a 999 call came through about the apparent murder of a young woman – I can still remember the address – in Stanhope. Probably illegally, he passed on the details.

The culprit had fled, handed himself in the following day, duly appeared in the insecure little court that more usually heard cases involving sheep.

On a Saturday morning about 15 years later I attended an even more improbable murder remand in Wath, a village of around 200 people near Ripon, where the monthly court sitting was said to boost the local economy, though no one explained how. The defendant might as securely have been there to pay the rates.

These days County Durham has just two magistrates courts hearing criminal cases. North Yorkshire has none between the Tees and York and Harrogate, Tyneside's criminals seem all to end up in South Shields, though that's not to traduce the Sand Dancers.

Bishop's two courts were usually busy, many faces familiar and none more so than that of George Henry Wilson (21 Lane Head, Copley.) Said to be a reliable farm worker when sober, George Henry would just as reliably pitch up in the cells after a weekend night on the town.

Frequently thrown off the last Lockey's bus out into the sticks, he'd make an accustomed Monday morning appearance in the dock – welly boots, battered mac, tie knotted somewhere around his sternum. Sometimes he got a short sentence – two weeks was a short sentence – sometimes a small fine. Nothing discouraged, just further dishevelled.

George Cosgrove, a privately avuncular chairman, eyed him one morning over his half-moon glasses. "Why now, George Henry," the chairman began, "what's tha been up to this time?"

George Henry carefully explained that it was the fault of the young pollisses. The old 'uns, he said, would take him home and let him sleep it off. The young 'uns wanted a notch (as it were) on their bedpost and locked him up.

So the conversation flowed. "Why now, George Henry," said the chairman after ten or 15 minutes, "we've had a bit crack and a bit carry-on but what are we going to dee with yer?"

"Dee?" said George Henry incredulously, "Tha's not going to dee nowt, is tha, George?"

Cosgrove probably recognised the futility of it all. "Bugger off, George Henry," he said, "and I don't want to see yer here again."

Bishop Auckland magistrates court, one of the last, closed in 2015. I attended one of the final hearings, the most noticeable changes that even the most minor cases seemed choked by paperwork and that none of the defendants had made the least effort to change out of their third-best jeans. Even George Henry Wilson used to wear a tie, and no matter that it was fastened around his sternum.

THOUGH no less an habitual criminal, as was said of Norman Stanley Fletcher, Ronnie Heslop – known as Rubberbones – was a rather bigger fish and from a rather bigger league. Back in 1961 he'd become the first man to escape over the wall at Durham Jail, a teaspoon used painstakingly to remove the grille from his cell floor.

Somehow squeezing through – hence the supple soubriquet – he'd dropped into the empty and unlocked cell below,

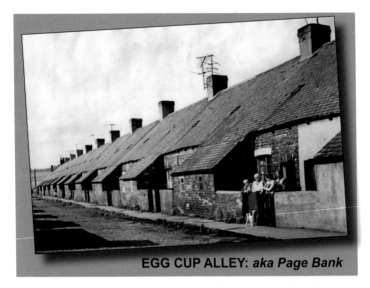

EGG CUP ALLEY: *aka Page Bank*

somehow got onto a low roof top and was away. Though the dogs soon had his scent, Ronnie was on the run for six weeks, escaping the hounds by swimming the swollen River Wear at Page Bank, near Spennymoor. The hounds couldn't follow, or were seriously disinclined to.

Page Bank was a former pit village of long terraces, known locally as Egg Cup Alley. Old Rubberbones knew almost everyone there, stayed one step ahead by commuting between the attics, though never quite above suspicion.

Years later John McVicar, an altogether nastier piece of work, claimed in his autobiography – serialised in the *Sun* – that he, McVicar, had been the first successfully to complete the Durham high jump. Ronnie, I guessed, wouldn't be best pleased at someone essaying grand larceny on his claim to fame. I at once headed to his house in Willington.

He wasn't, happily agreed to an interview for the *John North* column, accused McVicar of dishonesty – the nerve of it – but was rather reluctant to be photographed on the bridge at Page Bank beneath which he'd completed the great escape.

Finally he agreed, but only for a fiver. It remains the only occasion on which I've been tainted by chequebook journalism. Goodness only knows what the accounts department made of it, but still they paid up.

Ronnie's speciality, if that's the word, was village Co-ops, usually entering through the front door in the early hours and leaving it ajar. Just about the last time he was in the paper before his death was when commended by Lancashire Constabulary for his actions after coming upon an accident on the M6.

Like many of the villains who penitently paraded before Bishop magistrates, he was by no means as black as he was tainted.

As with the case of Ronnie's fiver, there's only been one example of what sport might call irregular payments and it happened in the first few weeks. The professional code of conduct, impressed upon all young reporters, forbade the receipt of any form of payment for publication. Some old doggerel put it more memorably:

> *You cannot hope to bribe or twist,*
> *Thank God! the British journalist.*
> *But seeing what the man will do*
> *Unbribed, there's no occasion to.*

GOLDEN weddings, sometimes even diamond weddings, were a fairly regular assignment, the happy couple always delighted to see us. It was a chance to remember – as to this day should never be forgotten – that while it might be bread and butter to us, for them it could be caviar, perhaps the only time between birth and death columns that their names might be in the paper.

Sometimes they had form, a yellowed cutting produced from the recesses of an elderly wallet – "that was the time I scored fifty for the second team..."

Hundredth birthday celebrations were much more rare

back then, an annual visit to old Mrs Sarah Green in St Helen's Auckland – she made it to 105 but was rarely able to leave her bed – the only one that comes to mind.

These days, happily, the milestone's much more familiar. The *Echo*'s classified deaths column, essential reading, recently recorded the passing of three centenarians on the same page.

For golden weddings, the only sweetener was usually a slice of cake and a glass of sherry – the reason that, to this day, I can't stand the blooming stuff. On one occasion, however – a golden wedding at Dean Bank, near Ferryhill – Bill Oliver and I were about to say our farewells when the old boy fished in a tea caddy on the sideboard and produced two pristine ten-bob notes.

He offered, we declined, he persisted. "You've just been so kind to us," he said. Finally, we accepted, for it would have been genuinely rude further to have held out. Crumpled almost to the point of disintegration, that ten bob note still sits accusingly in my own wallet – guilty but with mitigating circumstances. Bill's probably went on Capstan.

ANOTHER occasional experience, known by many young journalists but never welcomed by them, was what became known as the death knock – visiting the family of the recently and usually tragically deceased in the hope of some personal information – a story, in other words, and with luck a favoured photograph.

It would be stretching a point to call it bereavement counselling, though many welcomed the opportunity to talk affectionately – on or off the record – about their loved one.

One Monday morning the police reported a fatal road accident near Newton Aycliffe the previous Saturday evening. The driver had lived at Chilton, a few miles away. Off, anxiously, I went.

He'd been a factory worker, his family said, asked to put in an extra Sunday morning shift but declined because it would mean he'd miss Mass at his local Roman Catholic church. Then a gaffer remembered the Saturday evening service – the Vigil Mass – in Newton Aycliffe. It was on the return journey that the poor chap was killed.

It's true what the hymnist supposes, God moves in a mysterious way, his many wonders to perform.

LONG before laptops, stories for that evening's paper had to be telephoned, at Bishop magistrates from a little call box in a corner of the reception area, carcinogenic with the deep purple haze of Wills Woodbines. It was called ringing copy, the ladies who oft-truculently typed it known as copytakers. No matter how good the story, or how charismatic the story teller, the copytakers seldom made much attempt to hide their boredom.

Sooner or later, the first paragraph or the fiftieth, they'd querulously enquire "Is there much more of this?" It's a watchword of former times – no copytakers these days – and until circumstances suddenly changed in November 2019 it was long intended to be the title of this book.

A little while after leaving Bishop, I started walking out with – or, more accurately, buying lunch for – one of the copytakers. The liaison didn't last. "Is there much more of this?" may once again have applied.

6 : 1966 AND ALL THAT

NATIONAL politics didn't much poke its runny nose into our little patch around Bishop Auckland, save when they called a general election. My first was in 1966, the outcome in the Bishop and neighbouring North West Durham constituencies utterly predictable. It was the proverbial 'monkey with a red rosette' territory, or would have been had Labour in County Durham not inexplicably campaigned in green.

In Bishop Auckland, the Labour candidate and retiring MP was Jim Boyden, a decent and affable man who became a junior defence minister in the Wilson government but who lived 300 miles away in Sussex, with a constituency base in a caravan by the Tees at Winston. There should be a law against absentee MPs.

In North West Durham the Labour candidate and retiring MP was Ernest Armstrong, a former headmaster from Sunderland who'd been a Northern League footballer with Stanley United, a player so reputedly uncompromising that he earned the nickname Sikey (or possibly Psychie.)

Ernest, subsequently a good friend, also became a junior minister, a deputy Speaker of the House of Commons and Vice-President of the Methodist Conference, the highest office open to a lay person. He also lived on the patch. Both seats guaranteed 60-70 per cent of the total vote, the Conservatives often alone in opposition. Never in my life could I have imagined what happened in both constituencies, and elsewhere behind the Red Wall, in December 2019.

Back in 1966, the accompanying reports for the *Despatch*

GOOD KNIGHT: *Sir Tim Kitson*

were equally predictable, haltingly pedestrian and much, much too long. How different things must have been in the Richmond seat, across the Tees in North Yorkshire, where the monkey might have worn blue but the campaign was in glorious Technicolour.

The Tory back in 1966 was Tim Kitson – later Sir Timothy – an engaging landed gentleman who became Edward Heath's parliamentary private secretary during Heath's time as prime minister. More vivid yet, Labour's candidate was Pat Lisle – a 27-stone railway porter who drove a Bentley to work – while, most flamboyant of all, the Liberal was Keith Schellenberg, a tobogganist who'd twice represented Britain at the Winter Olympics and who in 1971 became the distinctly unpopular Laird of Eigg, a 7,400 acre Hebridean island which he'd bought for £600,000.

A more colourful trio may never have shared hustings. At the time I knew none of them but became acquainted with all three, especially the loquacious Mr Lisle, a man who could talk the hind legs off a cuddy, whatever its political persuasion.

Pat was born in Gateshead, attended a special school for kids with rickets, was evacuated to the Northallerton area during the war, became an artificial inseminator – though probably not for Tim Kitson's pedigree red polls – and was for 11 years the only Labour member of Northallerton Rural District Council. He campaigned under the slogan 'Never fear, Patrick's here.'

He'd been a signalman near Northallerton, was demoted for allowing two trains simultaneously onto the same section of track, was pursued around Richmond by BBC journalist Trevor Philpott, making a documentary self-fulfillingly called *The Losers*.

Pat was at his most emollient. "Can I count on your vote, sir?" he asked a tweedy Swaledale farmer. "Can thoo hellers like," said the farmer, who wasn't emollient at all.

After being declared bankrupt in 1970 – he blamed fast women, slow horses and booze, vowing thereafter to eschew all three – he became a bookie, owned a bakery and a ba-

WEAR A SMILE: *Pat Lisle*

by-wear shop in Catterick Camp, as then the Garrison was called, and ran several pubs including the Rookhope Inn in Weardale and the Tan Hill Inn, England's highest, in North Yorkshire's western wilds. In retirement he moved back to County Durham, fought Heighington parish council with the slogan 'Wear a smile, vote for Lisle' and promised to write an autobiography which, regrettably, never materialised. He died in 2010.

Tim Kitson and his well-heeled Liberal opponent had much in common – "He's a chum, he said I only did it to annoy him," said Schellenberg – while one of the few things which Labour and Conservative candidates had in common was that they both liked a bet.

Tim, who could probably afford it a bit more and who captained the parliamentary bridge team, had completed a high-priced double in 1963 on Lord Home becoming leader of the Conservative party and Scobie Breasley, at 49, becoming champion jockey.

One of Heath's biographies told the story of a prime ministerial visit to Singapore premier Lee Kuan Yew, on which our man was accompanied by his PPS. At the head of every formal menu was a statement that smoking was strictly forbidden. Halfway through dinner, Kitson was approached by an embassy flunkey bearing a note and at once excused himself, explaining that he had urgently to call London. He was absent for 20 minutes.

The same thing happened a little later, prompting Heath at the end of the evening to ask what on earth was going on. "Nothing," said Tim, "I was just dying for a fag." They based a *Yes Minister* script on it.

He'd also urged Heath, a leader with a reputation for being both aloof and grumpy, more assiduously to gain the support of his backbench MPs by fraternising in the Commons tea rooms and bars. The prime minister finally agreed; his aide eavesdropped. Heath fraternally addressed one of the junior members: "That speech you gave today was bloody

51

awful," he said.

Tim's campaign promises ranged from an end to sheep rustling to an end to outside netties, which if successful would have deprived my later columns of some of their best-read stories (but see under Marquis of Granby.) Perhaps most memorably of all, however, it was he who introduced the buxom American entertainer Jayne Mansfield to the Commons, a move which almost literally brought the House down.

Ms Mansfield had been playing the vibrant North-East nightclub circuit and staying in the Richmond constituency, which was how they'd met. For parliamentary purposes she wore a mini-skirt and a "striking" white blouse, seated by her host in the place in the gallery normally reserved for the prime minister's wife. It all came during questions to Denis Healey, then the defence secretary, about the cost of American F-111 jets. Ms Mansfield proving something of a side-show, the Speaker had several times to call for order, if not quite shoot her down.

THEN there was Keith Schellenberg – born in Middlesbrough, captain of the Yorkshire rugby team, owner of a successful motors business and of a Whitby shipyard, skier, motor racer, international car rally contestant, adventurer, charmer and extrovert extraordinary.

He may be remembered for nothing more indelibly than his purchase of Eigg, to the ultimate despair of most of the Hebridean island's 1,000 natives and amid unkind comparisons to Toad of Toad Hall. That he drove his Rolls Royce Phantom at high speed along Eigg's only road, wearing tweeds and goggles and with scarf blowing in the wind, may have accelerated the supposed similarity.

Nowhere, alas, is it recorded whether Keith simultaneously muttered "Poop, poop," as did the egregious Mr Toad.

Probably it didn't help landlord/tenant relations that one Christmas he sent the folk on Eigg a card depicting two of his burly bailiffs dressed as Santa Claus and carrying croquet mallets. "We specialise in recalcitrant tenants, squatters, weirdoes, junkies, hippies, new age travellers and reds," said the not overtly festive message.

Nor, in turn, was the laird much amused when a mystery blaze gutted a garage and the vintage fire engine which it housed. The Roller perished, too. Eigg, to a man, denied responsibility.

His big mistake may have been to sue the

GOOD EIGG:
Keith Schellenberg

Guardian for libel, a case too complex to revisit though the paper's comparison to Toad's skirmishes with the stoats and weasels wasn't at the heart of it. At any rate he lost, sold up and in 2001 moved back to Richmond with Jilly, his South Africa-born fourth wife. For £900,000 they bought a lovely house and gardens called St Nicholas which, idiosyncratically but lovingly and elegantly, they restored. It was there that I interviewed him in 2010.

Keith was 80 by then, still hitting the slopes and just back from Switzerland. He'd avoided Saint Moritz, though. "He thinks it's full of Russians wearing dead animals," said Jilly, who also admitted that her husband had quite liked the Mr Toad comparison – "it means he can wear his plus-fours."

Clearly eccentric, though with obvious early signs of dementia, he seemed to me delightful. "It doesn't strike me that I'd do anything differently at all. It's all been rather fun," he said. He died in October 2019, aged 90, just months after Sir

Timothy.

Tim Kitson, inevitably, had won the seat in 1966. Pat Lisle, probably picking up a lot of votes from the Northallerton area, came second with almost 25 per cent of the total. That must all have been rather fun, too, and an awful lot livelier than the banalities back in Bishop Auckland.

7 : THE GR CLUB

BACK in the formative, fumitive corridors of Bishop Auckland magistrates court stalked George Reynolds, safe-blower, the most incorrigible of them all. Though born in Sunderland and raised in sundry institutes of correction, George had settled in Shildon.

"Backward, mentally deficient and illiterate is what they called me. They hadn't invented dyslexia," he said, after – legitimately – making the umpteenth of his millions.

He'd had nowt, served time after time, made those multi-millions through a hugely and improbably successful work-tops business, owned a yacht and a helicopter, carried great wads of £50 notes wrapped in an elastic band, talked the hind legs off a cuddy, transformed one of County Durham's lesser stately homes into something much grander, became chairman and owner of Darlington Football Club, built them a handsome new ground – folly, perhaps, and in more ways than one – and at 83 still runs an e-cig business from Chester-le-Street, where he'll sometimes challenge customers to a game of chess. He learned it in prison, he says.

Though the Midas touch may have deserted him somewhat, George still has golden dreams.

We'd first met, almost inevitably, as he waited his latest presentation at court. Subsequently I was his best man – not the first wedding, long forgotten, but the second at Bishop registry office and afterwards at a local pub. The third was at the Castle of Mey, one of the royal residences in northern Scotland much loved by the late Queen Mother. I wasn't

KING SIZE:
George Reynolds,
then and now

even invited.

In those days George was trying, not always very hard, to go straight. There was a little joinery business in an old ice cream factory in Shildon, followed by a coffee bar – named The Dolphin after his beloved Alsatian – and then, above it, a cat-swinging nightclub called the GR but still known to older residents as Snowplough Hall because of the building's peculiar shape.

Back in the Bishop office of the *Northern Despatch*, the day's first job was to ring around the local police and fire stations to seek information on newsworthy events overnight. It was known as making the calls, greeted with differing degrees of civility but almost uniformly unrewarding.

One morning, however, Bishop Auckland police reported a burglary at a quarry explosives store at Bolam, near the A68 above West Auckland. Had readers seen anything suspicious?

When the paper came out, the police switchboard lit up like Blackpool illuminations. Lots of people had not only seen a blue Transit van parked on a road near the quarry but-further observed that the van had a large dolphin painted on the side and, for good measure, a Shildon telephone number (which, fifty years later, I can still remember).

Ever perceptive, the police went to George's bungalow, asked where he'd been the night before. George said that he'd been at home all night and (of course) had witnesses.

"Then what was your van doing outside the quarry store at Bolam?" asked the polliss.

"Someone must have nicked it," said George.

"Then what's it now doing back outside your house?"

"They must have brought it back."

That, pretty much, was the basis of his Crown Court defence. He was acquitted.

A 2am telephone call in the late 60s woke me, my mam and dad and very likely poor Mrs Gell, the manual exchange operator who in those days had, 24/7, to put it through. It was George. His mate Tony Hawkins had skipped bail – or in newspaper parlance was on the run – was keen to hand himself in but, first, to tell me his side of the story. No time like two in the morning, said George.

The Thames van pulled up outside the King Willie five minutes later. Hastily dressed, I clambered in. Where was Hawkins? A head emerged from beneath a well-trodden rug in the back – to some it might have been high drama, to me it recalled nothing more vividly than that bit in *Hancock: The Test Pilot* where Kenneth Williams knocks on the cockpit and says "Hello" in his best Snide voice.

George would have us go to Brusselton Folly, up a back road a mile above the town, where he half-hid the van and Hawkins got the story and some Woodbine fumes off his chest. Confessional over, we discovered that the van was stuck in the mud. Tony and I had to push it from behind while Lord Muck sat serenely at the wheel shouting instructions.

Covered in clarts, we arrived at Bishop Auckland police station about 4am. The young polliss looked casually up from his *Daily Mirror*. "Oh hello, Tony," he said, "we've been expecting you." Brusselton Folly could not have been more appropriately named.

ABOUT 11 o'clock one night in 1972 I was walking home when another Thames van, same shade of blue but sans Dolphin, pulled alongside. A chap in dark glasses wound down the passenger side window and sought directions to the GR Club.

I said I'd be passing it in a couple of miles. The guy budged up closer to the lady driver and offered a lift. It transpired not just that they were that night's cabaret but that they were Peters and Lee – Lennie Peters was blind – who from nowhere had hit No 1 the week previously with *Welcome Home*.

George, who'd booked them months earlier for broken biscuits, paced pregnantly outside the club. They were late, he said. Dianne Lee apologised, pointed out that they'd kept their side of the bargain despite being top of the pops, wondered if there might be a few quid more in it.

TOP OF THE POPS: *Peters and Lee*

58

George pulled a bit of paper from the inside pocket of his leather jacket. "What's it say on there?" he demanded.

"£15, Mr Reynolds," said Dianne.

"Then £15 is what you're getting," said the eponymous GR.

Thus it was that Britain's No 1 played Shildon, and that they probably lost.

INGENIOUSLY, enthusiastically and irrepressibly, George built up a kitchen worktops business, the Willie Worktop logo soon familiar on lorries throughout the land. When part of the business was sold for many millions, he bought Darlington Football Club – at the time close to extinction.

He substantially redeveloped the much-loved old Feethams ground, decided that he wanted something grander, commissioned a 25,000-capacity stadium on the edge of town. Initially it was called the George Reynolds Arena and it cost a fortune.

Upwardly mobile, George seemed particularly proud of the escalator and of the Italian marble fittings in the loos – "they do everything except pull your zip up," he said. When the stadium was almost complete, the Middlesbrough-born and now nationally celebrated artist Mackenzie Thorpe asked me if I could arrange a tour for him. George was happy to oblige.

We'd been there about a minute when George suggested a hurl on the escalator, its walls lined like the London Underground with framed adverts or artwork or whatever. His favourite, familiar at the time above a million mantelpieces, was that print of a black haired and vaguely Hispanic lass showing an inch of cleavage – Tina, she was called, painted by a mysterious chap called J H Lynch who at one time was rumoured to be a nun in New Zealand.

"Now that's what I call art, Mackenzie," said George.

"That's what I call shite, George," said Mackenzie. No matter that the escalator continued to rise, things thereafter went very quickly downwards.

CYNTHIA Payne, former owner of Britain's most celebrated knocking shop, seemed a right little madam – if not quite lying back and thinking of England then certainly bored stiff. It wasn't until I mentioned GR that her attitude changed completely.

"Lovely gentleman, completely misunderstood, we had a great time together," she said – though the time was strictly platonic, of course.

Taking the ceaseless search for a North-East angle to a distant extreme, we'd bumped into Madam Cyn – as the News of the World venally tagged her – in the year 2004 at Llanwrtyd Wells in mid-Wales, as impenetrable as it was unpronounceable.

MISS WHIPLASH:
Payne and suffering

Sharon and I were headed elsewhere – land of her father's – on holiday, Ms Payne was there for the dedication of a memorial to her friend Screaming Lord Sutch, he of the Monster Raving Looney Party, who'd polled 374 votes in the 1983 Darlington by-election, and much enlivened it. It's doubtful if Madam Cyn were a fully paid-up member, more an associate Looney.

It was also the day of the 25th annual Man v Horse race at Llanwrtyd Wells, an event won on each of the 24 previous outings by the hoss but on this occasion by a bloke who'd come fourth in the London Marathon – "smashed the equine hegemony," said the *Observer*. I always did have trouble understanding the *Observer*.

The guy who completed the 22-mile course on a pogo stick, a string of pasties round his neck, was unsurprisingly last. He was definitely one of the Loonies.

Famously convicted of what the charge sheet quaintly called keeping a disorderly house, Ms Payne seemed by then to be living more on her reputation than off her immoral earnings. How might we arouse – is that the word? – the First Lady of Streatham? By raising George, of course.

They'd met on a television show, at once hit it off – hit it off, note. Madame Cyn was invited to George's opulently restored pad at Witton-le-Wear, near Bishop Auckland, where she wondered if he were looking for business.

Business? What the lady had in mind was Madam Cyn's Show Bar, an 'upmarket' establishment in London in which the waitresses would dress as French maids and the male staff as Dixon of Dock Green. The menu would include lots of tarts and (of course) spotted dick.

George made his excuses and left her to look elsewhere. "He initially gave me the impression that he might be keen but nothing came of it. I always thought of him as a bit on the daft side, but he's a very careful businessman," she said.

"He had a poor upbringing, spent all that time in an orphanage and really had quite an unhappy life. He put all that money into Darlington Football Club because he wanted to feel loved, I sussed that out the first time I met him. We all need love in our lives."

She'd also been much taken by George's wife, Susan. "She talks so fast I couldn't take it all in," said the woman best remembered for imaginative use of Luncheon Vouchers. The show bar never went on.

Cynthia Payne died in 2015, aged 82, described in her

Guardian obituary as "an eccentric suburban brothel keeper." GR still tries to flog e-cigs, smoke but not the same fire.

GEORGE had two Achilles heels: one was women – though definitely not Cynthia Payne – the other the apparent need to surround himself with yes men. GR and consultation weren't exactly synonymous, though he'd had one or two partners in crime.

A 25,000-seat stadium for a town of Darlington's size and of the club's potential was just too big. George brooked no argument, paraded at the stadium opening in a convict suit with arrows, milked – and deserved – the supporters' adulation.

He'd also pledged, when the boat came in, to pay off the mortgages of his key and most loyal lieutenants. For reasons not wholly obvious, the promise was extended to me – something which I'd mentioned to Sharon.

One evening – I was out as usual – George rang the house, said that he'd sold part of the business and that he was going to be as good as his word. Sharon said that there was no need, George said a promise was a promise. The ball was biffed back and forth until George, reasonably, said OK then and put the phone down.

It made for an interesting conversation when I got home. He gave us a new front door, though, and some sawdust brickettes for the fire.

It was when he first tried hard to go straight, beginning with that little joinery business in Shildon, that he asked Shildon Football Club if he might pitch to fit out the small clubhouse proposed beneath the pagoda-like stand. The director to whom he spoke told him in strong terms that they wanted nothing to do with criminals. Like the elephant, and equally thick skinned, George never forgot.

Years later, the football club was in desperate financial trouble, close to going under. The late Mike Armitage, secretary for 40 years and my best friend since the first day at

Timothy Hackworth infants, knew that George had vowed to have nothing to do with the club but asked if I could intercede.

I went to see George. Within two minutes – and most of that time occupied in animated conversation with the cuddly toy pig in hunting pink which permanently occupied the chairman's seat in his boardroom – he'd written a cheque for £10,000.

He's now in his mid-80s, still trying to relocate the Midas touch and at the time that the book was being tucked up was bailed on charges which, if proved, could once again curtail his freedom. They'd also quite likely underline what many have long thought, that George is his own worst enemy.

I've always found much more good than bad about the guy – and, bottom line, a great many column inches. I'm pleased to say we're still mates. As ever, you speak as you find.

8 : INTELLIGENT LIFE

DISTRICT councils and their committees met from 6.30pm, requiring the young and keen evening newspaper reporter to head back to the office, write up proceedings immediately afterwards, shove the copy into a bright yellow envelope marked 'Important: News Intelligence' – which greatly over-estimated the contents – and then drop it at Bishop Auckland railway station. If the last train were gone, which often was the case, the news intelligence would await the first the following morning. Usually, if somewhat surprisingly, it had been delivered to our Darlington head office before the early birds flew in.

The only perk of regular late night appearances at Bishop Auckland station was that it usually brought a welcome warm by the porters' room fire. Goodness knows what sort of coal British Rail burned – the old waiting room at Thornaby might have been stoked by Satan himself, so incendiary the blaze – but if the LNER used the same stuff to fire its locomotives there's little wonder they broke all the world speed records.

Most council meetings were at best parochial, at worst stultifying, proceedings enlivened one evening when a Bishop Auckland councillor called George Steadman argued with a political opponent and suggested they meet outside afterwards. In the snicket by the side of the town hall, George pulled a gun.

Admittedly it was only a starting pistol, but the poor chap facing it wasn't to know that and it wasn't the sort of thing you expected at the works and health committee. It made the

BISHOP AUCKLAND STATION:

▲

Steam, smoke and a passing A4 loco

◄ *Waiting room*

A winter's rail
▼

Images courtesy of Gerald Slack

front page the following evening – and again when George stood in the dock.

The daily round was further leavened by what were called off-diary stories – not much sensation, lots of parish pump and flatulence – no event more memorable than when Arnold Hadwin rang in the middle of a cold November night to report that Page Bank, the village to whose bosom old Rubberbones had fled, was being swept away by a great flood.

I almost hadn't answered the phone; I thought it was GR again.

Memory suggests that it was Bonfire Night 1967, the situation so serious that I was allowed to forsake my dad's sit-up-and-beg bike – the usual means of transport in such situations – in favour of a taxi.

The scene was of true devastation, the story huge. Scores of families from those long colliery terraces were homeless, what hadn't been washed away subsequently demolished. Egg Cup Alley was smashed, and would never be rebuilt.

THOUGH I read the report now and shudder at its many shortcomings, it must have said something to Arnold. When Harrystottle decided to retire soon afterwards – word was that Millie considered him better employed making bacon and eggs for the lorry drivers – I was appointed the *Northern Despatch*'s chief reporter in the three-person Bishop Auckland office after just two years in journalism.

I rang the station master's daughter, then at university in Birmingham, singing the familiar ditty about what the working class might do in the event of such elevation.

The vacancy above the money lender's – neither usurer nor ornament, so far as we were concerned –was filled by Colin Randall, another Shildon lad, who despite his early tutelage was to become a highly regarded chief reporter, and Paris bureau chief, of the *Daily Telegraph*.

Colin's dad, Ernie, was a gaffer at a local clothing factory and secretary of Old Shildon Workmen's Club, entitled to suffix his name with CMD. Nothing to do with chocolate, it stood for Club Management Diploma. One evening, again with the station master's daughter, I'd bought drinks in the club lounge and then discovered there were no free seats.

A committee member indicated a notice insisting that none was allowed to stand, though the grammar might not have been so pernickety. I riposted that there were no seats, that women weren't allowed in the bar, that they'd completed the contract by serving me and that we were going nowhere. Ernie was summoned and put me on a fizzer, before the committee the following Sunday morning. Though it resulted in a famous victory, it seemed best not to put it in the paper.

AT the other end of the town was New Shildon Workmen's, promoted at the time as The Palladium of the North but now long demolished. One evening they'd booked Del Shannon, an American singer who not too long before had had several No 1 hits in the UK.

The concert hall was thronged. Jack Stabler, the club chairman, sat at the top of the stairs turning away all without a ticket – and that included Del boy. Shannon insisted that he was the star turn. "They all say that," said Jack, so firmly and so persistently that the American was headed back to the car park when intercepted by Peter Murphy, the club secretary.

"There's 500 people waiting upstairs for you," said Peter. That one did get in the paper.

9 : PARADISE REGAINED

MOST junior journalists in the 1960s fared from a staple menu of courts and council meetings, with the occasional car crash carelessly thrown in. In the Bishop office of the *Despatch*, Category D could be added to the almost-daily diet.

It was a Durham County Council planning policy, drawn up in 1951 and agreed without objection by every one of the authority's Labour councillors, which divided the county's village settlements into four groups, A-to-D.

The Category D tag applied ultimately to 121 villages. It stood, or might as well have stood, for doomed. Or damned. No further development would be permitted and existing property gradually acquired and demolished until the place was literally flattened and wiped from the map.

Among villages thus condemned was Stanley Hill Top, above Crook, a gloriously situated former mining community with a Northern League championship winning football team and, right next to the unique little ground, one of the warmest and most wonderful Methodist chapels in Christendom. The chapel survived until quite recently, the village is reborn.

Also on the list was Waterhouses, in the delightful Deerness Valley west of Durham – now a vibrant community with much new housing – Page Bank, where the great flood did the county council's dirty work instead, New Herrington near Sunderland, and Chopwell.

D-DAYS: *Witton Park in the 1960s*

Chopwell? Not far from the wonderfully named Victoria Garesfield, it's a village near Gateshead, known then as now as Little Moscow partly because of an incident during the 1926 General Strike in which the union jack was torn from the front of the council offices and replaced with the Soviet flag. Still there's a Marx Terrace and a Lenin Terrace. The county council knew how to pick its targets.

At the centre of the Category D campaign, however, was Witton Park, a riverside village three miles west of Bishop Auckland which in 1871 had a population of 4,313, about half of whom toiled in Messrs Bolckow and Vaughan's ironworks – many lodging in the already overcrowded two-up two-down terraces built to accommodate the industrial revolution.

The average, it was reckoned, was seven people per hencree-house. The record was supposed seven family members and 14 lodgers, the beds – day shift, night shift– never cold.

Back then the village had 15 grocers, 14 dressmakers, seven butchers, seven boot and shoe makers – and more than 30 pubs and drinking houses with names like the Puddlers Arms, the Welsh Harp and the Shamrock reflecting the origins of the workforce. The Welsh and Irish didn't get on, especially by chucking-out time.

Later the village became known as Jam Jar City – some say because jam jars were an acceptable admission fee at the Kosy Kinema, others because the Women's Institute preserved hundreds of the things – austerity, if not posterity.

I never did work out why Witton Park became the molten crucible of protest – perhaps because they squealed the loudest – but undoubtedly it did.

By the late 1960s, it was becoming the centre of worldwide media attention, no longer just from the Bishop office of the *Despatch*. The best remembered television documentary was called *The Village That Refused to Die*.

Witton Park grew up close by the banks of the Wear, and in 1820s was the Stockton and Darlington Railway's western railhead – though the eventual station, inexplicably, was called Etherley. Bolckow and Vaughan's ironworks opened in February 1846, workers at the formal ceremony feted with 'noble portions' of beef, bread and ale while gaffers and guests – whither Her Majesty's press? – were treated to 'an excellent collation with the best wines abundantly poured'.

In a speech which today might have been supposed disingenuous, Mr Vaughan said that Witton Park's location had often been commended for its beauty but that he could not help but exclaim that the smoke pouring from the tall chimneys left those beauties much enhanced.

The site upon which the belching, smoking, stinking, suffocating ironworks had been built was known, apparently without irony, as Paradise. Beneath the poison clouds of Mr Vaughan's utopia were long hours, wretched and unhealthy conditions and undoubtedly thirsty work. The men were paid fortnightly and on pay day, it was said, the gutters literally ran with beer. Blood, too, probably. There were several murders.

The ironworks closed after just 36 years, its slums and its workforce left behind. Unemployment rose to 98 per cent.

William Fordyce, the Newcastle publisher, wrote of conditions of "the most primitive rudeness."

None doubted that something needed to be done, or that the housing stock was deplorable. Few wanted to leave community and friends – especially not for new towns like Peterlee and Newton Aycliffe or the burgeoning Woodhouse Close estate in Bishop Auckland. The Reservation, they called it, unreservedly.

When the county council finally came up with its solution, 120 other County Durham villages joined Witton Park in uproar.

By the late 1960s the pace of protest had accelerated, led in Jam Jar City by an improbable trio of musketeers from Bishop Auckland Urban District Council. Allen Yorke was born and bred in the village, felt its pulse and knew its temperature; John Callaghan was a genial Jack the lad with a mischievous laugh and an eye for an angle; Harold Hutchinson, the quiet one of the trio, was to become a Church of England priest. All were media-savvy, especially John Callaghan. We were never short of a few column inches.

There were protests, demonstrations, high level meetings. What officialdom simply couldn't understand, or wouldn't admit, was the paradox that as much as residents deplored what had been allowed to happen to their villages, they didn't want to live anywhere else.

AMONG Witton Park's best known residents was Clarrie Simon, the south Durham coroner's officer and among the most industrious of a band known in the inky trade as penny-a-liners. An old penny was what newspapers then paid for every line of type from a great army of village correspondents; perhaps remembering the adage about counting your pennies, Clarrie did very well out of it. Many still keep his community-centred cuttings.

He was followed by his son David, usually happy to leave Category D to others and to major on the minor, the minutiae of community life. Clarrie would sometimes offer a lift, too, an offer best declined because his dogs – great moulting Airedales – had usually been sitting there first.

Tom Blenkinsopp, a Witton Park lad who was a post-war centre half for Middlesbrough and good enough twice to have represented the Football League, filled a couple of columns, too. Tom's reputation went before him, and snow-balled as it went.

Some called him Mr Bass, and not because of his singing voice, others knew him as Dirty Blenk and not because of his muddy shorts. Particularly he was said to have enjoyed a couple of beers before the match, though he always denied it – just two or three raw eggs for the wind, said Tom, and maybe a couple of sweet sherries with which to wash them down.

A former Green Howard, he'd still walk the three miles into Bishop for a pint in the DLI club – there wasn't a Green Howards club, not in County Durham – but in later life would catch the bus back. He died in 2004, aged 83. They probably blamed the drink.

The late Jackie Foster, an outstanding footballer at Northern League level, was also a proud Witton Parker. It might have been easier for that biblical camel to pass through the eye of a needle than it was to buy the beers in the Rose and Crown, if Jackie were in and liked you.

Others like Ron Tomlinson and Trevor Shaw had been born elsewhere but came to love Witton Park. Raised in West Auckland, two or three miles away, Ron was nine when taught by an uncle how accurately to blow darts from his mouth – "he said I'd thank him one day. He was right." He became known as Rondart, what show business called a speciality act, described in the papers as a modern William Tell. Christina, his wife, was Colombian, loved the old place equally. "They call me bonny lass," she said.

Trevor Shaw was a comedian, perhaps best described as

droll, a man who saved many a sportsmen's evening when the highly-paid main speaker had perished terribly. Though he came from Cockfield, he adopted the stage name Seth Shildon. Goodness knows why.

Trevor only once ran a joke past me to check if it were suitable – it concerned dear old George Reynolds in his time as Darlington FC's chairman and when former Liverpool player David Hodgson was manager. The gag had George keen to play an untried 16-year-old, Hodgson insisting he was too raw and inexperienced.

"Just leave that to me," said George and, half an hour before kick-off, brought in a hypnotist who told the lad that he had the speed of Thierry Henry, the balance of Ronaldo, the heading ability of Alan Shearer and the finishing of Gary Lineker.

It worked. After half an hour he'd scored a hat-trick but then suddenly left the field and was confronted by a manager anxious to know what on earth he was doing. "You don't think I'm going to play with those useless buggers," he said.

If Ron and Trevor were minor celebrities, another occasional visitor was perhaps in a bigger league. On a couple of occasions, the royal train had stopped overnight in what had been the ironworks sidings. Village historian Dale Daniel still has a photograph of the Queen Mother waving cheerfully from the carriage window – and if Witton Park were good enough for her...

CATEGORY D wasn't formally dropped until 1977, though Chopwell beat them to it when local government reorganisation in 1974 transferred the village to the Borough of Gateshead, who had a bit more sense. By then, however, it was obvious that Durham was bowing beneath the condemnation and the pressure.

In the year 2000 I joined a Memorial Hall reunion in Witton Park attended by exiles from around the world and co-organised by Phil Atkinson, a Witton Park native who was something very important in the government of British Colombia.

Abundant reminiscence included memories of long conversations across the three-holers at the bottom of the yard and of Tommy Judd, the hard-as-the-hobs village polliss in the 50s and 60s. On one occasion, it was said, a belligerent newcomer had sought out Tommy, stuck his face about two inches from the bobby's and announced: "I'm so-and-so."

Tom rose to his substantial black-booted feet, issued what might be termed a judicial review – probably around the left ear: "and I'm PC Judd," he said, "and divvent thoo ever forget it."

Dale Daniel recalled post-war days when Witton Park folk felt like rabbits in a cornfield. "We were chased from one house to another until finally there was nowhere left to go and we were taken off to Bishop Auckland," he said. In later years the village website compared it to the holocaust.

The village is now much changed – renewed, some might say. The last pub has gone, the last shop went decades ago, but there's a newish Methodist church, a Roman Catholic school and a much used and modernised Memorial Hall.

When in 2019 a vital bridge connecting the village to the west was closed for safety reasons, hundreds attended public meetings – and Durham County Council, pleading poverty, suddenly found £2.5m for repairs. Rob Yorke, a top class local Labour councillor of a wholly different stamp, had a lot to do with that.

When St Paul's parish church was threatened with closure – it still is – villagers sought to explore some sort of community ownership. Many might not live in Witton Park any longer, but they still wanted to come back to be married there – and to be buried in home soil.

The site of the Bolckow and Vaughan ironworks is now a greatly attractive county council nature reserve. Paradise has been regained, and it's lovely.

10 : HONOURABLE MENTIONS

S O Bishop burgeoned, familiarly and formatively. They even gave me a by-lined opinion column called *The Words of Amos* – the first four words of the eponymous Old Testament book. Cyril Fawcett, the seasoned chief sub-editor, preferred to call it *The Words That Shame Us* and may only have been half-joking. Maturity maundered.

Those three-and-a-half years had gone OK for all that, though we could never beat the *Gazette* to the story of pit closures – there were lots – on the patch. Charles Verdun Browne, the *Gazette*'s urbane old chief reporter in Bishop, had a mole down a mine, or more likely in the Coal Board's offices in Spennymoor.

Mostly it happened in Harrystottle's time, and always on a Thursday – convenient because it was both pay day and market day, all-day opening in the Cumberland Arms next-door-but-one to the money lender's. Charlie would play poor Harry dreadfully, tell him that there might be something of interest in that evening's *Gazette*, and when Harry was at his most mendicant, would accept another pint in exchange for the barest details to make the *Despatch*'s stop press column.

Thus it was that, on several Thursdays each year, news of the loss of another 250 jobs, another coal house door slamming, would appear between the results of the 2.30 and the three o'clock at Redcar.

Before the pits (and the pitmen) were utterly exhausted, it seemed a good idea to go down one. Some time in the mid-70s, County Durham's adopted minesweeper had moored at

SINKING FEELING: *Horden Colliery*

Seaham, among the visits laid on for the crew a trip down Horden colliery, a deep mine which stretched several miles back beneath the sea. Knee pads and helmet in place, I joined them in the cage.

Some of the homecoming matelots had been out on the town the night before and were awfully unwell by the time they even reached the bottom of the shaft. Good thing they weren't submariners.

IN February 1969, no longer given the Elba, Arnold had created a free-roving reporting job for me in Darlington. The exile was over. Before leaving Bishop Auckland, however, it's compulsory to tell the story of the Honourable Diana.

Diana was a trainee reporter on the *Auckland Chronicle*. Her father, Sir So-and-so, had been High Sheriff of Some-where-or-other, lived in a gated manor house with tennis court and. swimming pool In 1970, after I'd begun writing the *John North* column for the *Echo*, we started walking out – or, strictly to be truthful, going places in her 1966, D reg-Morris Minor.

The folks back home may perhaps have been intrigued,

more likely horrified. After I'd made two or three weekend visits to the family pile, wishing I'd learned more about table manners, it was deemed necessary that Diana's parents should pay a Sunday afternoon call upon mine.

We didn't have a manor house, of course, just an end-of-terrace place in Shildon, rented for thirty bob a week from old Joe Robinson. We didn't have a swimming pool or a tennis court, just a three-up two-down with me dad's old bike in the kitchen and a netty at the bottom of the yard.

Sir So-and-so and his Lady wife drew up outside No 30 Albert Street, and outside Nos 28 and 32, in their Daimler.

In those days if there were folk for their Sunday teas, County Durham families would open a tin of John West tuna and, in a good week, a can of pears in syrup. Me dad had gone further: he'd whitewashed the netty, put a little kelly lamp beneath the pipes to stop them freezing, even placed a toilet roll on the nail from which squares of the *News of the World* would more customarily hang.

All was going as well as might be expected until the dread moment that Sir So-and-so enquired the whereabouts of the lavatory. My dad, a wonderful man, directed him down the yard, past the old mangle. The guest ended up in the coal house, relocated, returned. My dad asked how it had been.

"Well, all right," said Sir So-and-so, "but it all seemed rather primitive. There wasn't even a lock upon the door."

My dad looked surprised. "We've lived here 30 years," he said. "and no one's pinched a bucket of shite yet."

When that story's told to the Women's Institutes, their almost inevitable response is to ask what happened next. The great romance lasted another day-and-a-half, that's what happened next. Parental guidance was strongly suspected.

11 : IFS AND BUTTS

THE new job in Darlington was pretty much what I made of it. Yet again I got lucky. Ted Fletcher, the town's left-wing Labour MP, had an agent called Jim Smith who liked a pint – Watney's Red Barrel back then – in the Imperial, a town centre hotel from which the youthful Jimi Hendrix had once had his guitar stolen. After a couple of looseners, Jim proved adept at bean spilling.

Soon afterwards he became northern agent for the newly formed Desmond Donnelly's Democrats, one of those short-lived breakaway groups, but continued to be a valued inform-ant. Ted was surprisingly helpful, too, so it seemed a bit un-grateful that – in a *John North* limerick competition during one of the 1974 general elections – the winner featured him. To the tune of Brahms' *Lullaby* it began:

> Go to sleep little one
> Or Fletcher will get ya....

Occasionally I'd wangle a trip to the House of Commons, too, one such dreary occasion enlivened by a coffee with Newcastle East MP Mike Thomas.

Mike liked to spin stories, among his favourites the tale of the North-East MP – let's just say of the old school – who, until the day it was announced that the biggest pit in his con-stituency was to close, had gone two years without making his maiden speech.

Urged into action, he creaked to his feet. "This here pit closure," he said in broad Geordie, "is ganna mean the crippilisation of my constituency."

It rather puzzled the clerk for *Hansard*, the parliamentary record, who the following morning knocked timidly on the member's office door and asked if he'd really said crippilisation.

The MP was a kindly old soul. "If thoo dissent understand lang words," he said, "just put it in invertebrated commas."

THE job lasted about six months. In September 1969 I was appointed chief reporter in the *Northern Echo*'s four-person office in York and the paper at once gained another sale as a result. My mam and dad, lifelong *Daily Mail* readers, got the *Echo* through the door instead.

Harry Evans had by that time left the *Echo* to pursue a stellar career nationally and beyond. He'd been replaced by Don Evans – no relation and not much similarity, either – who'd been the paper's industrial editor.

Don was lovely, loyal and probably long suffering, but his style was much more hands-off. Departmental heads were left pretty much to run their own shows and sales usually remained above 120,000, often the highest among English regional mornings. Like many more of us, Don also enjoyed a drink. In the early 1980s he was transferred to the parent

GOOD EVANS:
Sir Harry Evans and his successor, Don Evans

group's London office, just off Fleet Street, from which he retired fairly soon afterwards. The going-away party was in the Cheshire Cheese, an ancient pub legendary among journalists. He'd probably had a few too many when, at 8pm, one of the more patrician London office editors told me to get him home – deaf to pleas that I was down on the train from Darlington and that home for Don was in High Wycombe.

Happily the conversation had been overheard by Arthur Wilson, one of the London photographers, a West Ham supporter and a great guy. Together we got Don down the stairs and out into Fleet Street, where Arthur hailed a taxi with instructions not just to get his passenger to Marylebone but to pour him onto the nine o'clock train.

Don made it, or rather we never heard that he hadn't. I also never heard if Arthur had been reimbursed.

BACK in York there'd been another murder, only the second in my four years' inky trading. All three *Echo* reporters – the fourth staff member was Paul Hines, an ever-patient photographer – were together in the pub when the 10pm 'calls', the sort of thing that we'd done at breakfast time on the *Despatch*. turned up a police report that there'd been a suspicious death at 15 Rosemary Place, near Walmgate Bar in the city.

The Yorkshire edition was then the first of five or six, away at about 10 30pm. For the first and only time in all these years I rang head office and asked them to hold the front page – and no matter that the only suspicious element might have been that the poor chap had been caught out by the television detector van. Unsteady as you go, the three of us headed to Rosemary Place by taxi.

It was murder, as we'd guessed, the case unsolved for a week or so when at the routine police press conference I asked the head of North Yorkshire CID – perhaps having watched too much *No Hiding Place* – if there were any plans to call in Scotland Yard.

Yes, he said, there were. It was the last occasion on which

a provincial force asked the Yard to help with a non-terrorist murder and it worked. A few days later they had their man.

York's a lovely city, of course, its principal problem that it's not in County Durham. For the *Echo* it was a fringe area and a difficult one – the *Yorkshire Evening Press*, in whose city centre offices we had a room, sold to almost every home in the city and thereabouts and because of business sales had a saturation rate of more than 100 per cent.

Things weren't helped because the *Echo*, shortly before my arrival, had been banned from all city council commit- tee meetings – something to do with allegedly breaking an embargo – and because Chris Brayne, the *YEP*'s otherwise affable news editor, had similarly banned me from their news room over unfounded allegations of what these days might be termed industrial espionage. As if...

The patch extended for many a mile in all directions. My flat, not 200 yards from the Minster, was above a pub on one side and a fish and chip shop on the other, with – should the need ever arise – an Army and Navy store directly below. Wasn't it Charles Forte who talked of location, location, lo- cation? Usually helped by Paul Hines, who happily enjoyed driving, I got away with it for eight months until the job of writing the *John North* column became vacant back at head office.

At the end of April 1970 it was a thrill permanently to head back north across the Tees – but a final story before we leave the city.

Some time in the Spring of 1970 a little lad of two or three went missing from his York home, just wandered off, a huge police search ensuing. Eventually he was found hiding in a water butt, or some such, tearfully explaining that he was frightened of policemen.

The story made the nationals but one of the press agencies – a brilliantly run operation – had an idea for a follow-up. It was Easter time: they bought a huge chocolate egg and per-

HOT METAL WORKERS:
The 1970s Despatch newsroom

suaded the polliss to give it to the little lost soul, as if it were from them. The poor bairn wailed ever more loudly.

There's a point, however, when a child's screams can seem in a photograph to be laughter. That was the picture which in turn appeared in all the nationals, with the angle that he now loved the police. Almost five years into the job it was a worthwhile lesson: as in the case of the Queen Mother's ribbon, maybe you shouldn't believe quite everything you read in the papers.

12 : NORTH HOME SERVICE

THERE never was a John North, or at least not on the
Echo's leader page where a column under that by-line
had been the principal feature for 20 years or so. Perhaps the
best known incumbent had been Stanley Hurwitz, balding
and bearded but pretty much before my time. He left, memory suggests, after an elderly aunt bequeathed him a fortune.
Now it was my inheritance, and I relished it.

The danger with 'diary' columns was that they could become a sort of newsroom waste bin, a thinly-disguised receptacle for stuff which couldn't decently be accommodated
elsewhere, a journalistic doss house. I wanted my column
to be more distinctive and perhaps more idiosyncratic, too.
With luck there might even be a few half-decent exclusives.

A newspaper's primary role was traditionally and properly to inform, sometimes even to enrage. It seemed to me– still
does – that it should also entertain. The adage that news was
what people didn't want in the paper and that all the rest was
advertising seemed to me already to be out of date.

Though its author was based in Darlington, the column
embraced the North-East by whatever geographical deline-
ation, appearing Monday to Friday. Usually it was best to
work independently of others in the office – the waste bin
syndrome again – so satisfactorily filling the thing became
a bit like the legend of Sisyphus, the Greek king condemned
forever to roll a boulder up a mountain after falling foul of
the gods. Goodness knows what he'd done, probably complained about string in the cabbage. A few feet from the

summit the boulder, interminably and inevitably, would roll down again.

A more prosaic interpretation of tilting at a daily column was the recurring dream that there'd be a big white emptiness, just seven words, where the next morning's offering should have been. "He couldn't think of anything to write," they would say.

UPHILL STRUGGLE:
Sisyphus at work

It was new and it was challenging, as these days folk like to say, though some things remained the same. One of them was that the Darlington head office hadn't enough chairs, either, and that the plastic legs of those there were had long since buckled beneath the weight of too many liquid lunches.

At one point the publicity-seeking manager of a local Odeon cinema donated one of those double seats which used to smuggle snugglers into the back row. Kiss and tell, it was useless. We essayed an inky trade version of musical chairs, sometimes fiercely competitive.

Work was greatly convivial, nonetheless. We were almost all young, very often daft and I think most of us knew that we were very lucky to be doing what we were. Five years into journalism, there were also plenty of lessons still to be learned, among them to avoid making reckless and oft-unsustainable claims in print.

The J N column (as it became known) once featured the 86-year-old parish gravedigger in a Wensleydale village – Constable Burton, I think – supposing him to be Britain's oldest. I'd not been in the office 20 minutes before a call came from the sexton in the very next village, Patrick Brompton. He was 87.

Patrick Brompton may never have had a resident of that

name, incidentally, but Constable Burton in the 1980s really was covered by a rural police officer called PC Burton.

On one occasion, possibly after a couple of lunchtime liveners in the Red Lion, I'd been engaged in a newsroom fun fight – I think it was a fun fight – with an equally well-built reporter called Steve Harris and inadvertently knocked him into the glass partition which helped form a corridor.

Don Evans heard the shattering glass from his office down the way and at once called through to his secretary. "Go and see what Mike Amos has done now," he said.

One of Steve's jobs was to provide short summaries of every film in the region's cinemas – still quite a lot back then – for the weekend leisure supplement. One of the films was called *Do You Want To Remain a Virgin For Ever?* Steve's summary read "If so, apply E Heath, 10 Downing Street, London WC1."

He was fired, appealed, relocated to Bradford but was never again required to write pithy summaries of forthcoming films, and especially not that one.

Harry Coen, another much-liked colleague in the 1970s, was both proudly gay and an active drug user. The former could no longer get him into bother with the law but the latter did. Harry got 12 months, after which the firm, much to its credit, took him back. Mind, what was dabbling in a bit of pot compared to unkind remarks about Ted Heath?

The social highlight of the 70s may have been the Ales in the Dales outings, a bus-load of journos from all the company's Darlington titles headed into the wilds for a day out most kindly described as intoxicating. Almost always it was a Saturday, always it was men only.

Jon Smith, who so enthusiastically and expertly has edited *Unconsidered Trifles*, has a picture somewhere – I'm sure he'll find it – of one of those wanton wayzgooses looking greatly hirsute and in no need of the hair of the dog.

[See overleaf – Ed.]

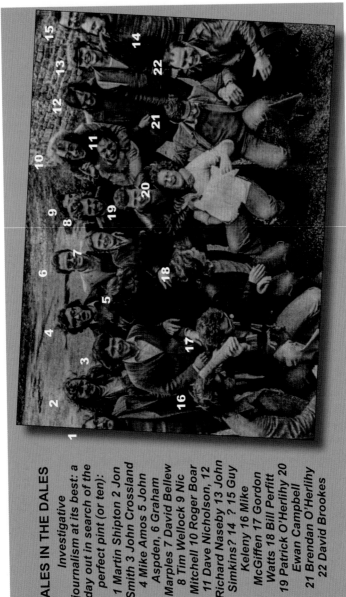

ALES IN THE DALES

Investigative journalism at its best: a day out in search of the perfect pint (or ten):

1 Martin Shipton 2 Jon Smith 3 John Crossland 4 Mike Amos 5 John Aspden, 6 Graham Marples 7 David Bellew 8 Tim Wellock 9 Nic Mitchell 10 Roger Boar 11 Dave Nicholson, 12 Richard Naseby 13 John Simkins? 14 ? 15 Guy Keleny 16 Mike McGiffen 17 Gordon Watts 18 Bill Perfitt 19 Patrick O'Herlihy 20 Ewan Campbell 21 Brendan O'Herlihy 22 David Brookes

Writing *John North* proved very enjoyable for all sorts of other reasons, though it's fair to say that some columns were better than others and some were borne of desperation. Conducting a telephone interview with Sooty, a glove puppet appearing at York Theatre Royal, may not have been my finest hour. Matthew Corbett had a hand in that, too.

Successive features editors became wearily accustomed to demands for yet more elbow room. Readers increasingly contributed, though not nearly so greatly as when email proved the instant enabler, and on one occasion it proved costly.

Someone forwarded a letter that had appeared in one of the left-wing magazines – *Black Dwarf* or *Red Mole* or some such – then peddled on the High Row in Darlington, and doubtless elsewhere. Of all things, it concerned the *Northern Echo* Nig-Nog Circle, a children's club formed before the war in a straightforward attempt to persuade more youngsters to read the paper. The Nig Nogs, said the letter, was a typical attempt by the capitalist press to ensnare the innocent minds of the young.

It had been written by a teenager in Durham, a young man subsequently and greatly foolishly described in the *John North* column as a juvenile subversive. His parents sued on his behalf and, inevitably, won. The gaffers were very good about it, but I didn't need telling that it had better not happen again. Touch wood, it never did.

13 : SOD'S LORE

CUSTODY of the column also offered the opportunity to meet celebrities at all levels, lists A to Z. They included George Romaine and Gordon Peters, both Shildon lads.

George had been a wagon works electrician before becoming the featured male singer on the *One O'Clock Show*, a half-hour variety spot almost impossibly broadcast live five days a week by the fledgling Tyne Tees Television. A delightful man and a good friend, George wore a toupee which, behind the scenes, he'd trail around the studios on a dog lead. He made records, appeared in cabaret, loved cricket, stayed in Shildon but never went back to the wagon works.

Born Gordon Peter Wilkinson in Highland Gardens, Gordon Peters was a comedian, a bit like Harry Worth it seemed to me though others saw something of Tony Hancock in him. He may also have been the country's unluckiest comic. In 1968, he'd been chosen to play the chief fire officer in the pilot episode of *Dad's Army* – a scene which writers David Croft and Jimmy Perry thought "hilarious." When the episode was played back, however, it over-ran by seven minutes. While almost everyone else went on to become much-loved household names, the fire chief's scene, without panic, was excised.

In the 1970s the BBC gave him his own six-week situation comedy run, the only problem that it was directly up against *Coronation Street*. That experiment wasn't repeated, either. Last time I saw him on television, he had a bit part fixing Mainwaring's door at the Walmington-on-Sea branch of the Swallow Bank; last time I saw him in person was in a Flanders and Swann tribute show at Darlington Arts Centre when he was greeted by a (very) old flame from the back row of the Essoldo. "Hello, treacle chops," she said, perhaps reprising a term of endearment from a more innocent age. Gordon was 94 in 2020, but appeared no longer to be treading the boards.

Then there was Macdonald Hobley, one of BBC Television's first on-screen announcers, who around 1947 had been given the job of introducing the first-ever party political broadcast. The speaker was to be Sir Stafford Cripps, the home secretary.

Hobley, black-tied and nervous, somehow got it wrong. "Ladies and gentlemen, it gives me great pleasure to introduce Sir Stifford Crapps."

Mostly, though, it was the common man – and woman – who made by far the most interesting interviewee. The celebrities, barely stumbling through the motions, had – then as now – done it all too many times before.The best example was the curmudgeonly Fred Emney, a monocled and overweight old comedian who, inexplicably, had pitched up at the Forum Theatre in Billingham.

Whatever the question, his answer was monosyllabic. Usually it was "Yes" or "No," occasionally "That's a damn fool thing to ask."

Exasperated, I finally asked what he'd write about himself if in my situation. He'd not heard that one before. "I'd write," he said, "that Fred Emney was a big, fat, bad tempered overpowering old sod."

The following morning's column said exactly that. The phone at home rang at 7 30am. "Emney here," said the old growler. "Finest interview with me I've ever read." It seemed wise, however, not to repeat the experiment.

The actor David Kossoff, himself in pantomime at Billingham Forum – goodness knows why – proved altogether more agreeable. How would he be spending Christmas, I wondered? "Like all Jews, I love Christmas," said Kossoff. It was many years before I realised that, far from exasperated teasing, he meant every word.

DARLINGTON had no greater local celebrity than Lady Starmer, daughter of a former Dean of Norwich and widow of Sir Charles Starmer, a former Echo owner, newspaper magnate and MP.

Lady Starmer was much loved and lovely. Somewhere near the opposite end of the town's popularity scale was George Pamler, leader of the local Hell's Angels chapter who'd legally changed his name to Jungle. Jungle was as scruffy as Lady Starmer was elegant, as anarchic as she was establishment. Jungle rode a large, oily and very noisy motor bike with sit-up-and-beg handlebars; Lady Starmer drove a Vanden Plas, and drove it, shall we say, idiosyncratically.

One day, quite forcefully, they met.

Though journalism's lawyers suggest that the preferred phrase in such circumstances should be that two vehicles "were in collision", thus seen not to be apportioning blame, there seemed little doubt that Lady Starmer had knocked Jungle flying from his chariot of ire.

FIRST LADY:
Lady Starmer

As he lay in the middle of a road near the town centre, she hovered over him solicitously. It was the start of an extraordinary friendship.

Jungle, not seriously hurt, was subsequently invited to tea at Lady Starmer's splendid home in the west end of town. He didn't wear his glad rags, the ordinary rags sufficed. They got on famously, nonetheless, so well that he became a regular guest, though one afternoon the visit coincided with one from her GP. "Ah, doctor," said Lady Starmer, "I don't think you've met my friend Mr Jungle."

I heard of the story some time later, visited Jungle's chapter house – is that what they called it? – rang Lady Starmer. Gracious as always, she confirmed the whole thing but gently asked that nothing be printed until after her death. How could anyone resist Lady Starmer?

She died in 1979 and was widely mourned, not least by me and by Jungle. The story appeared next day.

THE pseudonymous journalist whom most simply called 'John North' also became a minor, a very minor, celebrity himself. There were WI talks to give, first pints to pull, carnival queens to judge, fetes worse than death. I even got to do the old school speech day and to open the church garden party back home in Shildon.

The last pair fulfilled two out of three lifetime ambitions. The third was to write a story from the hamlet of Brotherlee, in Weardale, which legitimately might be headlined "Brotherlee love".

Despite all manner of public pleading, for golden weddings or fraternal affiliations, the third wish remained unsatisfied. I never did have very lofty ambitions, though it might never have been supposed that Alf Richardson, a former Hartlepool United footballer who lived in Coxhoe, would race a greyhound called Mike Amos. Predictably, it was useless.

John Pritchard, when Bishop of Jarrow, had a cat called Amos, though he pleaded that the name's origins were biblical. Insurance entrepreneur Brooks Mileson, of whom more later, named his new-born ostrich Amos – head in the sand, that was definitely after me –while Ward Allen, a ventriloquist, had a brazzened fond blackbird called Amos. Ward was from Littletown, an aptly-named place east of Durham which at the last count had just 54 houses but had still, happily, resurrected its cricket club.

Amos got into trouble, alas, after an appearance at the mayor's ball at Southport Floral Hall following which he was accused of homophobia, racism, sexism and anti-Semitism all in one go. I was obliged to deny paternity.

Birds of a different feather, the column also had a parrot story. Every old school journalist has a parrot story. This one lived in the Black Horse, a pub in Barnard Castle, and was given to advising customers as they entered that it would be a good idea if they left again. The parrot didn't quite put it so politely, of course. I don't think it was called Amos.

The column also organised both Over 60s running and Over 60s singing competitions – Over 60 seemed almost impossibly old back then – the former under the well-drilled auspices of the Black and Decker factory in Spennymoor and the latter held at Evenwood Workmen's Club, judged by Denis Weatherley among others and on one occasion won by a frail gentleman representing the King William in Shildon and singing The Holy City – you know, Jerusalem.

The concert hall was thronged like it was New Year's Eve; I swear there wasn't a dry eye in the house.

FOR someone hopelessly non-musical, thrown out of St John's church choir after one unenchanted evensong, I love all kinds of music – though nothing more than Simon and Garfunkel, later just Paul Simon, and Peter, Paul and Mary. Suffice that the late Mary Travers, a long-haired and long-legged blonde, had much for which to answer – and that I still wonder what Puff the Magic Dragon was all about.

Back in 1973 I was even on a record. Part of a campaign to save Hartlepool United Football Club – there've been quite a few of those – the players sang *Never Say Die*, backed (honest) with *Who Put Sugar in My Tea*. Arthur Pickering, who for many years covered the club as Sentinel for the *Hartle-*

pool Mail, joined me at the recording in Newcastle. What lyrics, what larks!

> *It's just because we're winning*
> *Or so the folks all say*
> *That they put sugar in my tea*
> *Because we won 2-0 away.*

Amazingly it got quite a lot of radio time, chiefly on *Children's Favourites* – perhaps renamed *Junior Choice* by then – when presented by Ed Stewart. It could only be assumed that the producer was a closet cloth-eared monkey hanger.

IN 1974 I'd been invited to open the carnival at Mickleton, in Teesdale, introduced by a chairman who vowed that they were delighted to welcome Mike Amos but admitted that I wasn't the first choice. The first choice, he said, was Mike Neville – for around 40 years a highly popular regional news anchorman for both BBC and Tyne Tees Telly – but Mike Neville was £50 and Mike Amos was nowt.

It made a piece for the following Monday's column – the poor man's Mike Neville, I said. Mike, a natural showman, rang about 10am to invite me to co-present that night's programme. The problem wasn't the stammer – have I mentioned the stammer? – it was the script, given me about 15 minutes before we were due to go on air and typed on jaundice-yellow paper.

Remember the bit about being colour blind? They'd to type it all again. Black on white and about 100 words a minute.

Long before television broadcast 24 hours, Tyne Tees ended the day's programmes with the epilogue, usually about 10 45pm. Peter Ridley, an assistant editor at the Echo, had been asked to interview a series of worthies – more of the God squad later – and asked if I'd record a five-minute slot with him.

It wasn't usually peak viewing. Tyne Tees put the average

audience at around 20,000, of whom half had probably fallen asleep in the chair and would be awoken by that high-pitched whine at the end of the day's broadcasting and the other half had taken the dog for a last walk around the block and forgotten to turn off the television. Memory suggests that my contribution was insufferably pious.

On the night that it was due to be shown, me and me mam still wide awake in Shildon, a continuity announcer popped up to report that the epilogue would be delayed because of some stellar happenings in space. Then it was further delayed and then again, finally cresting the airwaves at 3.45am.

Tyne Tees put the audience at two, me and me mam. It remains the lowest in television history.

AS with Mickleton carnival, no fee was asked for talks – the pay-off, it was always hoped, a paragraph for the insatiable column, the ever-open maw. A crescent-shaped notebook lived permanently in the back pocket, flying by the seat of my pants.

Rodney Wildsmith, the photographer on many of those

POOR DO: *With Mike Neville, circa 1974*

OTHER WORLDLY:
With Belinda Green and Rodney Wildsmith

John North jaunts, still keeps the picture above of me (and him) with Belinda Green, an Australian who in 1972 had been crowned Miss World.

The notebook's temporarily been transferred to the jacket pocket. "Is that what's called dressing to impress?" Rod wonders.

BROMPTON, a village near Northallerton, had a beck running through the village green. Locals had been getting cross, said the Women's Institute ladies, because Mr Edgar Hoare's geese had been doing whatever it is that geese do naturally and doing it in great abundance.

Talk completed, tea drunk, raffle drawn and competition judged, I was invited outside to view Edgar's answer to the problem. Each of the geese was wearing a disposable nappy. That went into the notebook, too.

Next morning a photographer went down to record the glorious scene. Giggle gaggle, the story and pictures went all over the world.

14 : SPEAKERS YOU FIND

THOSE talks continued for 50 years, the last at Howden-le-Wear Local History Society – it seemed wholly appropriate – in February 2020.

I'd addressed every kind of sports club, every voluntary organisation desperate for someone to fill an hour of their time, priests, people and even a couple of sermons. At Mowden Park rugby club in Darlington I was pelted with bread buns, saved post-prandially for that purpose – local tradition, apparently – but that was friendly fire compared to the annual dinner at cross-town rivals Darlington RFC.

The club had earlier catered for a lunch, the kitchen hopelessly unable to cope with both. Dinner was served about 10.30pm, the poor speaker rising to his feet shortly before midnight. Suffice that there was an attention deficit. It was the only time in my hind legs history that, prematurely, I've sat down and shut up.

The Crook Town Twinning Association (no less) may have had the best idea, inviting me to speak and then, inexplicably, forgetting to tell me that the venue had been changed. Perhaps they'd already heard the only joke I knew, the one about Fred Astaire and Ginger Rogers preparing for a posh dinner party.

Fred, inevitably, is first to be dressed. Ginger asks him to go downstairs and check on the food. The starters are fine, the meat and three veg are coming along nicely so Fred opens the oven door to check on the souffle. The resultant explosion brings Ginger tappy-lappy down the stairs, anxious to ascertain that her old dancing partner's all right.

Fred's picking bits of souffle from his hair and from his clothes. "Oh, I'm all right, Ginger, darling," he says. "It's just pudding on my top hat, pudding on my white tie, pudding on my tails."

It's no better for hearing at first hand. So far as the Crook Town Twinning committee was concerned, I went to the pub instead.

MERRY DANCE:
Ginger and Fred

I've also at least twice addressed the annual dinner of the Coundon and District Society for the Prevention and Prosecution of Felons, one of just two such bodies to have survived from lawless Victorian times. To invite Mike Amos once may indeed be supposed felonious – twice is positively criminal – though I was delighted when Bob McManners, the chairman and a local GP, gave me a lapel badge with the title Keeper of the Queen's Apostrophe.

Recompense has never been sought; very occasionally it would be received. Sometimes it might be a carrier bag which clinked – always welcome – perhaps a few local pork pies, no less gratefully received. Only once was there a toe in the financial big league – second division, anyway –and it was a disaster.

A group of Round Tables in south Durham had invited me to address their annual knees-up together. They offered £250, insisted upon it, accepted that I could give it to charity. Between cup and lip, booking and dinner, I'd also been shortlisted for a national sports writing award. The lavish lunch was in London,the dinner suit left hanging behind the door of my little bolt hole in Darlington.

I won. With my mate Mike Armitage we had a couple at the lunch, a couple more by way of celebration in Grays Inn Road and then joined the 4pm train, temporarily if rather unsteadily on the wagon and confident of sobriety by the time we crossed the Tees. At Alexandra Palace, about a mile out of Kings Cross, the train conked out and stood there for two hours – what was there to do but have another drink? We finally reached Darlington at 8.30, quick change and a taxi to be a rather shoogly square peg at the Round Table.

Sober, I'm OK; inebriated otherwise. Vainly I pleaded with them to keep their £250, until an improbable deal arose. The custom, apparently, was that the outgoing chairman should be feted – fated perhaps – by a scantily clad kissogram. The lady proved greatly enthusiastic and nor was the chairman obviously reluctant. With what little mental acuity remained, feet no longer beneath the Table, I pulled out a small camera.

The guys pleaded for the film. I refused, finally yielding on condition that they tore up their £250 cheque. Honours, dishonourably, were even.

AMONG the more surprising invitations was that in March 2013 to propose the toast to fox hunting at the Cleveland Hunt Club's posh, gentlemen only, red-coated, five-course and very traditional annual dinner. Presumably they'd confused me with someone else.

I had no great feelings about hunting, save that some of the antis had more against those who hunted – and what they were perceived to represent – than the welfare of the wretched Reynard.

Perhaps they remembered my attendance at the Countryside March in London, of which more in a later chapter, perhaps recalled my story of Major John Parry, sent in 1943 to command the Reeth Battle School high up in Swaledale and accepting on condition that his foot beagle pack could join him. The hounds, all 16 of them, travelled from Kent to

Kings Cross in the back of a London taxi and thence on the eight o'clock to Darlington.

Reckoned the world's oldest, the hunt club had been formed in 1722. Incoming members were required to lay their right hand on a hunting horn and to declare themselves "no enemy of cocking, smocking, fox hunting and harriers" and that they would endeavour to discover all poachers.

Smocking was smuggling, a staple industry around the Saltburn area. Clergymen were excused that bit of the oath but pursued the rest as vigorously as might a hound a dog fox with its tail up.

Histories told of a "merry pack", though whether a reference to hunters or hunted is uncertain, and of numerous annual dinner rules, not least concerning the consumption of copious amounts of alcohol. For the serious offence of "kissing or otherwise disturbing" those – presumably female – who waited upon them, however, members would be fined sixpence. From 1775, the words of The Hurworth Fox Chase had been recited at the start of every dinner:

> *Attend jolly sportsmen, I'll sing you a song*
> *Which cannot fail pleasing the old and the young,*
> *I'll sing of a famous old fox and his wiles*
> *And lead you a dance of at least 50 miles.*

They proved an affable and a boisterous bunch, doubtless aware of Jorrocks's observation that hunting was the sport of kings – "the image of war without the guilt, and only 25 per cent of the danger" – and none, so far as might reasonably be ascertained, at risk of being fined sixpence.

With an eye on the Hurworth Fox Chase, it seemed apt to end in similar vein, the eight-verse peroration beginning:

> *Give heed jolly sportsmen, I'll tell of a mystery –*
> *It's quite the most odd in 300 years' history,*
> *You've had peers of the realm, the rich and the famous*
> *So how come tonight you've copped for Mike Amos?*

In half a century of talks, that probably spoke for them all.

15 : IDLE WORKMEN'S

GONE are the days when an Over 60s singing competition might overflow Evenwood Workmen's Club, or queues form an hour before six o'clock opening to get a seat on New Year's Eve, or a place on a club committee represent not just a couple of beer tokens but a badge of honour as well. The clubs have collapsed like a pack of cards, trumped by changing times.

Once almost every North-East community had its own workmen's, the smallest in England said to have been in Mickleton, the village of the two-coppers carnival, where Sharon beat me at dominoes on our honeymoon. We don't talk about that; I don't. anyway.

Probably not much bigger, the club at Oakenshaw, a former mining village a couple of miles above Willington in County Durham, was run by the wonderfully named Henry Tudor, by day a senior lecturer at Durham University. Like Mickleton, like many more, it's long gone – though it might digressively be added that there really is an Idle Workmen's Club, near Bradford, and that it's still said to be putting in a shift. I've just never found it open.

Perhaps the most famous, and most feared, was Farringdon Club in Sunderland, where the audience might most kindly be deemed critical. Completing one spot was reckoned unusual, a veritable act of courage; surviving both spots was little less then heroic.

The clubs' greatest champion was fellow journalist Jack Amos – no relation, though we often cracked on that we were – a smashing chap who'd started on the *Consett Guardian*, became industrial correspondent of the *Evening Chronicle* in Newcastle and who for the *Sunday Sun*, the *Chronicle*'s garlanded sister, wrote a hugely popular column called *Jack of Clubs* which periodically promoted 'command performances' across the region.

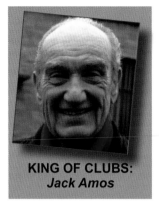

KING OF CLUBS:
Jack Amos

Once they even persuaded Princess Margaret to attend, Her Royal Highness spending several hours on the whisky and ginger. "She swore it was medicinal," said Jack, who also got himself into the Guinness Book for nominally buying the world's biggest round. It's much to be hoped that it was on expenses.

He'd been a full-time journalist until 1982, when he successfully stood for the secretaryship of the County Durham branch of the Club and Institute Union, gaining 70 per cent of the total vote in a field with 13 runners. He also served for 20 years on the CIU's national executive and for 21 as secretary of Shotley Bridge WMC, near Consett.

Jack did it all despite a medical history about which Simon Schama could have made a three-part documentary – and Channel 5 a 12-part series – not least the car crash in which he and his wife Flo received serious injuries on their 28th wedding anniversary.

"People talk about giving their bodies to medical science but I reckon they've had mine already," said Jack. "I daren't even go to the greyhounds any more, in case I catch distemper."

He was also partially deaf, bless him, blaming the proximity of the amplifiers at the many club evenings where, as guest of honour, he was seated at the front. Appointed MBE in 2004 for services to the workmen's club movement, he died three years later, aged 75.

MY old dad was never much of a drinker – nor much of a socialiser, come to think – only joining Old Shildon Workmen's so that his twins could go on the annual trip to Redcar, us and about half a million other North-East kids, or queue for the five bob given out every Christmas morning to members' bairns. Maybe on that occasion he'd have a half, probably shandy.

When we were a bit older, however, our parents would sometimes catch the Eden bus for a Sunday evening game of bingo at Newton Aycliffe WMC – known as the Big Club – from which they'd return with a couple of Jim's Pies for us two. Made in Aycliffe, Jim Whitton's pies were celebrated for many-a-mile around.

A couple of years back, first time in ages, I spent an evening in the Big Club watching an enjoyable film about long-serving (but latterly unseated) Labour MP Dennis Skinner, the so-called Beast of Bolsover. It was called *The Nature of the Beast*.

Many years after the Federation Brewery called time, precipitating difficult days for many workmen's clubs, Newton Aycliffe's had a room called House of Gin, also selling frozen cocktails and 'shots' like toffee apple and choc ice. On the walls were aphorisms like "Be thoughtful, be thankful." There appeared not to be any pies, Jim's or otherwise, and not all that many customers.

Perhaps the most dramatic – and successful – attempt to move with the times, however, has been at Hunwick WMC, another mid-terrace building, between Bishop Auckland and Crook.

Until early in 2019, the last time I'd been there was for a chat with Tommy Ward, who'd been secretary for 50 years and who became the first nonagenarian to win a game in the snooker league, using a 7/6d cue given him secondhand when he was 15. In 2019 he simply wouldn't have known the place: it had become the punk rock capital of the north.

Gimp Fist – a brilliant band, they reckoned – would give it what fettle in the concert room every Wednesday night. Two or three times a year there'd be a punk weekend, room for visitors to camp out the back, with bands like Pit Bull, Hospital Food and, wonderfully, Geoffrey Oicott. These days they'd have to be Sir Geoffrey Oicott.

So what on earth did the neighbours make of it all? "They all love it," said Lisa Hawkins, the stewardess. "The chap on one side's a little bit deaf, so he's not that bothered, but the people on the other side open their windows so they can hear it better. "

Club secretary Neville Blenkinsopp was equally enthusiastic. "It's an absolute no-brainer," he said. "We were paying £200 to people who were no more than karaoke singers and maybe taking £20 on the door. Now we don't have regular turns and on a punk day we can take £4,000 over the bar.The club's in a really strong situation."

In that terraced row in Hunwick, they were listening to the sound of the future.

16 : MEMBERS ONLY

JACK'S MBE was well earned, and not just for keeping Her Royal Highness in whisky and dry ginger, the manner to which by all accounts she was accustomed. In idler moments – a lot of those these days – I sometimes contemplate the formation of a North-East MBEs Society. However immodest, it would offer an excuse for a greatly diverse and potentially hugely enjoyable annual lunch. (Medals may be worn.)

Regrettably, it could never have included the late Tyneside industrialist Dr Ralph Iley, probably the only leek-growing pigeon fancier – same North Shields allotment since he was 13 – to be appointed CBE. Ralph would have been over-qualified, as would Bob Paisley OBE, a Hetton-le-Hole brickie who at Liverpool became one of football's most successful managers.

I interviewed him at his Merseyside home shortly after his retirement – charming, self-effacing and, with hindsight, already suffering from the early effects of dementia. We'd to wait until his wife Jessie came back before enjoying a cup of tea. Bob couldn't remember where they kept it. Not long afterwards I also attended his funeral.

MBE recipients like Ebac chairman John Elliott, snooker player Vera Selby – the Queen of Green – former *Echo* editor Pete Barron and former World Cup football referee George Courtney are saluted elsewhere in the book. Others, like retired Bishop Auckland GP and community champion Bob McManners – he of the Felons' Society – might only be allowed honorary membership since they're also higher up the roll of honour. Bob's an OBE, though might attend the bash as a guest of his wife Stefa, a retired head teacher and MBE for services to education.

Over another convivial lunch, Bob once proposed the formation of the Campaign for Real Authentic Puddings – the acronym may be imagined – in protest at all the modern muck on menus. It is not thought to have influenced the honours office.

Former County Durham police inspector Gordon Bacon, an old friend, would also have to be content with honorary membership after being appointed OBE in 1998 for leading the relief aid effort in war-torn Bosnia. Gordon swore that he'd been sustained by English beer – "I don't know who invented the widget, but if she's a woman I want to marry her" – and enjoyed further reward when, in later years, he became a manager of cricket tours to sunny climes.

Others eligible for the Members' Club, the MBEs' Knees, would include retired solicitor Jenny Flynn, who with husband John withstood for 39 years all that the Tow Law climate could throw at them – and that's an awful lot – before heading eastwards to Broompark, near Durham. "It's only 12 miles, but you can see the car thermometer edging up all the time," said Jenny.

Her MBE was for services to the community, ironic that she should need knee replacement surgery after a calamity at the community centre ceilidh. "I slipped and quite a few people landed on top of me, heaviest first," she recalled, painfully.

Her husband, 70 in 2019, continues to play 11-a-side football for Durham Buffs. "People call it walking football, which offends us because we're trying to run," he said. John's own medal may, as they say, be in the post.

Among couples who have both qualified are Peter and Sue Sotheran, each for services to the community in the Redcar area and Peter at the same investiture as I was. Among their numerous activities is bell ringing, knowing the ropes much trickier than it might appear. "It's like being able to rub your tummy and pat your head at the same time," said Peter, memorably.

We'd greatly welcome long serving former Darlington council leader Bill Dixon – not least because he owes me a pint – and John Culine, born in 1947 into a fairground family in a caravan on Jubilee Park in Spennymoor and until recently president of the Showmen's Guild, the national body representing the fairground industry. They've been on the road since the 17th century, an ancestor once crossing Bridlington harbour on a tightrope. "We're not kings, we're not queens, we're the marvellous Culines," said a Victorian promotion.

John and his wife Davina, whom he met at the annual Town Moor hoppings in Newcastle, still live in the luxurious static caravan on the edge of Spennymoor that, when not travelling, they've occupied for 40 years. "The Guild is there to regulate the profession, like doctors or whatever," he likes to say, and for John Culine MBE the shows must go on.

FAIR DO'S:
John and Davina Culine

John was in his 60s when royally recognised. Lt Col Mordaunt Cohen, the only person in this chapter I've not in turn been honoured to have met – since these things can be invidious, acquaintance must otherwise be considered a criterion for inclusion – was 101 and might reasonably have supposed that he'd never get the nod.

Born and raised in Sunderland and a solicitor in

the city, he was finally honoured for services to conflict resolution and for raising awareness of genocide. He died soon afterwards.

His wife, perhaps even more indelibly remembered in North-East England, was Judge Myrella Cohen QC – Cohen was also her birth name – who had a reputation for taking no prisoners (or whatever the direct opposite may be). Judge Denis Orde, also well remembered, once made a presentation at Durham Crown Court to a police officer retiring after 30 years service.

"Thirty years?" he said. "That sounds like one of Judge Cohen's more lenient sentences."

Former Darlington councillor Peter Freitag was but a boy of 86 when in 2015, for services to the community, he was appointed to the Most Excellent Order. Peter was a long-serving LibDem politician and president of the town's Hebrew Congregation, though he might also have been honoured for services to name dropping, at which he remains greatly adept. Like Jack Amos, Peter has a good Princess Margaret story. "I've a weakness for Elizabeth Taylor lookalikes," he insists.

There'd be places at the lunch for people like Anita Atkinson from Weardale, owner of Britain's biggest collection of royal memorabilia – and in the Queen's Diamond Jubilee year of a Stanhope coffee shop called Royal Teas – and for her delightful neighbour Judith Bainbridge, a retired teacher appointed MBE for services to the community in Frosterley but whose influence is felt many a mile beyond.

The toast to absent friends would include the late Father John Caden, a marvellously faithful Roman Catholic priest who spent four decades in Tony Blair's Sedgefield constituency, baptised all four Blair bairns and partnered the prime minister at tennis. Father John had also been a useful goalkeeper, persuaded while a post-war curate in Darlington to turn out for the Football League club's reserve side – on condition that he play under an assumed name, be back in church for 5.30pm confessions and that the formidable Bishop of

Hexham and Newcastle-should never find out. He was therefore much alarmed to find a reporter from the *Daily Express* on the presbytery doorstep.

The priest denied all knowledge. "As the reporter went back up the drive," he liked to recall, "I heard the cock crow twice."

Mike Adamson, Father Caden's late neighbour in Sedgefield, was a hugely colourful character who built up the Ramside Estates

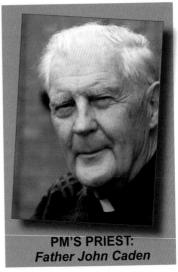

PM'S PRIEST:
Father John Caden

group which owns hotels and other hospitality venues across the North-East. Mike's MBE probably wasn't for services to dieting: he was one of two men I knew – Big Bob Scaife the other – substantially to gain weight while on a sponsored slim.

Ramside Estates is now run by Mike's son John, the flagship Ramside Hall Hotel outside Durham hung with original paintings by Norman Cornish MBE, an ever-unassuming Spennymoor lad and one of the original pitman painters. One of his pictures even included a newspaper, discarded on the floor but with a column by me – about him – clearly prominent.

Unlike Mike Adamson, Lez Rawe never had a spare ounce on him. An enduring all-round sportsman, he taught with distinction at Bishop Auckland Grammar School for 32 years, served for many more as a Methodist local preacher, was married for almost 75 years to Betty, a month or so older than he was. "For a few weeks every year I'm a toy boy," he'd insist.

At their 70th wedding anniversary party he'd pledged his

determination to live to be 100 – "even if I die in the process" – but was 98 when he died in June 2018, four months after Betty. His MBE had also been for services to the community, though perhaps not for services to sex education.

In the late 1940s, a reader and former pupil recalled, a clearly uncomfortable Lez had sat all the boys down to explain about the birds and the bees. "He spent an hour telling us in great detail about the amoeba. After that the experiment was abandoned."

Nor, come to think, did he ever teach me to master a forward roll.

We'd also affectionately toast the memory of Evan Bryson, acknowledged in 2004 after 48 years as secretary of Redheugh Boys Club in Gateshead, an organisation renowned for taking kids off the street through football. Formed in 1957, it had hoped to use an old double-decker bus as its first headquarters but had to rethink after scrap metal thieves stole the fittings.

Among the club's finds was the youthful Paul Gascoigne – "plump little feller, couldn't cope with the pace but you could see he was very special," said Evan. He lived in a first floor flat in Gateshead, gazed out of the window as we chatted.

"Maybe we taught them the wrong things," he said, perhaps echoing Lez Rawe. "You should see the number of young girls with prams out there."

Inevitably there'd be those who suppose the honours system a bit of a national lottery, and they'd have a point, but few may be undeserving and fewer yet not thrilled to have been invited to the Palace. It's a wonderful occasion.

Inevitably, too, my table would include quite a few other sports people, men like former Football League referee Terry Farley, long in Newton Aycliffe. Honoured for services to reffing, in 2020 he was still actively officiating – and devoting long hours to administration – at the age of 87 and nearly

20 years after a triple heart bypass. Lovely lad, Terry.

Raye Wilkinson, appointed MBE in the New Year 2019 honours, was based in Middleham – North Yorkshire racing territory – and had devoted much of his life to the needs of stable lads and lasses – described by former MP Alan Meale in a subsequent chapter as "those poor devils."

"I was a great believer in working late, leaving the light on," Raye once said. "Going home to their digs, often in the dark and after a long split shift, was when things would come to a head."

We were old friends, not least because he was an equally assiduous (and even worse paid) football scout, though what particularly distinguished Raye was that he may have been the only person in Britain with an office even smaller than mine.

Perhaps the most genuinely remarkable of that be-ribboned band, however, was Mike Findley, a former postal worker and union official from Marske-by-the-Sea in Cleveland. Told in 2005 that he had motor neurone disease, that hideous affliction, Mike was given between two to five years to live – and with progressive loss of physical abilities.

Instead of waiting for death, he determined to make the most of life. Mike formed his own MND charity, became borough mayor and had raised hundreds of thousands of pounds by the time of his eventual death in June 2019. I'd last seen him three years earlier, somehow still savouring his Saturday fish and chips – from the paper, of course.

"You just have to do what you can," he said and Mike, above all, truly deserved a medal.

17 : PLAYING THE BANNED

FOR everywhere that John North was welcomed, all about embedding the *Echo* in the community, there was somewhere else from which I'd be excluded. Few circumstances were more memorable than a December lunchtime at the Old English Gentleman, a pub in Darlington town centre.

In the office it was a mouse-quiet day, echoing and empty of ideas. Finally it seemed a wheeze, instead of spending lunchtime propping up the bar, to put in a seasonal shift working behind it. The Old English landlord, whom slightly I knew, was happy to agree.

What we'd both overlooked was that it was the last day of Christmas term at Darlington College, they of the world class chicken pie, and that the pub would be rammed. No problem when they were just drinking, of course – not unless someone asked to see their birth certificates – it was when the extra-mural activities began that things became a bit difficult.

Out in the corridor, a student couple were experimenting (shall we say) on the stairs, watched by an enthusiastic and fast-growing crowd. Goodness knows what they were studying, probably physical education. The landlord stopped the fun, closed the pub on one of the busiest afternoons of the year, threatened to write to their mums (or at least to the college principal.)

What had been seen as a quiet day column became a front page news story. Inevitably, I was no longer welcome.

The *Eating Owt* column, which kept me in hot dinners

from 1985 to 2011, inevitably proved contentious, too. Readers seemed most regularly to recall an excoriating review of the Kicking Cuddy, a pub in Coxhoe, though on at least one occasion I was barred without having written a word.

It was at the Four Alls in Ovington, a maypole village on the Durham/North Yorkshire border. We'd bought drinks, ordered food – the rabbit pie looked good – when the landlord came over, asked if I were Mike Amos and, told that it was indeed the case, advised that we drink up and leave.

Why? "You've had a go at all the pubs around here," he said, wholly inaccurately. He just didn't want the Four Alls to be next.

WHEATLEY Hill dogs proved a tail-between-the-legs job, too. The greyhound stadium in a former pit village near Peterlee was what's called a flapping track, taken to mean that they ran independently of National Greyhound Racing Club rules and had – how might this be put? – a few ways of their own. The first *Backtrack* column, November 1985, pondered the etymology of "flapping" in that context. All these years later, I still don't understand it.

County Durham alone may once have had a dozen flapping tracks – Coundon, Belmont, Spennymoor, Easington, Murray Park in Stanley where in 1947 annual takings were recorded at over £750,000. In 2019, Wheatley Hill was one of just four in the UK and in November of that year a serious fire again threatened its existence.

Until his death in 2005, Wheatley Hill dogs had been run for 40 years by Norman Fannon, a colourful character said to school dogs with innate Cruftsmanship. He'd also built a hare system – hare of the dogs – from a lorry load of ex-army beds. He was properly proud of it.

I'd first gone in 1986, even then a reincarnation of a half-forgotten world, wrote among much else that the atmosphere in the smoke-shrouded bar was "somewhat carcinogenic." Somewhat carcinogenic? The air was as purple as a pound of best plums.

Norman took exception, barred me. After his death I went back, obituary in mind, and was warmly welcomed by Jean Booth, his business partner. "Don't worry," said Jean, "there's not many through these gates haven't had a run-in with Norman at one time or another."

A few years later the distinguished journalist and author Matthew Engel was writing *Engel's England*, a carefully researched, stylishly written and delightfully quirky tour of the "original" 39

DOGS' LIFE:
Norman Fannon

counties. If he wanted to know where to go in County Durham, someone flatteringly told him, he should ask Mike Amos.

At once I recommended a night at the dogs. Engel ingeniously combined it with choral evensong, a glorious tradition, at Durham Cathedral. Down Black Lane in Wheatley Hill he found what he thought some of the ugliest buildings in the Palatinate and, at the dogs, "a system basically operating to rules that might have been understood, in some circles, at the time of the apostles."

It was part of a secret world operating in plain sight, he wrote – "as mystical in its way as choral evensong." He didn't understand the flipping flapping thing, either – "but essentially it's the greyhound racing equivalent of the Wild West."

Then there was the time that a photographer and I were

thrown out of a grouse beaters' ball in Swaledale, the head beater told by the chief toff to "send them orf with a couple of birds apiece." Dreaming of game pie, we got vouchers for Cherry Valley ducklings. For reasons forgotten I was also excluded from the Railway Institute in Shildon and from the Variety Club in Spennymoor, but that followed some unexpected revelations.

The Variety Club was a huge place which on Monday lunchtimes in the 1970s ran what they called shift workers' specials. What was so special for the shift workers – and, indeed, others of a less industrious nature –was that the shows featured an awful lot of strippers. Another day, another column.

One of the young ladies agreed to an interview in a diminutive dressing room. Diligently, myopically, I made notes until becoming aware that the lady, fully clothed at the start of proceedings, was now dressed as nature and perhaps her clandestine calling intended and was looking for what's apparently known in the oldest profession as business. Spice of life? In the phrase time honoured of the inky trade, I made my excuses, left and in due course revealed all, too. The ban followed within days.

18 : OUT OF THE HORDENARY

COUNDON Conservative Club was improbably located in a former pit village near Bishop Auckland and unlikely to have had too many true blue Tories hustled around the snooker table. Their exclusion order came soon after I suggested as much in print.

Horden Conservative Club, on the Durham coast and serving the region's biggest pit village, was more surprising yet and no matter that locals simply called it – still call it – the Tin Pot.

During the 1974 miners' strike, a notice appeared in the window to the effect that the price of a pint would be reduced by 10p for the duration of the Heath government's iniquitous actions against the poor colliers.

In October 1974 the year's second general election took place, improbably but vigorously contested for the Liberals in Bishop Auckland by the Honourable David Lytton-Cobbold who spent much of the campaign kipping on someone's bedroom floor.

David, then 37, was an Eton-educated international banker and heir to the Knebworth estates in Hertfordshire. His lovely wife Chrissie, with whom he sometimes shared the bedroom floor, was one of the last generation of debutantes to be presented to the Queen.

Though both professed, and doubtless meant, a love of the Bishop Auckland area, electorally it aided them little. David gained just 15 per cent of the vote, 19,000 behind the Labour winner, and returned to jousting – if not quite tilting at windmills – elsewhere. He's now Lord Cobbold, the second baron.

Some of us had got on so well with him that we were invited on a couple of occasions as weekend guests at Knebworth House, becoming known as a venue for high-octane music festivals. They had to meet the repair bills somehow. One or two slept in four-posters, all slept in style. David claimed, probably to all four of us, that Mick Jagger had occupied the same bed the weekend previously. We never got such treatment from the Tories.

Meanwhile back at Horden Conservative Club, someone broke in two decades later and stole the picture of Margaret Thatcher, her fate easy to suppose. Winston Churchill was unharmed. Saltburn Conservative Club, overlooking the ocean, had a picture of Elvis – never known as a Tory – above the fireplace. I never did find out why.

Elsewhere there were Constitutional Clubs, thought to have been formed with much the same principles; on South Tyneside there were Unionist Clubs – a throwback to an Irish workforce – and, in Hebburn, an Orange Unionist Club. Some survive still.

In the workmen's clubs, as in football, folk could be banned *sine die* – a Latin phrase meaning without limit, though victims just said they'd been sin died. Billy Gypp was luckier: he only got three months.

I'd first encountered Billy at a gurning competition – you know, face pulling – held at a Bishop Auckland nightclub and judged by me and Luke Casey, a delightful and greatly accomplished Irishman who'd himself begun in the *Northern Echo*'s Stockton office and worked at the time for BBC *Look North*.

That we named Billy the winner may partly have been because he had what might be supposed a head start. He lived in Cockfield, west Durham, where an oft-impecunious lifestyle led to complaints in the village workmen's club that he was forever pestering folk for the money for a drink.

He became the first workmen's club member in Britain to be suspended for cadging.

Luke went to London to work for Nationwide, the BBC's evening magazine programme, accommodated at the Corporation's expense at the Kensington Hilton. A couple of years later I spent a week writing the *John North* column from London, dined royally with Luke and ended up back in the residents' lounge at the Hilton.

It was about 4am when the night porter suggested that we might have had enough. Luke certainly wasn't banned, but they were probably very happy never again to see the noisy bloke from the *Northern Echo*.

BIG John Alderson, known since boyhood as Basher, strode into Horden Conservative Club like John Wayne come for his boy. He'd not been back for 30 years. His stetson was worn stylishly, his accent more California than Crimdon Dene. "Why yer bugger," someone said, "and that's swearing, mind."

A miner's son, almost inevitably, Basher had been born in

BASHER STREET KID:
John Alderson

Horden 86 years earlier, grew up in No 5 Eighth Street – netty out the back, tin bath in front of the fire – went on to feature in 150 films and television series, perhaps best remembered as Sgt Bullock in *Boots and Saddles*.

"I used to watch *Boots and Saddles* with me mam and she tellt us she went to school with Sgt Bullock," said a second Cons Club customer. "I used

117

to think she was mekkin' it all up. These was nee one from Horden talked like Sgt Bullock."

It was a wonderful story, a true exclusive, and like most of the best ones it owed almost everything to luck.

Back in the year 2000, Horden parish councillor Paul Stradling had produced a modest, 39-page village history to mark the millennium. Mentioned almost in passing, John Alderson raised inquisitive eyebrows in one or other of the columns and would probably have been forgotten again had not a letter arrived a few weeks later from Basher himself, by then resident in the Motion Picture Actors' Home in Hollywood. I rang him the next day.

"I blush with shame to see myself listed as Horden's film star," he said, but his career – usually playing villains – was truly extraordinary. He was the local lad made baddie.

He'd spent just two weeks down the pit, appalled at the conditions in which men toiled – "you'd not have got your free coals then," they said in the Tin Pot, sympathetically – joined the Army, was a sergeant at the outbreak of war and a major at the end of it. He married Mary Brown, the American general's secretary, was allowed into the US after being accepted as a war bride and confirming that he was no more than five months pregnant, yearned for an acting career.

"You can tell I was a good actor, the way I wriggled my way through the army ranks," he said over the line from LA.

Sir Aubrey Smith, a seasoned thespian, was looking to start a cricket team over there – Boris Karloff kept wicket – and seeking experienced players. Basher said he'd turn out if Sir Aubrey introduced him to an agent.

"He told me I was too big for an English actor, they were all supposed to be built like David Niven," he said, but subsequently attended drama school alongside men like Leonard Nimoy, who went star trekking, and Richard Chamberlain, who graduated as Doctor Kildare. "The worst actor in the class," said Basher, wholly affectionately.

So Basher went to Hollywood, appeared in *My Fair Lady* alongside Audrey Hepburn ("a lovely, charming and compassionate lady who I sorely miss"), in *Double Trouble* with Elvis Presley ("I never enjoyed working with anyone more"), in *Catch a Thief* with Cary Grant and Grace Kelly ("a wonderful pair of decent and good people") and in *No Name on the Bullet* alongside Audie Murphy.

"We spent all the time exchanging war stories and handicapping horses," he said.

John Wayne became a good friend after *The Hellfighters*, Angie Dickenson visited him frequently ("always good for a big hug"), Richard Burton three times shared a cast list, if perhaps in a slightly larger type size. Other television series, best westerns, included *Bonanza*, *Gunsmoke* and *Have Gun-Will Travel*.

One of the websites even had him playing a starring role in a 1976 version of *It Shouldn't Happen to a Vet*, but perhaps they meant John Alderton.

"My greatest achievement," he said over the phone, "was showing Catherine Zeta Jones around this wonderful residence of ours." The following year he was back among the Basher Street kids, exploring First to Umpteenth Streets, striding into the old Tin Pot like he'd never been away.

Why yer bugger (and that's not really swearing at all).

HE'D returned to England the previous day, was staying with his nephew Tom up the road in Peterlee – "I've seen my uncle Jack shot a canny few times," said Tom – planned a visit to Rome and an audience with the Pope ("it's not just me") on the return leg.

Pint or two in the Cons Club, stroll down to the once-blighted beach, dinner from the chip shop on Sunderland Road where he talked of himself as a limey cowboy and in a deep baritone gave the girls behind the counter *I'm Getting Married in the Morning* from *My Fair Lady* and said that he'd been in the film. "Nivver," they chorused, incredulously.

In the Tin Pot they'd talked of good old bad old days, of the 1925 eclipse, of frequent forays to the blast beach, of re-enacting *The Three Musketeers* ("Douglas Fairbanks was good in that one, we had bits of driftwood for swords") and of playing cowboys and Indians. "Never in my wildest dreams did I expect one day to be playing it for real, and getting quite well paid for it, too," said Basher.

His youthful best friend had been Skinny Martin, the pit manager's son, a frequent visitor to No 5 Eighth Street because Basher's mum made the best dinners in Horden. "If he's the gaffer's son," she'd been known to expostulate, "why can't the bloody gaffer feed him?"

He'd thought the beach particularly wonderful. "It gave you a sense of freedom away from the ever-present pit, which everyone hated. In the 1920s that was the furthest you ever got apart from the Sunday School trip to Redcar. You still don't get air like this in California."

TED Harrison was born just a few miles west of Horden, in Wingate, became a national treasure in North America – the Yukon, even colder than Crimdon Dene – was back visiting his twin sister in Wheatley Hill, next village along, when we caught up. He was a miner's son, his family accustomed to painting little more than the netty walls, wondered if he should be talking to the *Northern Echo* at all.

Before the war he'd won a colouring competition promoted by the Nig-Nog Club (which in equally ignominious but rather more costly circumstances has been mentioned in an earlier chapter.)

The prize was a big food hamper, including a turkey – "we could never have afforded it normally" – and just in time for Christmas. For some reason, alas, it was despatched by rail and finished up a junction somewhere. It was January before the hamper reached Wingate, and all bets off, as was the turkey. "It was one of the biggest disappointments of my youth," said Ted.

After school he travelled on the G&B bus to West Hartlepool Art College, happy on a brief return to County Durham to take the chance to relate the story of the bloke who tried to queue jump.

"Aa's fust," he shouted.

"I don't care which bit of you's first," said the conductress, "you'll wait your bloody turn."

Ted taught in New Zealand and Malaysia (and Middlesbrough), spotted an advert for a teaching job in the Yukon – "Weaklings need not apply," it said – got it and stayed for almost 40 years despite temperatures often so low that spit would freeze before it hit the ground.

In that time he only once encountered a grizzly. "I ran one way and it ran the other," he said.

It was the Yukon's snowy wastes which changed and inspired his painting, made him famous not least for his illustration of the epic poem *Cremation of Sam McGee*. He won the Order of Canada, the country's highest honour, had four honorary degrees, was even an honorary admiral.

Ted was back in 2006 to visit his twin sister, Algar – who still called him Eddie – and to celebrate their 80th birthday, particularly looking forward to some pease pudding and to a proper pork pie. He recalled hard times in the east Durham mining communities when families would spend summer in tents on Hart beach, because it was more congenial than the hovels in which they lived.

They'd moved to British Columbia when his wife became ill with Alzheimer's – "at first I was prostrate with homesickness," he said, and meant homesick for the Yukon and not Wingate. Ted died in Canada in 2015.

19 : PRISON SENTENCES

INSIDE stories weren't really my thing, they were for proper journalists, though as a kid on the *Despatch* I did once infiltrate a striking miners' meeting at Mainsforth, near Ferryhill, and stayed despite dark warnings that anyone not an NUM member had best get out sharpish.

Half a century later it seems so improbable. Anyone less closely resembling a rough-hewn collier it's impossible to imagine.

Nor might it ever have been supposed that I was much of a campaigning journalist, as opposed to a complaining one. I grumbled about everything from music in pubs to able bodied people pulling suitcases on wheels, now said by A&E departments to be the single biggest trip hazard that the fracture clinics encounter. There was a thing about cats, too, estimated to kill 55 million small birds – and a great many other creatures – every year.

Querulous columns also majored on the misuse of the apostrophe. A particularly peeving practice these days, much favoured by the *Northern Echo*, is the omission of the apostrophe s from names that themselves end in s. If in doubt, write it as you'd say it. If further in doubt, let the *Times* be your style guide. Nothing drew more correspondence, or is still more indelibly remembered, than the crusade against the aberrant apostrophe.

While there were no inside stories, however, there was quite a time spent in jail. HMP Northallerton, indeed, provided one of the two most profound quotes of a long lifetime.

In John North days I was writing an otherwise predictable series of features on how others would be spending Christmas, asked a (very) old lag what he'd most miss about being in prison on December 25.

"Being able to walk 100 yards in a straight line," he said.

The other quote, while we're at it, came from a Hartlepool chap who'd been a chef at one of London's top hotels but who returned to run a street corner pub in his home town. On the evening I visited he was cooking pie and peas for the Over 60s club, prompting the suggestion that there wasn't much he could do with pie and peas.

"Yes there is," he replied, "you can bugger them."

I'd also been to Northallerton jail to talk to an inmate who'd won a prize for making a gipsy caravan from matchsticks – times change – visited Durham prison and noticed how strongly it smelt of old cabbage, did time at the nearby top-security jail at Frankland and noticed how strongly it smelt of menace.

On a different occasion I was tipped off by Dave Thompson, a friend who officially and rather grandly rejoiced in the title of Frankland's governor of governors, that they'd hired a couple of hawks – jail birds – in an attempt to address the institutional pigeon problem. Better yet, the services of Ronnie and Reggie – night hawks, if ever – had been rejected in favour of birds more loftily named Zeus and Apollo. The initiative failed, the pigeons still ruled the roost, but for more effective services to HM Prison Service, Dave was appointed OBE.

Another Christmas I attended a carol service at Deerbolt Young Offenders' Institution near Barnard Castle where the lads had been taking liberties with *Once in Royal David's City*. Instead of "Mary was that mother mild, Jesus Christ her little child", the words were "Mary's mum and dad went wild, when they heard about the child."

Acklington prison in Northumberland had a policy of giving inmates nearing the end of their sentence what might be termed time out. One of the lads – let's just call him Gary – had reportedly played professional football in Scotland but burgled the club chairman's house when he hadn't been paid. "A simple balance of economics," it was said in court.

He got to play Northern League football for nearby Alnwick Town, no problem on Saturdays but a bit trickier for midweek matches when he had to be back inside by 10pm or else turn into a sort of penal pumpkin. Since the lad was forbidden from earning money outside, Alnwick paid him in big bags of chocolate biscuits, making him the most popular chap in the jail. That made a canny story, too.

THE most memorable prison sentences of all, however, came from Holme House, a £55m prison in Stockton which upon completion had drawn comparison in *Hear All Sides* – the *Echo*'s venerable letters column – with the nearby Swallow Hotel in the town.

Whether it was because the new jail was so swish or the Swallow Hotel the opposite is blessedly hard to remember.

The inmates had a football team – a Lags' XI, it might incorrigibly be said – which for perhaps understandable reasons had to play all its games at home. They won the fourth division of the Teesborough League, had a pretty good disciplinary record save for the unfortunate incident when the goalie was sent off in handcuffs and, having beaten four first division sides, reached the league cup final, too.

The only problem was that league rules said that finals must be played on a neutral ground. Not being free that day, Holme House were thrown out. Someone from the prison contacted me, I contacted the league, the league – much to its credit – waived the rule. The final, home from Holme, was played on the prison's artificial pitch.

It may also have been the only time in penal history that folk were charged to get into a jail, the £1 admission given to the league, the attendance restricted to 200 and the queue 30

INSIDE STORY: *Holme House*

yards long. They played Roseworth Social Club, also from Stockton, one or two of the visitors looking like they were already quite familiar with their temporary surroundings.

A sign read "Do not spit on the floor, thank you". It said nothing about the walls. The prison team included Mousey, Biffy, Fatty and Snagger. It wasn't hard to tell which one was Fatty.

Watching from a wing 15 yards behind the touchline – "the executive boxes," said Dave Watson, a senior prison official – the inmates seemed less than grateful for my intervention, though the abuse was no doubt scattergun in nature. At half-time it was 1-1, prison officers cheerfully talking about leading Roseworth into a false sense of security, but at the final whistle the Rosie had won 5-1. They planned a few beers back in the social club and then to paint the town red-and-white.

The Holme House boys got a cup of Home Office tea and were taken back to their solitary cells. The Swallow Hotel it wasn't.

20 : ARMCHAIR CRITIC

SO the diarist's days passed largely agreeably, little of the hard-nosed, hard news confrontation of popular journalistic myth.

The exception came one Wednesday afternoon at a pub in Barnard Castle – not, it might be said, that of the potty-mouthed parrot. Though it was market day the place was almost empty – quiet until the arrival of a psittacine pair who proved to be off-duty soldiers.

The landlord did little. His wife, upstairs with the children, came down to ask the soldiers to desist and was hit in the face for her intrusion. While her husband summoned the police, I and just about the only other able-bodied person in the pub manhandled the offenders onto the cobbles outside. A merry dance, though not what you'd suppose a military two-step, ensued.

We'd been followed by an old chap with a Jack Russell which may, in doggy years, have been yet more decrepit than its master. "Gan get them son," he told the dog, perhaps failing to realise that the average Jack Russell finds it quite difficult to differentiate between the goodies and the baddies.

Thus it was that I landed in Darlington Memorial hospital needing stitches in my backside, and that two of Her Majesty's finest spent a lengthy spell in the glasshouse.

MIKE McGiffen, the *Echo*'s much admired news editor, would sometimes ask me to cover major news stories – the IRA bomb at Claro Barracks in Ripon, the murder of a secu-

DISASTER AREA:
The aftermath of Dibbles Bridge

rity guard at a factory in Eaglescliffe, the terrible tragedy at Dibbles Bridge, near Skipton in North Yorkshire.

A group of pensioners from Thornaby, Teesside, had been enjoying a day out in May 1975 when brake defects led to their coach careering 1,400 yards down a bank and ending on its roof in a cottage garden. The coach sides also collapsed. Thirty-three people were killed and 13 injured. It remains England's worst road toll in a single accident.

Early that evening they sent me to Thornaby, to write a black-tinged colour piece. Chiefly it seemed to be based with anxious relatives in the police station waiting room – "the Salvation Army officer gave out cigarettes because there was little else he could give" – and the intended colour piece became the front page lead.

It brought appreciative notes – herograms, they're called – from the editor and others, and the feeling that perhaps the column writing days were drawing to an end. What I really fancied was Mike McGiffen's job. Alone in the newsroom, the news editor had a metal as opposed to a moulded plastic chair. Better yet, it was a chair with arms.

21 : CLOSED MINDS

IN the early days on the *Despatch*, the organisation of the local National Union of Journalists may most kindly have been described as ineffectual, a euphemism meaning chaotic. For a time I was the titular branch chairman without ever having been a member – and not much minded to let on.

By the mid-70s, however, the union had found itself a cause. They wanted provincial publishing houses – in union terms, chapels – to become closed shops, meaning that the editorial workforce would be 100 per cent NUJ. At Darlington the closed shop was declared unilaterally, management simply refusing to agree. Confrontation was inevitable.

I'd joined the union by then but with no great enthusiasm. The NUJ was most closely identified with the Labour Party and several years of covering local government, almost always Labour-controlled, had made me suspicious of much that went on.

The council members were often undemocratic, spent ratepayers' money on entertaining themselves, loved to attend conferences at southern seaside resorts at which the content must often have been way above their heads but the pillows below them were five-star.

It also seemed to me interesting how many key posts, particularly in education, were held by Labour Party members though there may well have been similar issues in Tory territory – and as wise old Arnold Hadwin pointed out, we'd need in each and every case to prove that the post holder got the job because of his politics. Exasperated, I stood in 1970 as an

Independent candidate in a Shildon Urban District Council ward with three seats and won more votes than the three Labour candidates put together.

NUNN SEQUITER:
Coun Walter Nunn

Labour retained 15 of the 20 seats. Each of the Labour members was elected to all committees, the Independents like me were placed on just two committees – one of which was road safety. It's a wonder they didn't make me dress up as Tufty. It did nothing to assuage those earlier suspicions of undemocratic activity.

The highest placed Labour candidate had been Walter Nunn – good bloke, not a very good loser – a teetotal, non-smoking, allotment-tending old school man of principle with an improbable claim to fame. Walter reckoned to know every word of *Eskimo Nell* – there must have been an awful lot of her – and to be able to recite the epic in precisely the time that it took to travel between council meetings in Green Lane, Spennymoor, and County Hall in Durham. Unfortunately I was never in his company on that journey.

So the closed shop posed a dilemma: support a policy with which I fundamentally disagreed or betray friends and workmates who, generally, were a very good bunch. Besides, we were young – some might say young and daft.

When a female sub-editor on the *Darlington & Stockton Times*– a top-selling weekly paper sometimes called the Farmers' Bible – joined the smaller and less militant Institute of Journalists, the NUJ duly walked out. The strike began in June 1977 – I distinctly remember the banners, 'Strike while the weather's hot' – and lasted until January of the following year. Production continued thanks to a small number of non-NUJ members and executives and a large police presence which thwarted attempts by late-night pickets from all over the land to block the narrow lane at the back of the head office in Darlington from which newspaper vans emerged. Many were arrested, locked up and gained a criminal record. Perhaps my heart or my back weren't in it, but my only criminal record remained that with Hartlepool United a few years earlier.

Publication only stopped when the powerful National Graphical Association printers' union called out its members in support. When it became clear that management remained unbending, the NGA went back and the NUJ should have read the message like a 96pt headline. They didn't, or wouldn't.

It became an international issue, but caused all manner of domestic agonies closer to home. David Kelly, then the *Echo*'s features editor but to become an outstanding and a caring managing director at Darlington, refused even to lean against the *Echo* wall while on picket duty. Others among us remained perversely grateful for its support.

Mike McGiffen was so dismayed and disturbed by all that

RUSTING RELIC: *The John H Amos (no relation)*

went on during those seven months in the cold that he never returned to work, leaving to train greyhounds in Somerset. For about a week before the strike I'd been deputy news editor, ending seven years as John North. When finally and forlornly we returned to work, Don Evans – his good grace memorable – offered me Mike's job.

No matter that a coincident if somewhat mischievous headline read "Rusting relic Amos must be scrapped" – it referred to the John H Amos, an elderly paddle-tug turned floating nightclub mordantly moored on the Tees at Stockton – I had the chair with arms.

22 : ALL THE NEWS

THOUGH sales figures inevitably dipped a little, the *Echo* retained its position among the top three regional morning newspapers in England, often No 1 and still above 100,000. When I became news editor in January 1978 – remember these stats – we had 35 reporters and 11 photographers in 16 offices across the North-East, serving six distinctly different editions.

Head office in Darlington had six or seven reporters, Middlesbrough had four, Bishop Auckland, Durham, Newcastle, Stockton and York found work for three reporters apiece and other areas had one or two, sometimes working from home.

Oscar, the district chief reporter's Airedale terrier, was also in semi-permanent residence in the Newcastle office opposite the Anglican cathedral, usually prone in front of the gas fire. Oscar's contribution to the nightly news list was limited.

Including York and Scarborough the North-East had eight evening papers, goodness only knows how many weeklies great and small and two more regional morning titles – the Newcastle-based *Journal* and the *Yorkshire Post*, which encroached from the south. All were our rivals, though the *Journal* more actively claimed the north of the region, its accent more vividly Geordie, the *Echo* what might be supposed the centre ground and the *Yorkshire Post* the greater part of the North Riding.

The difference was underlined by a case at North Shields magistrates court, after a burglar entering a pub in the early hours had been alarmed to find what folk call a lock-in – you know, a stoppy-back – in full vigour.

"They give us a good howkin'," the unfortunate villain told the court, a case of rough justice reported verbatim by the *Journal.*

The *Echo*'s sub-editor was more cautious, perhaps just more prosaic. "They gave me a good hiding," he translated.

The newsdesk also had control of several telephones, the office television and an old-tech bottle of Tippex. The only occasion that the last two were in unfortunate collision was on a Sunday afternoon when Somerset CCC, an improbable allegiance mentioned earlier, lost a John Player League match which they really should have won. Though the Tippex proved a well-guided missile, it wasn't my fault the bottle top came off. The Tippex didn't; even with the advent of colour, the newsdesk telly remained black and white.

The *Despatch* editorial team was on the other side of the second floor office, 30ft or more up, the rivalry usually friendly and on one occasion fortuitous.

Though we were the morning paper, I was usually in the office by 8am – before most of the *Despatch* staff. On one occasion only the evening paper news editor and his deputy had arrived, the latter cowering in terror on the window ledge as the former – known to be a little excitable – threatened to defenestrate him.

He'd missed a story, apparently. Fortunately, I was able to defuse things – the song about slack your rope hangman came to mind – before the poor No 2 could be well and truly Despatched.

DON Evans and I had agreed that Steve Hobman, the head office chief reporter, should become my daytime deputy while Joan Smith, as she became, continued to look after things at night. Joan was a greatly experienced and accomplished hand, but as midnight approached might still find time for a game of dominoes – "good enough to have played for the

NIGHT BIRD:
Joan Smith

Britannia," it's recalled – with the sub-editors.

Even that would periodically be interrupted, often around closing time, by calls from members of the public (best not say "readers") threatening to end it all. "It was like the local Samaritans some nights," it's recalled and Joan, bless her, never lost any of them. She herself died much too young.

Don had also agreed that an attractive blonde called Sharon Griffiths should join Northallerton office to replace a reporter who'd left in the strike to do a rural milk round instead.

Sharon still remembers her interview. "Oh, so you're Sharon, when do you start?" asked Don. She timed it at eight seconds. Subject to his final approval, Don also allowed his news editor to conduct most job interviews for reporters – usually in the pub, because that seemed to me more relaxing.

Peter Barron, a young applicant from the *Scunthorpe Evening Telegraph*, had heard about this admittedly unusual practice and was worried. He wasn't much of a drinking man: could he stand the prospective pace?

Much to his consternation, Pete was unable to finish his third – or was it the fourth? – pint. It didn't count against him: I admired his enthusiasm and local knowledge and recommended his appointment. He went on to become the paper's editor for 19 years, remained full of enthusiasm and local knowledge, fought valiantly for his people, cared greatly about the paper and the North-East and was rewarded with an MBE. He was still a bit of a half-shandyman, though.

SHARON Griffiths and I had met in June 1976 on a British Railways press facility trip – jollies, they used to be called – behind a Freightliner train travelling from Ipswich to Glasgow. Two coaches were attached to the end, one for the journalists and one for the food and drink deemed essential on such occasions. What you might term greasing the wheels.

Were such an invitation to arrive these days it's doubtful, such the industry's straitened circumstances, that there'd be a single acceptance from newspapers. In 1976, more than 30 newspaper and magazine journalists gathered in the bar of the Great White Horse Hotel in Ipswich. Only one was female and she well recalls that evening, too.

Sharon, who's Welsh, had read English at Bristol University, spent several years with the BBC – mainly at Radio Oxford – and was working her notice on a Teesside business magazine before joining Southern Television in Southamp-

MARRYING THE BOSS (pro tem):
Sharon on her wedding day, 1978

ton as chief press officer. "Everybody but one seemed quite nice," she'll tell anyone who'll listen. "One man seemed horrible, I asked who it was and they said he wrote the *John North* column on the *Northern Echo*."

Before the end of that two-day trip, I think we both knew that we'd one day be married. It probably helped that I was a Peter, Paul and Mary fan, eternally enamoured of Mary Travers as confessed earlier, and that Sharon was also a long-haired blonde. She in turn was a Rolling Stones groupie; my own resemblance to Mr Jagger (as then simply he was) perhaps a little less obvious.

That matrimony didn't happen until November 1 1978 – that November 1 is All Saints Day may be supposed co-incidental – was partly because she smoked like a Whitby kipper factory, fifty or sixty a day. The story was that if any at Southern Television saw her without a cigarette in her hand, they assumed she must have stopped.

I piously hated the habit, told her that if she gave up for ninety days we'd be married on the 91st. November 1 1978 also happened to be her 30th birthday, the wedding venue a portable building in the car park of County Hall, Northallerton, romantically decorated with a dead cactus.

It was by far the best thing I ever did. The pleasure of every day is chiefly down to her – and, of course, after passing the test at the ninth attempt she's always the designated driver.

It was also while in Southampton that she met someone from the North-East who happened to remember me. "Is his shirt still hanging out the back of his trousers?" he said. You can take the lad out of Shildon....

THE little Northallerton branch office was above a particularly bloody butcher's, confined quarters shared with Arnold Pearson, a delightful *Darlington & Stockton Times* reporter with a semi-permanent chuckle who'd been a navigator on wartime Lancasters, won DSO and DFC before he was 21 but never really wanted to talk about it.

Arnold was also a local county councillor, knew everyone in the Northallerton area, many of whom seemed to be called Clutterbuck, didn't so much run the office as hold court there – save on Wednesday, market day, when they'd decamp to the Golden Lion up the street. There can be no doubt that Sharon learned a great deal more from the *D&S Times* reporter than she did from the *Northern Echo*'s news editor.

Her huge patch matched her enthusiasm, her charisma and the speed with which she learned. There were even one or two of those herograms from the curmudgeonly old news ed.

In the summer of 1981, however, she left full-time journalism for the last time to give birth to Adam who, somewhat inconsiderately, arrived at 4am after a pretty hard shift in the delivery room. Not even his dad could find a pub open at that time of the morning.

Owen was born in April 1984, more conveniently at 4.10pm on a Saturday, just in time for the football results. It's possible a beer or two was drunk while his maternal grandmother held the fort at home.

Gratifyingly, both boys have inherited their father's football allegiance to Shildon and Arsenal – at a push in that order – though both have the advantage of being able to see the ball. Adam's a greatly successful area manager for the Enterprise car hire company, Owen a senior broadcast journalist with the BBC in London and sundry foreign fields – in most of which he can usually find an expats' team for a kickabout.

It may not be said that our tastes have always coincided, however. One day when Adam was at university in Manchester we arranged to watch a match in Cheshire, the plan that we'd travel by train from opposite directions and meet in the magnificent real ale bar on Stalybridge railway station, first there to get the beers in.

Adam's train edged it. He sat at the end of the bar, ten

brass-bright hand pumps, with a pint of something which in appearance fairly closely resembled the contents of a long-neglected cess pit. "It's diesel," he intoned and to this day retains rather strange tastes in alcohol.

They are great, great men.

23 : WEATHER VEIN

IF not exactly praying for rain, news editors on a quiet day are frequently grateful for it. Every cloud, and all that. The same might be supposed when heavy snow drifts in or in the event of a gentle gale. It's all ill wind. They're simply called weather stories and, as Dr Johnson suggested, among Englishmen can always start a conversation.

Inevitably that raises the journalistic moral dilemma of whether no news is bad news and, more crucially, if the opposite applies – but let's not get too philosophical. Weather stories can also be of the "Phew what a scorcher" sort, of course, but photographers are particularly fond of a cold snap.

If there's promise of a good sunrise they'll find themselves in front of St Mary's lighthouse at Whitley Bay, if there's a heatwave they'll be somewhere in the vicinity of the Black Midden rocks at Cullercoats, if it's snowing they'll see how far up the dales they can follow the plough and if it's especially stormy they'll point a long lens at crashing waves around Seaham pier, where a reputation for huge seas is tragically well known.

Usually dependent upon public transport, I'm happy in a downpour to hold to those wise words from *The Wind in the Willows*: "What's a little wet to a water rat?"

The great flood of Page Bank was revisited in an earlier chapter, the floods which ruined a sorrow drowning night in the Brit are mentioned elsewhere, too. One April Saturday in

YOUTH HOSTELLING: *With Sharon in Baldersdale*

1981, officially a day off between Friday and Sunday shifts on the desk, I'd arranged to attend the official opening of a new youth hostel at Baldersdale, on County Durham's wildest and most westerly extreme – Hannah Hauxwell country, as later it became known.

There'd been heavy overnight snow, several inches deep in Darlington and several feet on the fells. Sharon, five months pregnant, drove to within two miles of the new hostel and then had to abandon the car. Mike Cowling, an ever-amiable and greatly able photographer, followed. We yomped the last two miles, only to learn from the warden that the ceremony had been called off because of the blizzard and that they'd told everyone except us.

It was yet another case of cloud and silver lining. A buffet that might have fed the five thousand remained free to a good home. The four of us made valiant attempts to shift the lot – the cakes particularly memorable – before the warden took us back in his 4x4 to the cars. The official opening was re-scheduled for mid-summer, but I still made a point of sending someone else.

The most memorable weather story of all blew up between March 16-18 1979, when British Summer Time officially began. It was the weekend of the great snowfall – "the century's worst weather," the *Echo* confidently concluded on the Monday morning – and it caught the North-East cold.

It had begun on the Friday evening. By the following morning the scale of the white-out became evident. Stories that on a routine news day might have made half a page were lucky to get half a paragraph, the news desk engulfed in a great cascade of human interest and of heroism – and I was the news editor.

The storm had particularly affected North Yorkshire and County Durham. At Askrigg, in Wensleydale, every able-bodied male was out at 2am to clear a path for the ambulance, at Barnard Castle only one police car could be mobilised – and that not for very long – at Sherburn Grange, near Durham, an RAF helicopter had to fly a pregnant woman to hospital in Hartlepool and at Sedgefield teacher Jan Hutton found herself making shepherd's pie for 400 stranded souls.

Among the worst affected places was Shildon, towards which I headed with Mike Cowling – poor old Mike, it always seemed to be him – on the Saturday afternoon. The previous evening had been the Shildon policemen's ball – jokes of a vulgar nature may again be inserted according to taste – with all out-of-town guests obliged to camp down on the Civic Hall floor. Most were still there.

Still the snow fell. Soon it became obvious that Mike and I were similarly stuck. Newton Aycliffe, three or four miles away, was the home of energetic local councillor Tony Moore, an amiable Scouse exile who knew how to play the press for mutual benefit. I rang and asked if we might beg a bed – Tony at once agreed and arranged to meet us in the Southerne Club, close to his home and among his regular haunts.

Inevitably, unmissably, there were stories there, too – not least the wedding party for George Judge and Anne Pinkney

141

which went ahead, though they'd been totally unable to get to the register office in Bishop Auckland – eight miles away – to tie the knot.

The drifts were 15ft above our heads either side of Middridge Bank as Mike and I plodded in the face of the storm towards the new town. Tony, as ever immaculate in pinstriped suit with matching tie and pocket handkerchief, nobly got the beers in. Able to see even less than usual, I pinched his pristine handkerchief to clean and de-ice the glasses. That illegal use of the handkerchief was the closest I ever saw to the admirable Councillor Moore losing his rag.

A LOVELY follow-up to all those winter's tales arrived 30 years later – a bit of a lengthy gestation period, even for me.

Peter Brookes, a councillor for the Trimdon area, had been at a conference in London when he fell to chatting over lunch with Andy Rust, at the time an assistant social services director in Cornwall. Peter mentioned that he lived in Trimdon.

Andy at once recalled that as a young graduate in March 1979, he'd been travelling on a United bus from Peterlee to Middlesbrough when it became trapped in a snowdrift near Trimdon Village. There are at least four Trimdons, understand – Village, Colliery, Grange, Station – so it's necessary to differentiate. Unable to continue, Andy had been given shelter in the village by John Burton, another local councillor, who became Tony Blair's long-serving constituency agent, who'd scored a lot of goals for Stockton and for Shildon and has for 50 years led a greatly jolly folk band called Skerne – after the river which rises nearby.

It was three days before Andy could get on his way again. "If he'd stopped much longer I could have claimed family allowance for him," said John. "By the Saturday morning you could walk along the lanes and touch the telegraph wires."

Back at the conference, Peter Brookes listened incredulously. "So you're the Trimdon Refugee, you're legendary," he said. "Every time it snows in Trimdon, people talk about the Refugee."

Andy had been cold, miserable and broke, spent much of those three days checking on the old folk and visiting Trimdon's pubs – "I don't think I bought a drink," he said.

On that same weekend exactly 30 years later, he and his family were back in Trimdon to plant a tree on the green and to make a donation to the parish council in belated gratitude for their hospitality. The tree stands still, despite all that the North-East weather can throw at it. "I reckon I owed them," he said.

24 : MOORS MURDER

THE newsdesk day was necessarily and customarily sedentary, usually interrupted by a lunchtime stroll to the Britannia, a street corner pub where the publisher J M Dent was born and where, then as now, the Strongarm was kept in great good fettle. Brewed by Cameron's in Hartlepool, Strongarm was aimed at the town's steel workers when launched in 1955 – "beer for men who work hard," said the adverts. That was all right, then.

The Brit was immaculately kept for 25 years – to the day – by Amy and Pat Kilfeather, so traditional that on the second Sunday before Easter they still served carlins, cooked memorably with butter and onions, atop the bar. Everyone knows the legend of Carlin Sunday, don't they, and of the windy day which follows it? They do in Tynemouth, anyway.

Pat was a usually genial Irishman but with a tendency for refusing to serve folk without obvious reason. He wasn't obliged to give one, of course, but gum chewers had no chance.

Even in his last week, Pat served a couple of guys a pint and then asked them to drink up and leave. The offence is thought to have been that one of them had nipped out to place a bet. Perhaps he didn't close the door behind him.

There'd be an editor's conference at noon, another around 5.30pm, after which the pace would usually ease, for the news gatherers if not the sub-editors – all paper and pencil in those days, and an ash tray by many of the chairs. Sometimes if there were a late-breaking story, or if reporters weren't available on the relevant patch, Steve Hobman and I would head out and do it ourselves by way of keeping our hands in (and not having to bath the bairns.)

On one occasion we drove to rural west Durham, where a poor toddler had died after climbing onto a worktop, opening a cupboard door and swallowing an overdose of what she thought were sweets. Again we were immensely grateful that the devastated parents understood that we, too, had a job to do – and, in this case, a terrible warning to underline.

We went back to a pub in Cockfield, wrote the story, tossed for who'd find a call box from which to phone it over. As usual, I lost. Cockfield has a street called Bleak Terrace: that night it was easy to suppose how it came by its name.

The kiosk in question had few remaining panes of glass and in any case was occupied by a young lady in heated communication with the presumed love of her life. "But Tracey, I do love you," she finally pleaded. Steve and I had probably not come across that one before, and certainly not in Cockfield.

PERHAPS the most memorable late-breaker, however, was news that the body of Mark Johns had been dug up by police on the wild emptiness opposite the Bowes Moor Hotel, alongside the A66 near the Durham/Cumbria border.

Mark was a former Fleet Street journalist, chiefly on the *Daily Express*, who claimed to have been the world's first full-time television critic. Tiring of London and of the rat race, he said, he and his wife Jo had bought the Bowes Moor in the mid-70s.

Mark vowed to follow a countryman's lifestyle but soon missed some sort of association with newspapers and newspapermen. I'd originally been up to write the story for *John North* and was several times invited back as an overnight guest.

Mark meant well – faint praise, perhaps, but he did – his chief problem that he simply never stopped talking, and at about 200 words a minute. An awful lot of cuddies on Bowes Moor appeared to have no hind legs, an awful lot of visitors may have found themselves asleep long before being allowed to turn in.

The hotel didn't go well, few customers and rumours of big debts. Then one day Mark disappeared. When his car was found near Hull docks, it was assumed that he'd fled to Holland or somewhere to escape his creditors. Jo would quite have liked to get her hands on him, too.

Several years passed before a couple of lads were arrested in Darlington for a burglary offence. "While we're here," they told the polliss, "we might as well tell you about the murder."

The level of constabulary incredulity is unrecorded. Suffice that, finally convinced, they arrived in large numbers atop the moonlit moor – and that's where Steve and I finally pitched up, too. The culprits had worked at the hotel, thought little of their boss, finally blasted him from the top of the stairs with his own shotgun and interred him on the other side of the road. It was they who finally talked.

ANOTHER important part of the news editor's job, or so it seemed to me, was to maintain relations with the great and the good. Frequently that meant a Friday evening beer with Darlington MP Michael Fallon – later Sir Michael and Her Majesty's Secretary of State for Defence. He usually seemed to be famished.

On one occasion just about the only food the pub sold was Mars Bars. Overdosing on the adage that a Mars a day helps you work, rest and play, the honourable member had four pints and four Mars bars before we retired to our house for a nightcap. The bairns were then small. A doting grandmother had recently returned from holiday bearing large amounts of confectionery. Michael sat there wolfing pretty much all of it. The bairns may not much have noticed at that age, but their mother never forgave him.

They were the days of the Falklands War, the year-long miners' strike, of the Yorkshire Ripper and of the Pope's visit to Great Britain – including a Mass on York racecourse to be attended by hundreds of thousands of the faithful, most carrying little yellow and white flags, and covered by an *Echo* team of six or seven.

Coverage of the Papal visit took much planning across *Echo* departments. One meeting, for some reason at Teesside Airport, was interrupted by a message from my secretary – good old Julie – that a Darlington man had become one of the world's first heart transplant patients and my involvement in another planning session ended with news that a police officer had been murdered during a wages raid at a factory outside Bishop Auckland.

The new heart recipient was Joe Burnside, a carpet dealer who lived for another 30 years; the police officer was Detective Constable Jim Porter. Almost four decades later there was no need to check either name – you don't forget things like that – and on the second occasion I had to leave His Holiness to the Vatican.

I'd asked Dorothy Byrne, a feistily brilliant reporter in the Durham office, to write the main colour piece from York and can still remember how it began: "You must have seen me on the telly, I was the one waving the yellow-and-white flag." Dorothy became Channel 4's head of news, a post she has long held – no less feisty, it's reckoned, and doubtless no less brilliant.

They were also the dying days of old technology, of hot metal presses throbbing day and night, of pencil-chewing sub-editors – often with a cigarette in their free hand – of hard copy messages endlessly borne from the wire room, of post arriving twice daily and, of course, of cussed carbon paper. When the photographic department acquired one mobile phone between the lot of them, it was the size and weight of an Apollo astronaut's hand luggage.

The digital age was almost upon us, however; the age of

147

courses – courses for almost everything – was dawning, too.

On one of the first, somewhat optimistically aimed at those thought to have a bright future, a jumble of journalists of roughly my age and seniority gathered around a table in Hastings eyeing one another's prospects. The chief sub-editor from the *Basildon Evening Echo*, I concluded, looked the most likely to fancy a few beers when finally we were liberated

So it proved, but Drew Smith had a second agenda. He was desperately in search of jellied eels, a quest which took us to half the pubs in Sussex before his craving could be satisfied. Within a few years, Drew was a greatly esteemed editor of the Consumers' Association *Good Food Guide* and I was writing *Eating Owt* – a Geordie pun of which I was quite proud – for the *Echo*. Up our way, however, jellied eels were never likely to take the place of mushy peas, or indeed of Taylor's pies.

Another course extolled lateral thinking, along the lines of Edward de Baloneyo, those attending assured within five minutes that anything which took place in the days to come would strictly remain within those walls. Least said about that pledge the better.

A similar but more scatter-gunned course followed in the 1990s, everyone on the payroll obliged to attend for two days and with varying degrees of enthusiasm. The leader, a young man in sharp suit and shiny red braces, sarcastically observed one post-Brit afternoon that he was sorry to be keeping me awake.

"Not at all," I said, "the very opposite is the case." It remains my finest hour.

As the new age dawned, there were inevitably computer courses, too – why in Tring, for goodness sake? – and after long school days of never being able to see the blackboard, I instead found myself unable to see the whiteboard, sometimes barely even the keyboard.

The myopic slowness in embracing new technology stirred whispers of Luddism. Nothing could have been further from the truth – none could be more appreciative of all that innovation has made possible, not least for research purposes, but it may have sparked what happened next.

Allan Prosser, who had taken over as editor from Don Evans, had a very different approach from his predecessor. He was a big man, a hard man, a hands-on man who liked to remind us who was boss.

I still thought I was a pretty good news editor, knew the patch inside out, worked like stink, cared a great deal, generated any amount of stories and ideas, got on pretty well with most of the reporters – there were one or two snake-like exceptions – and enjoyed what these days is called creative tension with Jon Smith, the chief sub, with whom I'm still mates.

It was therefore a total surprise to be called into the editor's office one summer evening in 1985 and to be told that I was being relieved of the post. It transpired that the job – my job – had been anonymously advertised in *UK Press Gazette* and that a replacement had been lined up, if not then formally appointed.

The editor had no idea what I should do next, but did – extraordinarily – offer a £1,500 pay rise for not doing what I had been doing in the first place and for doing something else, anything else, in the future. A cynic might call it a sweetener.

There'd not been a word of advice, much less of encouragement, admonition or explanation. I simply hadn't seen it coming, but that's myopia for you. It was to be the start of something big.

25 : NO SMOKE...

SO what would happen next? Constructive dismissal? It seemed possible but just not worth the hassle. Besides, I was a North-East lad who loved the job, the region and the paper – and who else would employ a journalist who'd never be able to drive? The firm was always greatly understanding about that.

The editor seemingly having no idea what to do with me, save offer a substantial pay rise, I floated phantasmagorically for a fortnight after relinquishing the chair with arms and then made some proposals.

Since it seemed to me that our sports coverage was too pedestrian, too "professional" and too predictable – the editor at once agreed – there'd be a fact-based bi-weekly column to be called *Backtrack*, concentrating on the grass roots, the offbeat and the improbable.

It was to be self-generated, in no way a convenient receptacle for sports desk overmatter. As with almost everything else, 90 per cent of the content would never otherwise have found its way into the paper, much less on the back of so idiosyncratic a vehicle. As with everything else, it would be people and not opinion-based and as with everything else it would maintain barge-pole distance from the burgeoning public relations industry.

The trade likes to call such stuff human interest stories, presumably to differentiate them from those of no interest whatever, or of interest only to the dog.

The column lasted for 34 years, covered everything from hurling to kurling and from rowing to wrestling – I once saw Big Daddy's bare backside, the things that happen when you haven't a camera to hand – but majored on grass roots cricket and football. It won very many regional and three national awards, attracted huge feedback and offered its author untold enjoyment.

Backtrack readers would even learn in time that the bowling for Benwell Hill Cricket Club in Newcastle was opened by Shiraz Khan and Tom Cant, that Subbuteo once had an angling version and that a peckish bat can get through 3,000 midges on a good night. We never did work out, any of us, why it was looking so black over Bill's mother's.

From the autumn of 1985 there'd also be that *Eating Owt* column, combining food reviews with news from the region's food and drink industry, particularly when seen through the bottom of a pint pot.

Then the editor came up with the *Gadfly* column – nice title, nice pesky logo to follow – which reasonably he imagined would chiefly oversee and occasionally undermine the region's politicians, local and national. It developed into something broader but, it was to be hoped, no less biting.

The columns were born and the columnist reborn. I even found myself a little broom cupboard of an office, stocked it with books and frequently closed the door. Thus began a sort of semi-detachment from much of the rest of the newspaper which lasted until I retired from full-time journalism in 2011. Working from home thereafter, the only reason for me to close the door was when Sharon was listening to *The Archers*.

JUST when things seemed to be returning to an even keel, however, the editor had another idea. He wanted me to write a "Village" column.

The *Village* column would appear fortnightly, requiring me to book into a North-East pub or hotel around Friday teatime, to absorb as much of the community atmosphere as possible and to leave again after Sunday lunch – pretty much a 48-hour shift on its own and with around 2,000 multi-faceted words to write thereafter. That Sharon was being left with two very young children every other weekend hardly helped matters. It continued for seven or eight columns until, late one Monday evening, I was admitted to coronary care at Darlington Memorial Hospital.

Save for the unfortunate business of the lawnmower a couple of years earlier, I'd always been pretty healthy, and even the lawnmower incident could be attributed to chronic stupidity and not physical (or electrical) malfunction. I'd been cutting the grass about 30 yards from the house and out of sight of it, a lovely summer afternoon with Adam, then three, playing at my feet. Probably quite a lot of people slice through the cable; rather fewer may pick up the live end to check what's wrong.

The live wire wouldn't put me down. "Get help," I shout-ed to my elder son as consciousness faded. He ran scream-ing towards the house, his mum – looking after his sleeping baby brother – able to discern just one word through Adam's panic. It was "wires."

Anyone else would have wondered what it was all about, perhaps ran up to the top lawn to find out. Sharon at once thought "My exceptionally foolish and wholly impractical husband has plugged himself into the National Grid," pulled out the extension lead plug in the sitting room and then – only then – went to see what the matter was. It saved my life.

After initial tests at the Memorial, they asked if she could drive. It was necessary to have specialist attention at Mid-dlesbrough General (as then it was) and, then as now, there was a shortage of ambulances. Adam was rewarded with a bottle of Coke.

Coronary care was different. After 24 generally sleepless and fairly anxious hours, I enquired of a nurse if I might have the ten o'clock news on television. She, in turn, asked the chap in the next bed if he minded. "It's mint imperial to me," he said, a memorable example of Cockney rhyming slang.

It was a family joke that I could never stay awake during the ten o'clock news. So it proved, At 3am they stirred me because someone who was properly poorly needed the bed. Mine wasn't a heart attack. Save for all sorts of theories about extreme stress they never really got to the bottom of it – but the *Village* column, if not the *Village* columnist, was quietly laid to rest.

THAT column still had some memorable moments, not least in Wheatley Hill – home of the east Durham flapping track – where I stayed with Tom Thubron, an old friend and former Bangladesh missionary who was then the vicar.

Joined by Mike Cowling, poor old Mike yet again, I headed about 11 o'clock on the Saturday morning for the bar of the workmen's club. As we headed in, the crowded bar – almost to a man – hurried out.

It was Mike's photographic gear that had spooked them. "We thought you were the Nash," they explained later, the further explanation that in those parts "the Nash" is still the term for the National Insurance, which became the DHSS and is something just as frugally tight-fisted today.

The Wheatley Hill lads, at any rate, were far too dependent upon the black economy to be wholly comfortable when someone with a camera saw them with a table full of beer (and especially if a clock were in the background.)

Another weekend was spent in Fishburn, a third at Jolly Jack Robinson's pub in Mickleton – where the carnival had unceremoniously been opened a few years earlier– a wintry couple of nights in Rookhope, high in Weardale.

Perhaps best remembered for the Rev Arthur White Officer, a slightly strange vicar to whom we shall come in another chapter, Rookhope was also home to a chap of 90-or-so called Wilf Swindell-Brown, who lived an almost hermitic existence up a stony path high above the village. As Hannah

Hauxwell did a few years later, he'd have made a great book.

It was Reeth, however, which provided the most memorable and the most colourful weekend of all – and, praise be, with a fire brigade angle, too.

I'd always enjoyed fire brigade stories, right back to the time at Bishop Auckland when the local firefighters complained to the gaffers in Durham that the watch room was, rather appropriately, hot enough to grow tomatoes. Headquarters, you might say – but probably shouldn't – poured cold water on it.

Unknown to the bosses, but not to the ever-curious columnist, the lads grew some rather splendid tomatoes in the watch room. Once Bill Oliver had got his pictures, the firemen got their ventilation.

Then there was the 1970s night that the Cosy Cinema in Middleton-in-Teesdale burned down and the village's part-time brigade were summoned by their pagers. Two of the lads were in the middle of a hand of dominoes at the Over 60s club, one 73 and the other 67. They did a magnificent job, none doubted it, but thereafter it was decreed that even retained firefighters must retire at 55.

REETH's in Swaledale, North Yorkshire, a delightful spot which also has a retained – part-time – fire brigade and where in 1977 I'd run with the story of the firemen's ball.

The problem was Fireman Simon Coates, a lively character who'd been banned from the Buck – the Top House – after an incident at a darts match. The Buck was where the fire brigade held its annual dinner dance: on no account, said the landlord, could they have it again if Fireman Coates were in attendance.

Passing the Buck – or not, as the case may be – they'd held a secret ballot. Should they stick with the Buck but without Simon, or move the knees-up elsewhere? The brigade voted 11-1 in favour of the status quo. Simon was the one.

The long-time sub-officer in charge was Tom Guy, a local garage owner with a wealth of stories like the time they rescued a goat from up a tree.

In the great floods of July 2019, the firemen of Reeth and of Leyburn – a few miles across the top in Wensleydale – took 115 calls for assistance in just a few hours. When I settled into the Buck Inn that Friday evening in 1986, there'd not been a shout of any sort, not even a goat up a tree, for 11 weeks.

Tom was in the bar, expecting nothing to disturb the weekend peace.

GOOD BET:
Tom Guy at Reeth

Serendipity squared, I bet him £10 that there'd be a call.

The full English that sunny Sunday morning was interrupted by the klaxon of Tom's fire engine, a two-tone ode to joy. Fifty yards along the road, the tail-end Charlie left at the station offered details of the emergency: cow in ditch at Grinton, half a mile down the hill.

It was an 8ft dry ditch, more of a moat surrounding a farmhouse. If that's what they call a haha, then the cow – down there all night – seemed distinctly unamused. "I didn't like to disturb you," said the farmer. Tom was first down a ladder to see what was to do. "Which one's Tom and which one's t'cow?" someone asked, insubordinately.

"Tom's t'one in't 'at," replied another fireman. (It was Simon Coates.)

While rescue plans were successfully being drawn up,

155

Tom glanced down dale and saw another fire engine, blue lights flashing, heading in their direction. He hadn't asked for reinforcements, told one of the lads to radio in and find out what on earth was going on. Another cow in another ditch, this time on the far side of Reeth, and a crew sent up from Richmond – 11 miles away – to extricate it.

Then they saw the third fire engine. This one was from Northallerton, it transpired, sent to rescue the second which had become stuck in the mud. The village fire brigade which hadn't had a shout for 11 weeks had effectively had three inside an hour.

I gave Tom's tenner, and mine, to the fire service benevolent fund. Never mind the *Village* column, they again had to hold the front page.

26 : HILLSBOROUGH

REQUESTS to supplement what's known as hard news coverage became much less frequent after 1985 – maybe they realised I had quite a bit on as it was – an exception the Hillsborough football ground disaster in April 1989. The Saturday evening had been the annual Tom Cordner Awards, for North-East journalists and in memory of a much respected news editor of the *Hartlepool Mail*. While there, I was asked to go to Liverpool, a city in mourning, the next day.

Sharon came, too, the abiding and overwhelming memory the dignity, the humanity and the helpfulness of Liverpudlians in the face of a terrible and almost corporate tragedy. They

FOOTBALL TRAGEDY: *Hillsborough*

were incredible. Even when our old car broke down in the middle of the road near the Anglican cathedral, the crew of a passing bin wagon stopped to get it going again. The Scousers were, and are, wonderful.

The other memory, I suppose, is that the editor suggested that my front page piece might have been too short. No one before or since has accused me of under-writing, but he was absolutely right.

A postscript came on Friday May 26 that year when Arsenal, my team, went to Liverpool needing to win by two goals to take the old first division title. Failure to achieve that, and Liverpool were champions. The Arsenal players handed 25 bouquets around the ground before kick-off.

Lacking the courage to watch at home, I took myself to the Raby Hunt in Burnthouses, an interestingly named little hamlet near Raby Castle in County Durham and one of the few pubs which didn't have a television. Owen, just turned five, had to his eternal chagrin been packed off to bed by his mum. Adam, seven, was allowed to stay up to watch.

Shortly after word arrived in the Raby Hunt that an up-for-grabs added-time goal had given Arsenal a 2-0 victory – and that Adam had broken down in tears – my old friend George Parkinson walked into the pub. He was a police inspector, several times the British police weight-lifting champion, and a true gentle giant.

Familiar in pubs around the area, George could usually be discerned amid a thick cloud of purple pipe smoke, observing – as was his wont – that there was no fear of steady men. The Anfield crowd had again been magnificent, acknowledged Arsenal's right to celebrate one of the most memorable victories in football history.

In the Raby Hunt at Burnthouses, and in the company of the local police inspector, we celebrated long into the night as well – and raised a glass to the City of Liverpool, one of the best places on earth.

27 : HATCHED, MATCHED...

A MONG the saddest things I wrote in these early days
back constructing columns was an obituary of the *Despatch*, the evening paper where it had all begun. It folded in
1986 after a gallant fight for survival, though the Saturday
sports edition – the florid *Pink* – had gone several years earlier.

Always the *Echo*'s younger sister, sometimes perceived
as the poor relation, the *Despatch* had been launched in 1914,
two or three times switched masthead between *Northern* and
Evening, concentrated its coverage on Darlington and the
south-west of County Durham. For many years the papers
had a joint staff.

Arnold Hadwin, editor when I joined, fiercely championed the paper's place in the community and its editorial
independence from the *Echo*. He was a great editor. Robin
Thompson, the last incumbent of that chair, was perhaps
even more passionately committed.

Robin was an exuberant Geordie with a fondness for deck
chair blazers who fizzed through those difficult days, used
always to accentuate the difference between the morning and
evening papers – not least that the *Despatch* was younger at
heart – and was devastated when the closure decision came.

He also nourished and motivated a great galaxy of future
journalistic stars, including news editor Tony Watson who
went on to edit the *Yorkshire Post*. I was therefore pretty
disappointed that many who read that valedictory column
seemed to think it unsympathetic. Some even supposed it

159

SAD NEWS: *The last edition of the Despatch*

schadenfreude, a term we used all the time in Shildon. The kindest comment I can find on-line is that the tribute was "neat", encapsulating all that's said about damning and faint praise.

Maybe I didn't feel it as much as those whose jobs had been threatened, or lost, but the *Despatch* was the mother ship, the paper which afforded some of the happiest days of my life. Certainly they were the most educational. Few, even then, may have foreseen how many titles would follow its demise.

It had been printed in-house, presses rolling between producing the *Echo* and a great stable of weeklies, the eagerly awaited first edition usually on the streets by about 1.45pm and updated thereafter, not least with the racing results (and maybe a pit closure in south Durham.)

These days, 2020, there are almost no 'evening' papers. Though the titles are similar – the *Chronicle* in Newcastle, the *Gazette* in Middlesbrough – they're usually printed over-night, often many miles from the conurbation with which they were traditionally associated, and are usually in the shops –

none is sold on the streets – by breakfast time. Sales have almost always plummeted, sometimes to just a few thousand, hope and resources still invested in a second coming on-line.

Times change. A final chapter will look at some of the reasons for newspapers' decline, though they're rooted in the generalisation that the younger generation doesn't buy papers (and the older generation, inconsiderately, dies.) In the case of Robin Thompson and his talented team on the *Despatch*, the failure certainly wasn't for want of trying.

28 : WILL POWER

AMONG the contrasts between writing self-starting columns in the 1970s and those from around 1990 onwards
was that some genius had invented the world-wide web,
email and sundry other miracles. The chief and abiding difference was that readers could instantly be drawn into the
newspaper's family circle. It was mutually beneficial.

In *John North* days the reader relationship was conducted
either by telephone or by post. Telephone communication
was sometimes unsatisfactory because so many older people
still seemed uncomfortable with it – or didn't usually have
access to it – and the Royal Mail's chief shortcoming was
that I almost never found time to reply.

Personal callers were generally not welcome, largely
because they'd found themselves in Darlington with nothing better to do and assumed that I hadn't either or because
they'd just been poured out of the pub. The reception staff,
bless them, would ring upstairs to ask if I were in. Usually
I told them I wasn't. They became proficient, if vicarious,
fibbers.

The heaviest response to a *John North* column had been
when I wrote about Harry Cox, the hirsute and vividly colourful landlord of the Marquis of Granby at Byers Green,
near Spennymoor, who'd fixed above the bar what folk formerly called a two-holer.

Two-holers had been part of the North-East social fabric.
They were neighbouring toilet seats – netties in the vernacu-
lar – usually found in a gale-tossed brick outhouse at the bot-

tom of the garden, oft surrounded by great clouds of horse-flies and the further from human habitation the better. Folk didn't just do what was necessary, they made an occasion of it and with little thought, or need, for privacy.

The netties were emptied by night. In early days attending the works and health committee of Bishop Auckland Urban District Council, I recall references to "midnight soil", a glorious if slightly time-specific euphemism. Was there an etymological link between middens and midnight men, they with the horse and cart and the long-handled shovels? I never did work it out.

Harry's two-holer stirred memories. Readers recalled three-holers, then four, claimed five. Six may have been apocryphal, just like the memory that it was always a warm summer evening and that the horseflies were the size of spug-gies. Mostly they had to write their memories down, and not just on old squares of the *News of the World*.

Maybe there were 20 responses. In the digital age there'd have been 100. In the e-mail era *Gadfly* particularly benefit-ted, the column frequently composed from reader reaction as one thing led happily, serendipitously, to another. Maybe it was a rag bag, but it was my rag bag, and it would have made a canny proggy mat.

Where else but the *Gadfly* column might readers have learned, or contributed, that newts can live to 27, or that 34,000 vehicles a day used the Tyne Tunnel, that "traffic calming" was thought Britain's biggest oxymoron or that a poster proclaiming "Redcar: Yorkshire's last resort" had been withdrawn after further consideration.

It was also a pleasure to share the news that, in a fit of pique, Darlington council official Bill Lawrence had hurled a coffee cup through his fourth floor office window. Bill was the health and safety officer. He took it in commend-ably good part. Seeking lunch one day, I was also aghast to discover – and this must have been 20 transgender years ago – that Thomas the Bakers was selling "gingerbread persons."

Generously, the gaffers even allowed a little in-house teasing. Alan Titchmarsh hadn't really been dive-bombed by a flock of skewers, as the *Echo* had supposed, but by skuas. If the *Echo*'s weekly prize crossword really were number 17,025, as we said, then it had been going for 327 years.

Particularly, however, Gadherents majored on their punctuation, their aberrant apostrophes, their typos and their artful Oxford commas. All columnists love feedback; I gorged. Such the burgeoning relationship that several readers, on visiting America, would return with packets of Famous Amos cookies – a national delicacy over there though, truth to tell, I didn't much care for them. Until Harry Whitton died, and in the absence of Famous Amos pork pies, they remained just about the biggest bounty.

HARRY was among the most valued correspondents and telephone callers – valued not least because he could always be relied upon to fill a few gaping column inches – a Dunkirk veteran and retired electrical shop owner from Thirsk in North Yorkshire who himself was an author, historian, raconteur, racehorse owner and greatly entertaining speaker.

What particularly distinguished Harry, however, was that he was an incorrigible name dropper. "I enclose a letter from Sheikh Hamdam Maktoum," he'd write or "Here is a photograph of me with Princess Anne." Or "Lord Howard de Walden once told me that his father occasionally dined while wearing a suit of armour."

Ribbed rotten in print, Harry simply came back for more,

BEQUEST FOOT FORWARD
Harry Whitton

might sling in the story about the time he appeared on stage in Bradford with J B Priestley. "You'll always be an enthusiastic amateur," Priestley had unkindly observed, but was clearly right about the enthusiasm.

Harry's last letter, in December 2004, concerned his vow never again to enter St Mary's parish church in Thirsk after being told off for photographing its pulpit. It was simply signed "Adios."

He died a few weeks later, aged 86, but it was several months before the solicitor's letter arrived – a heartsink moment as GPs are reputed to say of the appearance of particularly pesky patients. This one, however, advised that Harry had left me £500 in his will and wondered if I'd be inclined to accept.

We blew the lot on a weekend on the Northumberland coast, probably including fish and chips – among the very best – at Seahouses. I teased readers ever since, but there was never so much as a brass button.

29 : IN THE WASH

MY own switch from carbon paper and cussing to a rudi-mentary understanding of new technology was greatly helped because my little cupboard of an office was next to what newspapers called the library.

For more than a century the idea had been that every worthwhile story, and many that were utterly inconsequential, should be cut from the newspaper, pasted onto another bit of paper and filed in an appropriate packet in an appropriate place in the library. Photographs, still hard copy, were similarly treated – which is to say that the filing process was frequently a year behind and that the searcher might more easily have found a needle in a cobwebbed haystack.

The classification was arbitrary, some might suppose eccentric. The story persisted around the *Echo* that the reason cuttings on a particularly heinous killing couldn't be found was that the foolish reporter hadn't looked under N. N was for naked murders.

All that was changed by Peter Chapman and his team. Appointed head librarian to drag the *Echo*'s archiving into the digital age, Peter succeeded wonderfully – always patiently on hand to help the poor bloke in the cupboard in exchange for a cup of tea (and no matter that Peter usually made that, too.) Best of all, he was a railway enthusiast, and no matter that his preference was for what Thomas the Tank Engine called diseasels.

Gasping to maintain the pace of change, I was also invited

about 1990 to join the line-up being presented to the Prince of Wales when he visited a hospice in Bishop Auckland. To this day I've no idea what I was doing there and the heir to the throne, happily, didn't ask.

The thing which really raised the profile of all those columns, however, was a piece of good old fashioned journalism which started one Saturday morning in the bath.

Stuck for something to read, I fell to perusing the shampoo bottle. It was a product called Tricelle – "a mild shampoo with a rich, luxurious micro-lather" – which I think had been one of Sharon's freebies. Beneath the company logo was the boast "New York, London, Paris, Rome, Tokyo" and, on the back, another logo with the inscription "A product of Tricogen Laboratories, DL1 1HL."

DL1 1HL was none of those fascinating and no doubt immaculately coiffed world capitals. It was a little industrial unit on a litter-strewn industrial estate near Darlington railway station. Tricogen Laboratories, not listed in the phone book – unless, of course, it was the Tokyo phone book – was across the road from a scrapyard.

So why hadn't the shampoo people come clean and admitted that their product was made in Darlington?

A walk up there revealed that it was next to a hairdressers' supplies cash and carry called Ray and Co. Both were owned by the same chap. He admitted that Tricelle wasn't made in any of the places in the bottle, nor had they agents there. They did, he insisted, have agents in Middlesbrough and Newcastle. "It doesn't imply that it's made in those places, it implies that we hope to sell it there," he added, disingenuously.

Hitherto I'd never entered journalism competitions but that story, however immodestly, seemed a pretty compelling example of what can come out in the wash. On the back of that and other examples of what I was doing, I was named North-East Journalist of the Year in 1989-90, the first of seven such accolades in 16 years.

There were to be three national sports writing awards, numerous other regional awards, a place in the inaugural Provincial Journalism Hall of Fame, two Lifetime Achievement awards and, of course, that memorable day at Buckingham Palace (and afterwards in the Coal Hole). I stopped entering things after that.

There must have been more than 40 awards altogether – and Sharon's much-loved columns in the *Echo* deservedly kept on winning things, too.

How different things might have been if, in 1989, our house had had a shower and not a bath.

AFTER one or two hiccups, Peter Sands had been appointed editor, succeeded by Andrew Smith and in turn followed by Peter Barron, he who not many years earlier had so greatly fretted when unable to finish his third pint at interview.

All three took the view that the guy in the cupboard – it was a different cupboard by then, though much the same size – should be left alone so long as the columns kept appearing on time and in decent fettle. It seemed to me a very agreeable arrangement; the door remained ajar.

Pete Sands was an amiable and greatly able Geordie who'd been chief sub on the *Despatch* and who was destined for yet higher things. Pete Barron, a Teessider with the advantage of being an equallyimprobable Arsenal fan, occupied the editor's chair for 19 years, cared greatly, championed causes, fought tenaciously for his paper and his people and was himself appointed MBE.

For much of Pete Barron's time the MD was David Kelly, the features editor who'd so patiently sifted my stuff in the 1970s and got through a great many French fags, pungent old things, by way of calming his nerves. David, a man of great vision, also fought tirelessly for his people – who knows what odds he sometimes faced. We remain friends.

Somehow – and I really can't remember how it happened – two more columns, multi-faceted and people-based, had joined the weekly omnibus. I felt like a good Catholic mother who patiently kept adding to her offspring and vaguely wondered how it had all come about.

So for about 20 years there were two *Backtrack* columns each week, *Gadfly*, *Eating Owt*, the new Thursday column and *At Your Service*, which I enjoyed as much as any of them. More of that a little later.

30 : PROS AND CONS

FOLK in North-East England tend not to say that they're from Shildon, or wherever, but that they belong Shildon. It's a usage of which I'm greatly fond. The *Backtrack* column belonged sport's roots, maybe even its byways, seldom striving for the big league or to have dealings with those who sought to control, corral and ultimately to emasculate the media.

These days, particularly in professional football, it's almost impossible to have truck with players and managers save on semi-formal occasions or through an oft-obstructive army of press and public relations people. An early example of how things were different came around 1986, with a young man called Paul Gascoigne.

Gazza was just starting to attract attention at Newcastle United, a casual topic of conversation with Alastair Garvie, a taxi driver on a short journey from Durham station. "Oh, I'm his agent," he said and, honest, he was.

A one-to-one chat was set up after training – no minders, no pesky press officers, no taxi driving agents – in the Newcastle Arms, a traditional pub across the road from St James' Park.

We both had two pints and two cheese and onion toasties, partly because Gazza insisted on standing his round. He was brilliant, greatly friendly, but the column's one of the cuttings which has vanished from the library.

We only ever met on one other occasion, several years

TOASTIE GUY: *Gazza*

later. "You're the guy with the cheese and onion toasties," he said – a lovely and (obviously) a rather tragic man.

1986 was also the year of the Commonwealth Games in Edinburgh, which the editor decided we should cover in some depth. Three of us – sports editor Jeff Todhunter, photographer Mike Cowling and I – were booked into a spacious apartment overlooking one of Auld Reekie's grassy strays.

Transport was chiefly provided by Mike's motor bike, or it was until someone nicked it. Memory fails in any case to suggest how he managed with three of us, unless motor bikes did croggies. Jeff would provide the event reports, I had to write a daily *Backtrack* column focusing on North-East based contestants and on the queer and the quirky, trying to avoid too much about deep-fried Mars Bars and motor cycle thieves.

Had mobile phones been invented then? Probably, though I'm pretty sure we didn't have any. No such luxury as laptops, either, the column still had to be phoned each evening to a querulous copy taker. Much more of this? Och.

PRESS and competitors mixed much more freely than these days is permitted, even ate together in the athletes' village though none ever mistook me for a competitor. Among those who could never be supposed anything else was Charlie

171

Spedding, an international distance runner who kept a pharmacy in Ferryhill and was also an enthusiastic member of the Campaign for Real Ale.

Charlie sorted me squatters' rights in the Nike House, where many of the North-East contingent were based and where we'd meet in the evenings over an orange juice. Most were greatly agreeable – one who notoriously wasn't was the great Daley Thompson, who simply wouldn't talk to the press.

It seemed almost too good to be true, therefore, that one morning I found myself behind him in the athletes' village cornflake queue (a sentence which simply couldn't be written today.) Politely, apprehensively, I introduced myself and asked if we might have a chat. "No," he said, and that was my Commonwealth Games exclusive.

Though the word is egregiously abused, another *Backtrack* exclusive – there were precious few – was denied by the kind of corporate close control which now bedevils professional football. For a fairly sociable soul, I've never really run with the press pack and certainly not been herded as now, alas, they are.

It was the spring of 2001, foot and mouth disease stalking the countryside, one of its more inconsequential effects felt in the Crook and District League second division where the grounds of both Stanhope Town and Wearhead United had been ruled out of bounds as a precaution.

One team was seventh, the other eighth. There only were eight clubs. Since both grounds were closed and since they'd to meet in the season's final game, Stanhope chairman Clem O'Donovan wrote – "audaciously," he admitted – to Bob Murray, his opposite number at Sunderland FC.

The 50,000 capacity Stadium of Light was also by the Wear, said Clem. Might they use that instead? When Murray agreed– incredibly, instantly – Clem was straight on the phone to me and I to the PR department at Sunderland for a comment on what was intended both as a front page story and as incontrovertible evidence of the North-East maxim that shy bairns get nee sweets.

The PR department said that they'd break the story in their own good time, not in the *Northern Echo*'s. If we ran it before they were ready, the clubs' invitation would be withdrawn. For their sake, I had to back off.

Weardale, it might in passing be added, was clearly the place for bright ideas and brazzened bairns. When Wearhead United celebrated the club's centenary a few years later, someone spotted that it was the same weekend as Sunderland Air Show and asked if the Red Arrows might just pop by in salute.

The squadron leader rang to say no problem, the club asked what time the Arrows might be expected – thinking maybe between two and three o'clock. "15.21," said the air ace and at 15.21 precisely they looked skywards to see a formation of wing-dipping Arrows coming over the Pennines in tribute. No one said we couldn't put it in the paper.

It was also in Wearhead that, when the village's new sports pavilion was completed, they invited not the parish council chairman (or someone) to perform the official opening but Field Marshall Lord (Peter) Inge, the Chief of the Defence Staff. One of the lads had been a corporal in his regiment. The sports Field Marshall said he'd be delighted.

These things may also have made the *Weardale Gazette*, a community newspaper which served the whole dale but which a couple of years earlier had carried Stanhope Town's 12-1 defeat beneath the headline 'Stanhope in 13 goal thriller.' The *Gazette*, sadly, folded in 2019.

Clearly, at any rate, Sunderland FC knew that they'd had us by the sheep and cheerfuls, but the event was well worth it. It was the May bank holiday, all that marred the occasion the sight and smell of animal pyres as the team bus moved down dale. You could tell it was a big game, one of the lads had forsaken his pre-match pie in favour of a banana.

Goodness, they even wore ties and had arranged for someone to sing *Abide With Me*, a rendition abandoned after the intended singer wrecked his vocal chords on the workmen's club trip to Redcar – like Sunday School trips, always Redcar – the day before.

Eight other buses followed – seen off outside Stanhope club by the world, his wife and a three-legged dog –the Stadium of Light attendance put at 913. "Usually we don't even get two men and a dog, just the dog," said Stanhope secretary David Bee, as Stadium of Light became Theatre of Dreams.

The match ended 2-2 but the score didn't matter a jot. Light fantastic, if ever.

31 : WRIGHT AND WRONG

A NOTHER favourite story came from the Darlington and District Cricket League Division D – there wasn't a Division E – Trimdon Colliery and Deaf Hill playing Yarm fourth team. Grass was rarely more deeply rooted.

Facing a Yarm bowler who appeared to pose little threat, a home batsman prepared to smite a particularly gentle delivery into the next parish when the ball deviated prodigiously and uprooted his middle stump. Closer inspection revealed that the agent of deviation – some phrase – had been a swallow, and that the poor creature lay dead about two-thirds of the way down the wicket. The wretched victim unceremoniously interred in the hedge back, conversation turned to what the umpire's decision should be.

On the Monday morning, there was a call from Paul Trippett, one of the Trimdon lads, who was also a member of Tony Blair's team. I rang Dickie Bird. Who else? The celebrated test match umpire, a proud Yorkshireman, didn't charge but didn't really offer an opinion, either. Try the MCC, he said, which is where former England batsman John Jameson – then MCC's assistant secretary – gave the verdict that since it was a dead bird it should also be a dead ball.

It might not be said that one swallow made a summer, but – bless it – it didn't half make my day.

THE Durham clergy cricket team quietly married two of my interests, cricket and the Church. A post-match pint might be considered a third.

The *Church Times* runs an annual cup competition for diocesan clergy teams, Durham's frequently on its knees in terms of both resources and results. When cricket enthusiast Michael Turnbull was named the new bishop in 1994, I felt compelled to ring him – the first call I ever made to a phone in a car – to ask what he was going to do about it. He professed interest but doubted that he'd have time for a game himself.

Still they were habitually caught short, as a cricketer might suppose. A *Church Times* Cup match against the diocese of Bradford in 1997 seemed almost a re-enactment of the Parable of the Rich Man's feast ahead of which, it will be recalled, all with one consent began to make excuse.

The star bowler's wife had inconsiderately gone into labour, three more team members claimed funerals, a fifth had taken his dog to the vet's. "That dog's the most important thing in my life," he pleaded.

"What about Jesus?" someone replied.

By the appointed hour, Durham had just seven men and no sign of their bishop appearing over the hill with the Calvary cavalry. When the game began 45 minutes behind schedule, some of these guys late for other people's funerals, numbers had swelled to eight.

The Rev Jonathan Lawson, vicar of Usworth, Washington, was scorer. In the space where it said "Date of match" he had written St Boniface Day. Boniface was the patron saint of lost causes.

The match was at Masham, a charming North Yorkshire village best known for its breweries. My offer to help make up the numbers having faithfully been turned down – rules ordained that it should be ministers only, orders is orders – I offered instead to stand the beers in the event of a surprising, some might say miraculous, victory.

Such fixtures, apparently, were not always characterised by fraternity. Philip North, a Sunderland priest who once had a letter in the *Guardian* defending his beloved Arsenal, was said to have been formally warned by the York umpire for what might best be termed youthful over-exuberance. Father North became a bishop.

Despite a difficult start, the eight men reached 157 in their allotted overs against opponents for whom batsman Bradley was reckoned a particularly formidable opponent. Bradley was indeed going well in reply until a ball pitched a good two feet outside off stump, struck the boot which the batsman had carelessly left in the vicinity and rolled without word of contrition onto the stumps.

"Well, bless my soul," said one of the Durham number.

"Bugger me," said a West Yorkshire opponent.

It was one of those seminal moments when it's possible not just to believe that God's in his heaven and all's right with the world but that the Maker studied theology at Cranmer College, Durham.

Bradford collapsed to 76 all out, the biggest slaughter since the Children of Israel had that little set-to with the Midianites. It was a happy band of pilgrims which retired to the pub and, good as my word, I stood the beers. I always did believe in giving to the church.

For eight years thereafter the Durham team didn't win another match – that's when they could raise a side – a concern I eventually raised with Tom Wright, Michael Turnbull's successor as bishop. "As you would expect of me, I am not without hope," he said – but the team gave up the ghost soon afterwards.

TOM Wright, an academic with little or no parish experience, was Durham's bishop from 2003-10 – a man who got through so much work, said Archbishop John Sentamu at the bishop's farewell service, that he was suspected of being a consortium. At the press conference to announce his appointment, he'd spoken of the need to "engage with the post postmodern society." They talked of little else in West Cornforth,

I felt obliged, in print, to observe.

Ever trying to keep the region's feet on the ground, the subsequent column also noted Mrs Wright's "vertiginous" heels. Thereafter we were frequently acquainted, both Sharon and I several times guests at functions at Auckland Castle – then home to Durham's bishops – and entertained not so much episcopally as royally.

Nothing proved more memorable, however – nor more newsworthy – than the new bishop's first Sunday service in his new diocese, in the small west Durham village of Hamsterley.

Hamsterley was unusual in that it still retained three churches – Anglican, Methodist and Baptist – not to mention a social club, a pub, a community tennis court and a village hall which staged film shows among much else. Though unlicensed, it clinked agreeably on such occasions.

WRIGHT REVEREND:
Former Bishop of Durham
Tom Wright

Bishop Tom's visit was less than a fortnight after his enthronement at Durham Cathedral, the new man toting just a small attaché case in which a more secular soul might have carried his cheese and pickle sandwiches.

A few minutes later, he re-emerged in full episcopal fig. Had the name Marvo the Magician been inscribed on that little case, it could hardly have seemed more improbable. It was something of a disappointment to learn that his chauffeur had arrived before both of us, bearing a portmanteau of fortnight-in-Blackpool proportions, but that wasn't the story.

His 13-minute sermon, lucid and compelling, was based on a letter he'd received a few days earlier from "David, aged eight-and-a-half", in Oxford. David was one of those young men who knew clearly what he wanted. "If more people pray for the same thing, is God more likely to answer?" he asked. "If so, will you pray that I get a go-kart for Christmas?"

The writing was child-like, accompanied by a couple of winsome illustrations which the bishop eagerly showed his congregation, quoting the example of Aslan in *The Lion, the Witch and the Wardrobe*. "Aslan was powerful, wise and loving but not tame," he said. "The question was not how to get Aslan to do things for you but could Aslan enlist you in his service."

Bishop Tom was convinced that the letter was genuine. I wasn't. Was he the intended victim of a sort of ecclesiastical Henry Root, seeking material for his next book?

The following March he received another letter from David, who had indeed had a go-kart for Christmas. This time the child, perhaps nine by then, had another dilemma. His friend Sanjeet had stolen his bongies – Oxfordshire for marbles, apparently – and was unrepentant. "Should I forgive someone if they aren't sorry?" he wondered. "He doesn't give a dam (*sic*) but still wants to hang out with me."

Bishop Tom had mentioned it at a primary school talk in Middleton St George, near Darlington, remained convinced of the letters' authenticity. "I have about a ten per cent suspicion that there is an adult standing behind," he said. "The question was succinct and clearly put but it could easily have been a bright six-or-seven-year old."

By then I was much more suspicious. It was all too profound, too clever by half A colleague on the *Oxford Mail*, part of the same newspaper group, agreed to call at David's address to see what could be discovered. He'd not been able to get there by the time that the column went to press. It was headed "The bongies dilemma and other theological questions."

By the following week, the *Mail* man had delivered. The guy who'd answered the door was aged 28, also called David, married but with no children. Though he declined to answer further questions, the truth soon became clear.

For once Bishop Tom declined to talk to me directly, but sent a message through his chaplain saying that it was a great shame. "The biblical text about forgiving seventy times seven doesn't mean you stop forgiving after 490 times but that you keep on forgiving," she added.

The scripture about out of the mouths of babes and sucklings? "Children are very intelligent, you should never underestimate them," the chaplain added.

Nor should we, but on this occasion the luminously learned bishop had not just been taken for a ride, but taken for a ride on a go-kart.

32 : BOXING DAYS

BOXING had grass roots, too, never more incorrigibly promoted than by Paul Hodgson, the showman secretary of Spennymoor Boxing Academy. Never a boxer himself, Hodgy still held the UK All Comers' Dole Drawing championship, having not officially worked for more than 40 years and none from the Nash able to lay a glove on him – though goodness knows they tried.

On one occasion he was hauled in after I'd reported, pretty much in passing, that he and his family were back from a cruise down the Rhine. The dole office manager demanded to know how they could afford it. Hodgy at once retorted that his journalist mate was going a bit deaf. "It was a cruise down the Tyne," he insisted.

All those years of window cleaning, he added, was just an unpaid favour for a friend.

Hodgy had also made the column after a wager with Gary, one of his sons, over who could grow the tallest sunflower. The lad seemed distinctly to be heading towards the heliotropics when one morning he woke to find his prize bloom mysteriously deflowered. His dad pleaded innocence. "It must be that acid rain," he said.

Had he been a bit more conventional, sported fewer tattoos, worn a tie, toed a line or had better taste in caps – those he wears are the size, shape and probably consistency of a Grandma Batty's Yorkshire pudding – Hodgy could have made a fortune in public relations. He simply fizzed with good ideas, rarely more memorably than the day the club or-

181

ganised a trip to the Millennium Stadium in Cardiff to watch Lennox Lewis fight Frank Bruno.

We'll come to Mad Frankie Fraser in a moment.

The coach, said Hodgy, would pick me up about 6am at Scotch Corner, a mile from our house. It proved not to be a coach but what folk call a crew bus, and on this occasion a distinctly motley crew bus. They'd already started on the supermarket lager.

BUCKET BRIGADE:
Hodgy with boxing academy coach Robert Ellis

Breakfast was taken at a motorway services somewhere north of Birmingham, after which it seemed wise to have a little shut-eye before the day's further rigours. Waking an hour later, I was momentarily surprised and soon greatly alarmed to see a motorway sign reading 'Milton Keynes 6.'

Milton Keynes is not notably near Cardiff, nor was it remotely en route. Innocents abroad, they'd taken the M1 instead of the M5 and might have ended up beneath Marble Arch before anyone noticed. The hotel, belatedly reached – and via the Severn Bridge – was in Merthyr Tydfil. That's where the motley crew bus had a collision in the car park.

Finally we made the fight, seats so far from the action that we might have been in orbit. Hodgy, for whom the phrase about getting where draughts cannot might have been coined, somehow found himself at ringside.

It ended after midnight. As the bus passed Cardiff railway station I asked to be dropped off in the hope that there might be a milk train to somewhere, pretty much anywhere. Thus it was that, via London, I was home by 9am – and probably in bed before that lot.

MAD Frankie was Hodgy's idea, too. Then in his 80s, an occupational pension unlikely to have been available, the former East End gangland enforcer was trying to supplement his income with personal appearances. Hodgy got him to do the club's annual presentations, in a marquee at Whitworth Hall.

"Frankie said he didn't want to do Spennymoor, it would give him a bad name," he said.

He turned up with Marilyn Wisbey, his girl friend, whose father had been a Great Train Robber. Frankie, still barrer boy Cockney, reckoned they'd met when he heard her singing at a nightclub. "It was that song *Crazy*. I fort is she getting at me or what?"

Would it be OK to put something in the paper? "For a fellow Arsenal fan, anyfing," said Frankie.

He'd spent 42 years at Her Majesty's displeasure, some of it up the road in Durham, been certified four times, been given penal servitude – though transported no further than the Scrubs – done more bread and water than any man then alive and was old enough, or young enough, to have received 18 strokes of the birch while handcuffed over a penal barrel.

MAD FOR IT:
Frankie Fraser (front) with son David

"Right on me deaf and dumb, that's me bum," said Frankie, keen to give his County Durham audience a rhyming slang primer.

183

"I once heaved a brick through a jeweller's Tommy. That's Tommy Trinder, see."

He wore the soubriquet of insanity almost as a badge of honour, like Chopper Harris or Bomber of that ilk but presented the awards almost diffidently, like a public school speech day guest reluctant to ask the fearsome headmaster if the bairns might have a half holiday.

Though not all approved – there were letters to the paper – the old lad insisted that his message was that crime didn't pay. "I was one of the failures," he told the kids. "For God's sake don't follow me."

Long queues formed for his autograph, each signed in the same way: "Be good – Frankie Fraser."

After the unfortunate business of the ASBO in his care home, he died in November 2014, aged 90. Hodgy, happily, is still with us – still wearing his daft cap and still, of course, gaining the benefits of the doubt.

33 : OUR MAN ON THE SPOTS

PARTICULARLY with cricket, it's now the case that those who write about sport in the national papers have usually themselves played at a high level. Some of them can even string a sentence together. Stephen Brenkley, one of those who succeeded me as custodian of the *John North* column, became a top-class cricket correspondent for the *Independent on Sunday* though he'd not played at a higher level than keeping wicket for Barnard Castle – though Barney, it should swiftly be added, was a pretty high level, anyway.

I'd not really partaken at any level at all, though there was always the time in 1982 when I kept goal for the *Echo* against the *Evening Gazette,* from Middlesbrough. Julie, my secretary – I was news editor at the time – had somewhat insubordinately sewn an absurdly corpulent flying pig onto the back of my goalie top. Football followers should think Tommy Lawrence and at once get the picture.

Sharon and Adam were in what passed for the crowd, he in a baby buggy. After precisely one minute I was in collision – as the court reporters still have it – with Doug Moody, the opposing centre forward, driven to the Memorial Hospital and thoroughly examined in casualty.

Finally the doc pronounced the all-clear – "but if you want to keep fit, Mr Amos," he said, "in future I'd stick to jogging."

A few years earlier, there'd been a 'novices' cricket competition at Coundon in which I'd been invited to enter a

185

Northern Echo team. Rules stipulated that none should have played league cricket in the two previous seasons, which didn't explain why the *Echo* side included Tim Wellock, a fully paid-up member of the sports desk but also a formidable opening bowler for Darlington in the North Yorkshire and South Durham League.

Nor did it immediately explain why we'd all agreed to call him Jack.

All went well, or as well as guilty consciences might permit, until a skyer was lofted towards our right wrong 'un on the boundary. "Catch it, Tim," we shouted as one. The organiser was umpiring. "I thought that bloke seemed familiar," he said. Though the story never got in the paper, we were thrown out in disgrace.

It may therefore be unsurprising that further recreational activity has been confined to 5s and 3s, a form of dominoes said to demand a modicum of skill but which additionally requires great barrow loads of luck. Immodesty compels the observation that I once won 24 successive games, league and cup, almost certainly an all-time league record. I probably lost the next 24.

For 40 years I've spent wintry Monday evenings in the Darlington and District 5s and 3s League, a usually agreeable outing though numbers tumble as old age and infirmity knock spots off all of us. Seeking to address the decline, the league committee even proposed that women be allowed to join in, a move I opposed so vigorously in print that Tyne Tees Television came out to the male chauvinist pig sty (aka the Brit) to do an interview on that one, too.

Happily, the proposal was defeated at the annual league meeting (and the one after that.) What's wrong with a lads' night out – or a lasses' night out, either?

BACK in 1960, Houghton-le-Spring MP and former miner Billy Blyton – later Baron Blyton of South Shields but simply Baron Billy to his friends – had raised in the Commons the matter of cheating at dominoes. He sought to have side betting, as opposed to a few bob a corner, criminalised.

The amount of tic-tacking and skulduggery was terrible, said Bill; some leagues even had check markers, the check marker to ensure that the marker wasn't himself fiddling.

"If a man pulls out his handkerchief it might mean he has double six, if he scratches his nose it's double five." Bill lost, as usu-

SPOT ON:
Lord Blyton

ally do the Britannia B, but at least we lose scrupulously.

We're a fraternal bunch, team membership remarkably constant down the years. An unfortunate exception occurred before an away game at Middleton St George when Peter, a team member known to like a pre-match drink – starting about eight hours earlier – was loudly complaining that he'd been dropped.

"It's that blooming Mike Amos," he protested to the chap sitting beside him, "he's useless but he gets picked because he works for the paper."

It was only then that someone pointed out to Peter that the chap to whom he'd been complaining for the previous ten minutes was, in fact, Mike Amos. We never saw him again. It was also at Middleton St George, come to think, that someone threw an egg and tomato sandwich at me – and he was a member of our own team.

DARLINGTON was reckoned 5s and 3s capital of Great Britain, the Grey Horse the greatest. Five times in seven

187

years they won the UK 5s and 3s championship, pretty sound proof that dominoes is a lot more than fortune. Only white horses are lucky.

"There's a magic, an aura about them," said Keith Masters, the tournament organiser. "You'd expect a really good team to win maybe 65-70 per cent of their games but these lads consistently win 80-90 per cent. You can't cheat at singles, they're the best in Britain."

The finals – 64 eight-man teams from up to 1,500 hopefuls – were held each November at the better-days Spa Royal Hall in Bridlington, an annual outing for Grey Horsemen like Colin Stainsby, Tony and Derrick White and Norman Kent. Norman was also an accomplished musician and, whisper it, a member of the Magic Circle. Sleight of hand, he insisted, never came into play at 5s and 3s.

I joined them on finals day in 2005, the lads having stayed overnight and so keen to keep themselves right that they'd all been in bed by 4.30am. Norman, alas, had had an early hours fall, wrecked his knee – "I wouldn't care, it was my good knee, I've just had an operation on the bad 'un" – and so badly damaged his hand that he had to stand his dominoes on end, like the kindergarten cup.

You could tell he wasn't himself, he was drinking Lucozade Sport, though his hands were so mangled he had to get someone else to open the bottle. He'd just overbalanced, said Tony – "all those double sixes he keeps in his trouser pocket."

Derrick White believed that they wouldn't win as regularly if the finalists were the last 64 teams in Darlington– "there are more good players in Darlington than the rest of the country put together" – his brother supposed that the joy of dominoes was akin to the joy of sex.

"It's just that these days dominoes takes a little bit longer."

As almost always was the case, the *Backtrack* column alone represented the nation's media, though Tyne Tees had once sent Wincey Willis, their weather girl – well remembered, christened Winsome as earlier noted – to ascertain that all was set fair. "She took me down to the sands," Derrick recalled. "Unfortunately she only wanted to talk about anticyclones."

A competition that began at 10 30am ended almost 12 hours later, the Grey Horse again first past the post after coming from 3-1 down to beat a pub from West Bromwich 4-3. After that they went for a drink.

34 : COLUMN INCHES

THE publishing group which owned the *Northern Echo* and many other newspapers had a training centre at Hastings, on the south coast, the place where once we'd gone fishing for jellied eels.

One year, only one, they asked me to present the passing-out prizes and to address the young aspirants on the craft of column building. The cement which held it all together, I told them, wasn't stylish or even idiosyncratic writing. Nor was it outrageous opinions or endless exclusives – the term 'exclusive' being, in any event, the inky trade's most insolently over-used.

The key, day after day and year after year, was simply filling the damn thing, avoiding those seven dreaded words "He couldn't think of anything to write."

Broadly there are three kinds of newspaper columns. 'Opinion' columns are coveted but rarely coruscating, 'light' columns make a lot of money for guys like Giles Coren but oft prove indigestible in other hands, and fact-based columns, sometimes called 'diary' columns, which are a greatly endangered species.

Sharon compares my stuff to Autolycus, a comic thief in the Shakespeare play *A Winter's Tale* who was said to be a snapper-up of unconsidered trifles and thus not to be confused with the mendicant columnists who'd sit by the newsroom wastepaper basket in the hope of unwanted scraps for a dog's dinner daily.

Though *Unconsidered Trifles* eventually became the title of the book, Autolycus is an appealing but not wholly accurate analogy. The character from literature who most closely mirrors column writing – column writing based on people and events – is Mr Micawber, who always believed that something would turn up.

It was greatly to tempt fate, but something always did. Prattle of Hastings, I left them with those thoughts as the train headed back towards Darlington.

SUCCESSFUL fact-based column writing needs much more, of course. It needs ideas, it needs contacts, it demands endless out-of-hours socialising – hopefully on expenses – and most of all it needs serendipity, a long word which basically means good luck. It's probably my favourite word – euphony second, threnody third – and I've had serendipity in abundance.

Some columns would need just one idea a week. Others, like *Backtrack*, were always multi-faceted – not world exclusives, of course, but usually quite capable of holding their heads up in polite company.

The weekly *Backtrack* column ended up as 2,000 or more words but for many years appeared on both Tuesdays and Saturdays, about 1,500 words a time and sometimes seriously short on information and ideas. Monday mornings were worst, stretching Micawber's maxim to the limit. Why else but by way of crisis management might a sports column's readers learn that on a good night a hungry bat can feast on 3,000 midges? Usually, though, the columnar cavalry would be awaiting the penultimate trumpet, if not quite the last one.

Often it was in the form of a telephone call from Kip Watson or a handwritten fax, for he was a bit old-fashioned that way, from Hails of Hartlepool. When Ron Hails hadn't much to say for himself, their dog, Patch, would sign on instead.

Kip Watson was co-founder and secretary of the North-East Over 40s League, a football success story that had grown from six clubs to more than 70. He was a retired teacher, lived in Sunderland, had gained a spurious theology degree which (apparently) entitled him to be called "the Reverend" but was a thoroughly good bloke without all that. Unlike a great many journalists, Kip knew a story when he saw one – and when he saw one, he was straight on the blower.

He also loved his nicknames. Jackie Wilson was The Flying Window Cleaner, Maurice Flint – landlord and player/man-

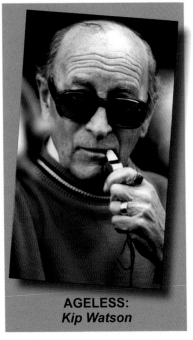

AGELESS:
Kip Watson

ager of the Masons Arms at Middlestone Moor, near Spennymoor – was Captain Flint and his team the Pirates. It was to prove apt.

The league's players had simply to sign a declaration that they were indeed forty years old. All went well until someone put an advert in the paper congratulating Maurice on his own 40th – a year-and-a-bit after he'd made his debut. Kip pounced on the story, his committee pounced on Captain Flint. The buccaneer was banned indefinitely and, possibly for other reasons, sailed off for sunny Spain. Last I heard, he was still there.

Kip's only problem was that he could talk the hind legs off a cuddy – I often wondered who paid his phone bill – but there were an awful lot of pearls among the oysters. Rarely a Tuesday column appeared without mention of the Phylossan Forties.

Ron Hails, a retired welder or some such, was so greatly on the column's wavelength that we might have been tuned to the same transistor. He also had an Amstrad when most people still thought it was a street in Holland. An enthusiastic member of Hartlepool Indoor Bowls Club, he was a lifelong Hartlepool United supporter, seemed to recall just about every match he'd ever seen and had been a canny cricketer, too.

His memory was extraordinary, his writing style delightful, a man who could turn a phrase on a tanner. Faxes in those days arrived elsewhere in the *Echo* building in Darlington, Ron's Monday missives borne almost triumphantly by dear old Tom Middleton, the chief telegraphist, from the wire room.

"Here's tomorrow's column," he'd proclaim and, very often, he was right. A truly lovely man, Ron died shortly before Christmas 2019.

ANOTHER morning, while I blankly contemplated the empty expanse of that Saturday's *Backtrack* column, a book called *The Far Corner* landed in the post. Sub-titled "A mazy dribble through North-East football" it was by Harry Pearson, of whom I'd not heard, but was clearly up my alley – so much so that I arranged to meet him that tea time at a pub in Hexham.

Harry was from Great Ayton, south of the Tees, had been a barman before becoming a writer and had moved to the Tyne Valley. The subsequent column forecast that *The Far Corner* would be named sports book of the year – it wasn't, it was runner-up, but Harry's deservedly won an awful lot of awards since.

I didn't often write about books – there was rarely time to read them – and even more rarely became excited by them. Another exception had come in the early 1970s when Alf Wight, a middle-aged veterinary surgeon from Thirsk in North Yorkshire, produced under the pseudonym James Herriot a semi-autobiographical and gently amusing account called *It Shouldn't Happen to a Vet*. Again I immediately arranged to see him – the most charming of men – again he signed a first edition and again I forecast great things. James Herriot proved animal magic.

Perhaps the only other example of literary love at first sight was when Jack Chapman, a retired English teacher and long-time club cricketer from Hebburn, sent a copy of *Cream Teas and Nutty Slack*, his gloriously anecdotal, wonderfully quirky and deeply knowledgeable history of club cricket between Tyne and Tees. Once again, an immediate meeting was arranged. The book's still around on eBay and is warmly recommended. Jack, a true gentleman, had a serious stroke in 2019 and, time of writing, was in a care home in Jarrow.

Allowed three books on a desert island, those might well be the pick. Mind, I quite like the cut of this one, too.

35 : OLD, OLD STORIES

WHAT readers like Kip Watson and Ron Hails had in
common – save for their kindness and an almost sym-
phonic harmony with the guy who wrote the column – was
that word "retired". They were getting on a bit and that en-
capsulated provincial newspapers' greatest dilemma, which
none has been able to resolve: their readership is ageing, in
truth it's dying.

Whenever a name appears in the classified deaths column,
the chances are that it represents another cancelled newspaper – and with none forming a queue at the other end of the
age spectrum.

Though I was but a bairn of 39 when the *Backtrack* column began – almost half a lifetime ago – it seemed always
to attract the older reader. Was it me, was it the eternal mag-
net of nostalgia, or were they already the only ones who remained?

Where else might regulars have read about Charlie Walker, the Demon Donkey Dropper of Eryholme – more of Charlie shortly – or of 73-year-old Tommy Stafford, the wicket-
keeper with the WD40 knees? Where might they keep track
of Ian Barnes, the UK Over 80s 5000-metre champion, of
Tom Smith, into his 80s and still being stotted off the five-a-
side wall bars by footballers half his age, or of former England amateur international footballer Dave Rutherford, still
playing well into his 60s and still terrorising grab-a-granny
night on Whitley Bay promenade?

Whether grab-a-granny night can properly be designated

a sport, even in Whitley Bay, is a matter for the International Olympic Committee, not me.

Even the column's mountaineers had peaked, in age if not in achievement. Alan Hinkes OBE, still the only Brit to have reached all 14 Himalayan summits of 8,000m or more – the Death Zone, they call it, unequivocally – was 66 in 2020 but still aiming high. He lives near the Durham/North Yorkshire border where sometimes we simply raise a glass.

Alan also set himself the challenge of reaching the highest point in each of England's 39 former administrative counties, still a bit of a climb in Cumbria – and in County Durham since the 1974 Local Government land grab left the county with Mickle Fell – but perhaps less hazardous elsewhere. The highest point in Middlesex was the traffic lights on Bushey Heath; in the former Huntingdonshire just 250ft above the briny. Perhaps appropriately, it was called Boring Field.

What, too, of Dave 'Fingers' Morrison, the wicket keeper with the mangled metatarsals and a man who himself epitomises one of the problems facing this book? Dave was a wickey for fifty years, mostly at a high level in the North

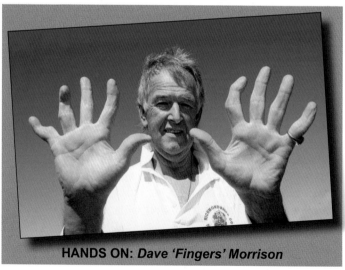

HANDS ON: *Dave 'Fingers' Morrison*

Yorkshire and South Durham League, his prowess behind the stumps reckoned considerably greater than his ability with a bat in front of them.

What really distinguished him, however – save for the tartan trews ("two pairs for £13 from Catterick market") and the T-shirt with the message "Cricket is life, everything else is detail" – was his hands. Five decades of broken bones and battering had made them resemble a relief map of the Andes.

The doctors marvelled at his juxtaposed joints, begged him to let them deliver learned lectures about them, to x-ray and to x-rate them. Vainly they urged him to take up a gentler sport. The first time that the column told the story, accompanying photographs of black-and-blue hands taken against a bright blue sky, the national media pounced upon it before ultimately it winged its way around the world.

The dilemma, unresolved at the time of writing this chapter, is whether the book should include photographs at all, with the resultant likely increase in cost and in cover price. If it does, and it probably will, Mr Morrison's mitts will be at the very top of the pile.

THE *Backtrack* column also carried an awful lot about scouts – though not, of course, about boy scouts. Much too young. This was the old boys' brigade, the men who'd spend endless hours at football matches, either eyeing up the opposition or, ever more improbably, seeking a pearl among the adolescent oysters.

The hirsute Owen Willoughby, known to Paul Gascoigne as Dr Who because of a perceived resemblance to William Hartnell, was still sedulously scouting for Spurs when he died at 84 – only a couple of days before he was due to be a guest when Tony Blair entertained US president George Bush to lunch at the Dun Cow in Sedgefield.

Though left permanently and painfully on crutches after a car accident, Owen was not only among the most trusted scouts but was much involved in running youth football in south-east County Durham. An all-weather facility at Trimdon – one or other of the Trimdons – is named in his memory.

Jack Watson, once said in the *Backtrack* column to be the most assiduous scout since Hawkeye, still worked daily as Middlesbrough FC's recruitment coordinator when he died in 2013, aged 90. He was also a leading Minor Counties cricketer for both Durham and Northumberland, once took 6-23 against India and was 71 when he claimed a hat-trick on his debut for Bearpark. "I was so old that the other players were calling me Mr Watson," he said, not entirely regretfully.

Mind, Jack was still but a bairn compared with fellow Shildon lad Bob Murton, with whom in the early years of the 21st century he enjoyed a weekly game of bowls. Bob, a former band leader, was still bowling when he was 100 – up and down like a green baize bluebottle. Not unreasonably, but mindful of the lesson of the Patrick Brompton gravedigger, the column supposed him Britain's oldest active sportsman; no less unreasonably, the club gave him life membership to mark his 100th birthday. He died at 104, having taken them up on it.

For all that those guys made very good copy, I was aware of the age curve, what clever folk like to call the demographic, and concerned about it. When newspapers desperately needed to attract younger readers, did it help that *Backtrack* was increasingly about older sports people, or about times past?

The best argument I could come up with was that most of the other reporters and writers were young enough to be my grandkids and that they might reasonably be expected to tilt the age balance back again – besides there were some agelessly wonderful characters about.

AMONG the most remarkable was John Dawson, a retired Hartlepool postman, who became known as King of the Ground Hoppers. John was a Newcastle United fan – a bachelor, perhaps inevitably – who became disillusioned with professional football and decided to concentrate on what folk call the non-league game. In his most prolific season, he watched 280 matches, sometimes two or three in a day.

By the winter of 2019-20, John was 78. Still once a week, sometimes twice, he'd catch the overnight coach from Middlesbrough to London – a great deal cheaper than the train but a lot less comfortable – and, fortified by the eat-all-

HOPPING MAD:
John Dawson

you-like breakfast at Victoria coach station, fit his appointed match into the next 16 hours down south and, seldom sleeping much, be on the midnight coach back home.

As a bit younger man he rode a small-engined motorbike, little more than a scooter. On one occasion he'd watched a Friday evening game at Scunthorpe and then at little more than 40mph headed through a particularly stormy night to a Saturday afternoon fixture – in Portsmouth. The bike finally gave up on him somewhere in the Reading area – but John found a train and still made the match.

Inevitably he's fuelled by the sort of food, and not just the dawn fry-up at Victoria coach station, which a chap with his cardiac history might best avoid – eyebrows once raised at his double helping of jam roly-poly. "The fruit salad's off," he explained. His aim's to visit every ground – thousands of them – at the top six levels of the non-league game and no matter that clubs persist in upping sticks. He's also a very nice guy.

Mick Henderson refereed football until 2019, when he was 86 – sometimes twice a day – swore that he was happy so long as he got a plate of chips afterwards. A Sunderland fan, he'd been a linesman at a Northern League match at Evenwood in 1972-73 – a season not to be forgotten by the red-and-whites – and deemed it prudent to have a radio on the half-way line to keep up with events elsewhere.

Sadly for Mick, fearsome league secretary Gordon Nicholson was also there. While Mick was down the other end, Nic switched the wireless off. The linesman looked puzzled. "Just concentrate on the game, Mr Henderson," said Nic.

Readers might also never otherwise have heard of Seaham lad Leo Smith, then 70, who toured Holland with his local football team, becoming so upset at being dropped that he set fire to his boots in his bedroom. Unfortunately he as near as damn it set fire to the hotel as well.

Margaret Horn had turned 70 when still fourth team coach at Darlington Rugby Club, familiar thereabouts since the days when her father was a first team man and the players changed behind a hedge. "They told me to turn my back. I peeped, of course," she said.

She professed formidableness, her players swore affection. "They phone up on a Saturday morning and say they're a bit injured," said Margaret. "I tell them that if they're dead they're injured, otherwise they're playing."

It was for services to the community in Sedgefield, not to Darlington's fourth team, that she was appointed MBE. For years she'd guarded her age as the elders might have guarded the secrets of Joanna Southcott's Sealed Box, so the marvellous Margaret might have been miffed – mortified, even – when her death notice, in 2013, revealed her to be 93.

John Armstrong was just 61 when, fielding on the boundary for Etherley second team near Bishop Auckland, he was flattened when the sight screen blew over onto him. After several weeks out injured he still finished top of the bowling averages and still offered up the story. As the chapter on meteorologists supposed, you know what they say about an ill wind.

LEAPS AND BOUNDS: *Len Watson*

Arthur Puckrin and Len 'the Leap' Watson were among the most amazing of all. Sharon Gayter will get a chapter all to herself.

LEN Watson lived in Trimdon Village, County Durham. Built like a roll of barbed wire, he'd been a professional foot runner – the breed said to have had lead in their pumps – held the world record for the Over 75s long jump, 4.13m, and the British record for the Over 70s 100m and 400m, 14.4 seconds and 77 seconds respectively.

His secret, he insisted, was a noxious embrocation called Watson's No 6 – none ever knew what happened to Nos 1 to 5 – compounded to an old family recipe, rubbed deep from a dark red bottle and with a smell akin to a pox doctor's back parlour. None knew the formula, but Len seemed to spend an awful lot of time in the hedge-backs, decommissioning dandelions.

"There were seeds in it and all sorts," recalled Barry Parnaby, with whom Len trained up and down Kelloe pit heap. "I don't know what it was doing to Lenny's arse, but it took all the skin off my fingers."

Len also sold the stuff at a local painter and decorator's, on a shelf next to the turps and probably with much the same effect. "The miners would come in for a ha'porth or a pennorth, especially after working in Trimdon Grange wet seam," he said.

He died in 2005, aged 90, having reluctantly spent the last few years of his life in a care home. "The trouble with retiring," he said, "is that people give you a stick and expect you to fade away."

At his funeral, his mate Barry recalled the time that Len had been chased out of a pub in the Borders for the mortal Scottish sin of eating his own sandwiches. "Mind," said Barry, "they'd never, ever have caught him."

ARTHUR Puckrin, an athlete who took extreme sport to extremes, would wholly have endorsed Len's retirement philosophy. "If ever we have a power cut on Teesside, all we need do is hook up Arthur to the National Grid and his energy levels will do the rest," Ray 'Robocop' Mallon, the former Mayor of Middlesbrough, once observed.

Arthur was himself a Boro boy, left school at 15 with two O-levels, became a police officer and later a barrister, represented Britain at seven sports – including bridge – but was best known for his irresistible attraction to "iron man" events, ferrous for 15 minutes.

The basic iron man discipline was a two-and-a-half mile swim, a 112-mile bike ride and a quick marathon with which to wind down. Arthur did them in multiples – quad, tetra, deca. For Arthur a double-deca was a busman's holiday. At one stage he simultaneously held three overall world records and 30-odd age group records and also came second in the world coal carrying championships, held (of course) at Guisborough gymkhana. Eleanor Robinson, his sister, was a former women's 1,000-mile record holder.

When 75 and seriously ill – fitted with a pacemaker,

though goodness knows it hardly seemed necessary – Arthur finally proposed from his hospital bed to Mary, his partner of 35 years. They married three weeks later, the honeymoon spent less than coincidentally in Aberdeen because the city happened to be hosting a veterans' swimming championship. He came back with a bride and five golds.

He died, aged 80, in 2018. Had it all just been an exercise in hanging around with his mates? "Exactly," said Mary. "he knew all the crazy people."

In the nuptial gestation stakes, however, Arthur probably came second to Roderick Burtt, a former Darlington councillor, chartered surveyor, outstanding raconteur and national Round Table president who proposed to the magnificent Judith Kent after a "particularly good party" on Midsummer's Day 1969.

Judith spent all her working life at the same Darlington primary school, appointed MBE for services to education, if not for patience and long sufferance.

The engagement announcement had appeared a few days after his proposal in the "forthcoming marriages" section of the *Daily Telegraph,* though it didn't say anything about forthcoming any time soon. They moved in together in 1978, finally married in 2004 after Rod had himself been diagnosed with terminal cancer. He upheld a long-standing promise to give me the story, which subsequently went worldwide. "If I'd known a day could be so happy, I'd have got married more often," he

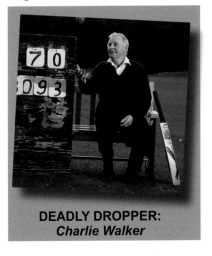

DEADLY DROPPER:
Charlie Walker

said. Sadly, he died soon afterwards.

ANYWAY, the Demon Donkey Dropper of Eryholme was so nicknamed because of a bowling action which, like the Lorelei, lured the unsuspecting into a false sense of security. Eryholme's a small village near the Yorkshire bank of the Tees, its cricket team sustained for more than half a century – on and off the field – by Charlie.

He'll be 80 in the summer of 2020, has claimed well over 3,000 wickets – and counting – led the major restoration work when the flooded river swept away much of the ground. "I only play when they're short," he now insists. For some reason they seem almost always to be short.

The most gentle and most unassuming of men, he still runs a grass-cutting business and rears turkeys, a 20lb special delivered here each Christmas. Whatever it is that turkeys vote for, you'd always vote for Charlie – old uns and best uns every time.

36 : SELBY DATE

VERA Selby, queen of green, was getting on 50 when first she won the women's world snooker championship. Forty years later, her feet remain – however metaphorically – firmly beneath the table. "It's a wonderful game, I like the peace of it," she says.

With much charm and no little allure, Vera has also helped exorcise many of the ghosts of male chauvinism which haunted North-East workmen's clubs – not least when she and snooker partner Ray Lennox turned up at Shiney Row, near Houghton-le-Spring, for the North-East semi-finals.

The doorman, forever Cerberus, said it was men only. When Vera persisted, he said he'd have to find a committee man. What happened next was recorded in one of Vera's many delightful poems:

> *They took it to the secretary*
> *His voice could not be clearer –*
> *No women are allowed in here*
> *We only let in Vera.*

She had also become the first woman to pot black, or any other colour, at venues ranging from St Peter's Social Club in Byker to the sumptuous snooker palace in Nairobi. "Good God, it's the end of empire," someone is said to have observed.

She was born in Richmond, North Yorkshire, her father-manager of the local branch of the Freeman Hardy and Willis shoe shop chain. In 2009 she became the first female master

QUEEN OF GREEN: *Vera Selby*

of Richmond's ancient Fellmongers Company in its 400-year history.

She'd started pottering around a snooker table when just six or seven but was in her 30s when spotted by Alf Nolan, a former British champion from Newton Aycliffe.

Ever elegant, she won a second world title in 1981 and was five times British billiards champion, an achievement which earned her a place in the Guinness Book. "They used my age, I can't lie about it any more," she'd gently complain.

She became a television commentator, referee, referee instructor, retired at 53 from lecturing in textile, fashion and design in Newcastle and remains an enchanting speaker and raconteur, usually with the title "Woman in a man's world."

Once or twice it seemed to me that she bore a resemblance to Anne Robinson, queen of mean not green, though without the bitter-lemon smile.

Once I heard her at Tow Law football club, and while Tow Law may be the last place on this sainted orb to require a breath of fresh air, that's precisely what she provided. Vera addressed a hall as she might a ball – coolly, precisely and with much success.

Long widowed, long in Gosforth, she was appointed MBE in 2015 for services to her sport, was 90 in March 2020, professed to being bored to tears if just sitting round the house all day. The Selby date may still be some way off.

37 : FEVERSHAM PITCH

NOTHING in sport is more grass-rooted than the Feversham Cricket League, though quite often the grass may be obscured by sheep muck (or that of the bovine kind.) Nor may anything be more joyous.

It's centred around Helmsley in rural North Yorkshire, destination of an annual *Backtrack* column outing for getting on three decades – a sort of journalistic Sunday School trip, though without the egg and tomato sandwiches – and is village cricket at its most bucolic, its most boisterous and its most blessed.

"The Feversham is but a distant cousin, a high country cousin, of those cricket leagues which snarl and scowl, bark, bite and regard the umpire's decision as an invitation to eyeball-to-eyeball arbitration," I once wrote. No more excoriating expletive is heard than "Oh, s**t", and that's probably a reference to what the guy's just stood in.

Its territory is also greatly undulating. Had the Ancients played cricket in the Feversham League they could never have believed that the earth was flat.

Local rules abound, usually unwritten, not least that if a game starts it would take some pretty fearful weather to stop it. Mr Kenneth Grahame probably had something similar in mind in *The Wind in the Willows* – that adage about little wet and water rat – though Magnus Magnusson understood the principle, too. They've started so they'll finish.

There are (or were) glorious grounds like High Farndale,

NOT ON THE LEVEL: *Spout House cricket pitch*

deep in daffodil country and with a ramshackle pavilion from which even the rats may have absconded, like Rievaulx, in the shadow of the great Cistercian abbey, and like Spout House, in Bilsdale, where the pitch sloped like a Grenadier Guardsman. The *Darlington & Stockton Times,* bless it, once described Spout House cricket ground as "unusual". It was like calling Mount Everest biggish.

High Farndale's glorious ground has a 1-in-6 descent from hut to wicket – were it a metalled road they'd have to have grit bins alongside – topography like a relief map of Tibet, a scoreboard that resembles a rusty bedspread and a cast of characters as colourful as the springtime floribundance for which the dale may marginally be better known.

After my first visit, in 1996, the *Daily Mail* pinched all my pictures and devoted a page to the fantasia that is Farndale. The cheque must still be in the post.

Spout, sadly, are no longer in the league – impossible regularly to raise a team amid acres where sheep out-number humans about 1,000-to-one – though they still contest one or two cups. On the first visit I'd rung to ask the times of buses from Stokesley up the dale. "Friday," said the lady.

209

Since that was the day of the match, 6.30pm start, I said that it appeared to be my lucky day. "Friday, ten o'clock," she added, "then ten o'clock the week after."

Spout also had the league's first female player, an artificial inseminator called Rachel Godschalk who worked that way but made the 100-mile round trip from near Barnard Castle. "I look at the cows and I can see them thinking 'Daddy'," she said.

Rievaulx could count among former players the England test batsman Graham Roope, though his impact may have been limited. "He wasn't as good as't local lads and even worse at getting his hand in his pocket," Frank Flintoft, involved for more than half a century, had recalled. Johnny Wardle, another ex-England man, also had Rievaulx connections and a similar reputation for what Yorkshiremen call being careful. "Wouldn't spend a penny but expected everyone else to," said Frank by way of translation.

The Feversham, what's more, has playing connections with royalty – more of which shortly – though the gentleman in question always stood the bar.

PERHAPS the most remote ground of all was Bransdale, about eight uphill miles from the nearest bus stop and with horse flies – clegs, they call them up there – like midges on marijuana. One hot summer evening they staged a final there, the necessity to hoof up from Kirkbymoorside. Bransdale was at the end of the road and the first sight upon arrival seemed surely to be a mirage.

It was Ann Willis, a greatly attractive blonde, probably 6ft tall, who'd had the next office when I'd worked in York getting on 30 years previously. Ann was seated on a rug with a cool box, a picnic and a great many cans of beer. That her husband was there could do nothing to spoil either the moment or the taste of a can of Fosters.

On the occasions that there's cause to doubt that God's in his heaven and all's right with the world, I recall that double vision in Bransdale and am agnostic no longer.

Almost always the Feversham jaunts are joined by Charles Allenby, the faithful and indefatigable league secretary, who's also a volunteer signalman on the North Yorkshire Moors Railway and, like Ivor the Engine, sings in the choir. Sometimes Mrs Allenby will even lay on tea. "Killing the fatted calf, eh?" I once observed. "Quite a small pullet, actually," she replied.

Once league membership fell to three, now it's back up to five – Glaisdale, High Farndale, Lockton, Rosedale Abbey and Slingsby, probably the only one of the five which might gain provisional membership of the Flat Earth Society, and only then if the theodolite's on the blink. Slingsby's also the only ground with a little clubhouse – great burgers, too. The church beyond the boundary once had a resident jackdaw, which would peck the Victorian rector's sermon notes for want of something more valuable to thieve.

On one occasion, it's said, the rector was obliged to rebuke a parishioner who wanted shot of the bird. "Probably there are jackdaws in heaven, too," he said.

UNTIL a few years ago there was also Gillamoor, locally pronounced almost to rhyme with Fred Flintstone's wife Wilma. On one Gillamoor visit, Charles having taken to his bed, I was picked up at Thirsk railway station by his lad Nick, who's a fireman. We talked, as you would, about rescuing parrots from trees. "They get out of the house, somehow find a tree and short of saying Pretty Polly have no idea what to do next," said Nick. "I get the distinct impression they'd have been happier in a cage."

The occasion on which sub-officer Tom Guy helped rescue a goat from up a tree has, of course, been recounted in an earlier chapter.

Gillamoor's a stone-built village, smelling of cows and of contentment, a place where barn dances are still held in barns, where the parish church was built without north and east windows because the prevailing winds would have blown them in again and where Hen House Cottage leaves little doubt about its previous incarnation (or incubation, perhaps) but which now has five stars from the English Tourist Board,

The cricket pavilion, come to that, rather resembled a hen hut but was set alight – fired, as was said of Mr Graham Kelly, with enthusiasm. The cricket club unfortunately folded a few years later. Valiantly and incomparably, the Feversham bats on, the annual excursion joined in recent years by one or both of my boys – train along the Esk Valley line followed by a moors walk and, just possibly, a pint or two. Adam, to his manifest delight, has even had a couple of games, and a couple of wickets.

There's an additional, and again immodest, benefit. Whenever the subsequent column has seemed particularly refreshing, or quirky or just unmistakably glad to be alive, it's formed part of the entry for regional and national press awards in the hope that anecdote will also prove antidote to the judges' accustomed heavy duty diet. In the days of entering press awards, quite often it seemed to go down pretty well.

I OWE the Feversham Cricket League some very happy days – and some pretty rewarding nights, as well. William Ainsley, licensed to retail British and foreign wines, spirits, ale, porters and tobacco – or so it rather breathlessly said above the door of his remote country pub – was the eternal essence of Feversham League cricket.

In the Ainsley family since 1823, the Sun Inn was next to the Spout House ground – bordered it and latterly infringed upon it. Possibly even before William's time, an ancestor had once caused a stir, it's said, by increasing the price of ale from 1/3d to 1/6d – a gallon.

William had made his cricket debut when he was nine, supposed that the men must have been off haymaking, played on 62 different grounds, turned to umpiring thereafter and in being club secretary for 66 years fell short by six years of his grandfather's record tenure.

DAYS IN THE SUN:
William Ainsley

He loved and nurtured the place, never wanted to leave, championed its integrity. To the delightful William Ainsley, rejecting suggestions that the vertiginous ground might somehow offer home advantage, may be attributed one of the all-time great cricket quotations:

"It's t'same for both teams," he insisted. "If it lands in't cow clap for one, it lands in't cow clap for t'other."

The story's also told of the time William spent a few days in the Friarage Hospital at Northallerton, given an injection by a nervous student nurse who asked if it had been OK. "Certainly," said William kindly, "much better and I'll let you inject t'sheep." In more recent times it was the sheep which principally claimed squatters' rights, however. "People complain about t'sheep shit," said William philosophically, "but they complained even more when it was't cows."

He and his forebears were also farmers, worked with Clydesdales. He still kept a 1954 Ferguson tractor. "Starts first time," he insisted.

William had even shed blood for Spout, his cheek bone shattered when the ball seemed to run all the way up the handle of his Len Hutton bat. He spent another three days in

213

hospital. "I doubt if Leonard himself could have played the shot any different," he said.

Folk also recall that a handsome stranger was once seen buying drinks in the bar. Afterwards they told William that he'd just served His Royal Highness Prince Harry. "Oh," said William, "does he play for Spout House, as well?" If he didn't, he certainly played against them on at least two occasions.

In bachelor boyhood Harry had been a house guest of Lord and Lady Mexborough, a few miles down dale at Arden House – wasn't that where Dr Finlay compiled his casebook? – in Harmby. On August 11 2007, entered in the scorebook as Spike W – Spike was his nickname, W was said to stand for Wells – the prince made his Arden House debut at Spout House. In March 2009 I finally got wind of the story. That was quite quick for me.

If not exactly sworn to secrecy, the players had accepted Harry's right to privacy, something rather more greatly infringed in later years. The usual crowd, the self-styled Sid and Doris Bonkers over from Thornaby on their motor bike and sitting on a rug in front of the big barn, were nonetheless advised that if they kept a sharp eye on the players they might get a surprise. Subsequently they were asked if they'd noticed anything unusual.

"Oh yes," said Sid, "you have a lady player" – the enthusiastic artificial inseminator, aforesaid.

"No," said his informant, "the guy in the khaki shorts is Prince Harry."

"There you are," said Doris, "I told you that chap looked just like Harry."

He struck two fours in an innings of 16 – showed a liking for the mid-wicket whack, always a profitable Spout stroke – but was then clean bowled by 12-year-old Peter Thompson, a farmer's son from near Helmsley. "The Taliban couldn't get the prince," said Spout player Chris Brass – a reference to the royal's RAF days – "but young Peter did."

A plaque above the family fireplace recorded the feat: "HRH Prince Harry, b P Thompson 16." Beneath it someone had added "Middle stump, as well."

Several years later, the *Telegraph* ran a piece headed "The mysterious Spike Wells who looks like a prince." It wouldn't have been a mystery to the good folk of Bilsdale, or to *Backtrack* column readers, either.

GROUND and pub are alongside the main road from Stokesley to Helmsley, a television transmitter high on the hill beyond. The original Sun Inn, cruck-framed and now a National Trust property, was opened in the 1760s. The successor pub –"a peaceful drinking Arcadia," the *Guardian* once observed – was built in 1914, closed in 2011 when William and his wife Madge were no longer able to run it.

The wicket may have been the only flat – flattish – 22 yards for many a mile around. The roller, filled with concrete, took eight men to budge and had SHCC engraved upon its wooden handle lest anyone try to flog it at a car boot sale. "Helped build t'Pyramids did that," someone said.

William was also keeper of the local rules, and of the records. Who else might authoritatively have averred that John Willie Wood, the 28-stone Fangdale blacksmith, bowled W G Grace for a golden duck in an exhibition match at Newburgh Priory? The triumphant bowler's response – "they came to watch W G Grace, now they'll have to watch J W Wood" – may be supposed a little more apocryphal.

Local rules were largely unwritten, though never disputed. Like the great Canterbury oak, Madge's clothes line was within the third man boundary though nothing would be scored if the ball hit it (or, for that matter, if a chasing player were garrotted by it). The hen house was four, but batsmen might continue running to try for five.

The little changing hut, perhaps never once called a pavilion, had itself been a hen cree. When finally it was replaced, by a shed bought secondhand from a fertilizer factory, the Countess of Mexborough – she who had entertained the future Duke of Sussex – was called upon to cut the ribbon. The six pebbles which the prince had shifted from hand to hand in his obligatory spell as umpire remain framed on the wall, alongside the playing record of Spike W.

A six might only be scored by clearing the ancient dry stone wall at the top end or, it was claimed, by striking a passing motor cyclist burning the Helmsley road at the bottom. Those gentlemen, truth to tell, had enough ways of causing their own premature recall to the celestial pavilion without worrying about flying cricket balls.

Since the resident sheep were rather less efficient than the average Flymo, there were also rules about lost balls – accounts might further be considered fanciful, but once they ran 23. William himself was umpiring at square leg against Rievaulx when a Spout batsmen hit the ball no more than 20 yards. "Slips must have been asleep," he said. "T'ball stopped in't long grass just yonder but all of them chased towards the boundary. I could have told them where it was, but it wasn't in my interests, was it?"

Spout had made their first final, up at Bransdale where the horse flies were thoroughbreds, 35 years after he joined the colours. It wasn't until the year 2000, however, more than 150 years since cricket was first played at that rural Ruritania, that Spout itself was awarded a final. "Do you know," said William. "I thought it was never going to happen."

He died two days after Christmas 2012. Harry Mead, his eulogist, recalled that William had loved farming and loved his little dale –"but his absolute overriding passion was cricket."

38 : GOLDEN GAYTER

BENEATH the sort of harvest moon made for lovers, Sharon Gayter jogged gingerly, jubilantly, into John o' Groats. It was 11.23pm, Friday September 15 2006, precisely 12 days, 16 hours and 23 minutes since she'd set out on foot from Lands End – and it was another world record.

Sharon, a chronic asthmatic, was 42 and had averaged four hours' sleep each night. Her support team had stretched toilet roll across the finishing line, placed a chair (and a blanket) two feet behind it. There were no pipes and no drums, no media save the bloke from the *Northern Echo* and the photographer we'd hired from Thurso.

The occasion notwithstanding, the photographer thought we were best seeing John o' Groats by night. "It's a horrible, terrible place," he said.

Mrs Gayter, probably the most extraordinary athlete from the crowded field with whom the *Backtrack* column long ran in tandem, took a sip from a Tesco champagne bottle. "When (triple jumper) Jonathan Edwards claimed his world records he was literally jumping for joy," she said.

"With me it's just the knowledge that I won't have to wear a pair of shoes tomorrow."

She was raised in Cambridge, came north because there were more hills, met her husband – the brilliant Bill, at the time recently demobbed – when both were driving buses on Teesside but quit after being beaten up by a drunken passenger. She became an athlete who took ultra running to ex-

217

JOURNEY'S END: *The magnificent Sharon Gayter*

tremes. "There's a lot of improvement still in me," she said, prophetically, when first we met in 1993.

For more than a quarter of a century I've followed her, very much in her wake, including an event around east London, sponsored by the Flora spread folk, in which it was required to run a mile in every hour for 1,000 successive hours and then finish the job with a quick dash around the London Marathon course.

She'd fancied herself in that one, backed herself at 9-2 – is that what's known as spread betting? –thought she might get a new van out of the bookies. She came second, her 3 hours 34 minutes for the marathon not quite quick enough.

Then there was the Commonwealth 24-hour event, forever around a happily pretty park in Keswick – views of Skiddaw – in which she took drinks on the hoof, swallowing them at an angle like an Orange marcher playing a tin whistle. 138.8 miles gave her gold. "I'm so excited I won't sleep," she said.

Bill usually led the support party, his wife grateful for his loyalty if not for his cuisine. "If it isn't out of a kettle or out of a microwave he's had it," she said. When she ran hundreds of miles across the Libyan desert, or the Himalayas or through the Grand Canyon, someone else usually had to heat the beans.

When somehow she found time between running and training, Sharon studied for an MA in sports studies and physiology at Teesside University, is now a lecturer there and is close to completing a PhD.

By way of a change, no doubt, she'd also essay world records for running on a treadmill – 517 miles in seven days among those waiting to be overtaken by those anxious to go nowhere fast.

When injured she tackled jigsaw puzzles – not titchy little 1,000 piece jobs, not footling five-thousanders but 35,000-piece giants – and she did those methodically, and against the clock, too.

"The Wicked Witch of the South," Bill will sometimes call her. "Grumpy Gayter," she retorts. They make a wonderful team. That night in John o' Groats was particularly memorable because I'd reached the end of the road first: dawn train from Darlington to Edinburgh, another from Edinburgh to Inverness, a third – there are precious few – up the east coast spur to Wick, arriving at 10.30pm.The taxi from Wick overtook her two miles from journey's end. It was as if, 830 miles earlier, I'd asked what time she'd be finishing and she'd replied "What time can you be there?"

John o' Groats was near-deserted, save for a couple of dram-and-blasters locked into the gloomy pub and a kind gentleman from the Highland Council who gave Sharon a certificate. The pub door stayed resolutely fastened.

Meticulous in every last detail, she'd been planning the record attempt for two years. She'd snatched those four hours sleep each night, seen her feet expand from size five to size seven, lost six pounds from an already spare frame, used ten pairs of running shoes and made it with 37 minutes of Bill's

45th birthday remaining.

"When most people break world records they do it in big stadiums with cheering crowds," said Sharon. "It would be nice to have had a few people here, but it's the record that matters."

One of the support vans had had "World record attempt" emblazoned on the side. Approaching midnight, one of the crew found a piece of duct tape and carefully excised the word "attempt."

They gave me a late night lift down to a campsite in Wick, the offer of a sleeping bag declined because the first train south was at 6am and the next not until 12.15pm. It was while on the third or fourth nocturnal lap of Wick's wonders that I was stopped by two Scottish police officers – do they have courses on dour? – who enquired what on earth I was doing.

"Waiting for a train," I said. They were unamused.

Bare footed but otherwise fully clothed, the new world champion had herself snuggled down into a sleeping bag in the back of a van. I can still see the smile on her face, still hear her final words before blessed sleep. "I wondered what had happened to my bog roll," she said.

ALMOST 13 years later, August 2 2019, the reception party at Lands End was rather bigger when Sharon, by then 55, ran triumphantly home to knock more than four hours from the women's world record for completing the epic in the opposite direction. Her time was 12 days, 11 hours six minutes and a few seconds.

No offence to Bill's baked beans, but she'd been fortified for the final run-in by a Big Mac and chips– though not a Cornish pasty – about 20 miles out.

Officially the distance was 822 miles, in truth rather longer because of a major navigational issue involving roadworks in Preston – Preston! – and one or two other glitches. She'd sometimes survived on three hours' sleep, on one late-night occasion simply collapsed in the road.

A sign of fast-changing times, hundreds had followed her every step on social media, shared her agonies and her frustrations, perhaps even chipped in a few quid for MIND, her chosen charity. Since neither logistics nor expenses ran to my presence at Lands End, she was on the phone within five minutes of arriving, just as she'd promised. "I'm pretty pleased," said Sharon and soon afterwards hit the sack.

In 2020 she was planning to beat the men's world record for a 500-miler in northern Scotland and to attempt a million metres – around 620 miles – on a treadmill at the university. Unless beaten by the coronavirus, few doubted that she'd achieve both. This one really could run and run.

39 : TRANPORTS OF DELIGHT

WHETHER to Wick or to Whitby, Penzance or Peterlee, public transport has usually been the vehicle for my journalistic journeys. Buses are simply a means to an end, trains a continuing if sometimes masochistic pleasure. Let's begin on the buses.

Back in the 1960s, when the school bus fare from Shildon to Bishop was threepence, every town seemed served by a multi-coloured myriad of bus companies. From Bishop there'd be the Bond Brothers service to Willington, Shaw Brothers to Byers Green and places out Spennymoor way, the Favourite to Sedgefield, the Eden – that was Summerson Brothers – to Newton Aycliffe, the OK to Durham and Newcastle, Lockey's out towards Cockfield – Lockey's buses ended up in Malta – dear old Weardale Motor Services faithfully headed westwards to the sticks and the United Automobile Company almost everywhere. Where did the Heather Brae run, then?

They were the days of clippies – sometimes tickets, sometimes the ears of the juvenile recalcitrant – of inspectors, feared by schoolboy swizzlers, of open platforms and of duplicates. When last did a bus company run a dupe? None may then have heard of health and safety – how else might the buses have countenanced all that standing room only? – or, for that matter, of senior citizens' bus passes, one of the perks of advancing years, that and getting half price into the match.

If the question's where would we be without them, the answer's probably sitting at home watching *Countdown*.

The buses may now be fewer, especially at night, but they're generally cleaner – save for the windows – and the drivers scruffier but less blooming miserable. The maxim, as with much else, is use it or lose it – and then don't come whinging to the papers when they're gone.

Weardale's among the independent survivors – a friendly, almost neighbourly service which still runs up towards the Cumbrian border and then stops at Killhope Wheel lest, as the flat earth folk imagined, they fall off the end of the world.

I was once on a Weardale bus when the driver stopped by a roadside cottage near Frosterley, let his dog out of the house for a run round the garden, continued the journey a few minutes later but presumably repeated the exercise on the return leg. None minded a bit; it was all part of the service.

Hodgson's, Barnard Castle based, runs a similarly scenic service four times a day between Barney and Richmond, sometimes driven by Talite Vaioleti, a Tongan rugby international who's 6ft 4ins and 18 stones and presumably not a shrinking Vaioleti at all. "When people first see me they probably think I'm a bit scary," he admitted, but a gentler gentleman never squeezed behind the wheel.

The man they simply call Vee may not stop to let his dog run off steam round the garden, but is so popular that regulars buy him Christmas presents.

ELSEWHERE in County Durham there were Gillett Brothers around Quarrington Hill – clearly bus operation was a pretty fraternal business – Gypsy Queen north-eastwards from Durham City and Trimdon Motor Services, known universally and affectionately as Trimdon Muck Shifters, serving the south-east corner and beyond.

TMS had been formed by a trio of pitmen in the 1920s, mostly running better-days double deckers until bought in 1959 by Bob Lewis, a Hebburn-born philanthropist and businessman. The transformation which turned the Muck Shifters into the biggest and most profitable private bus company in the country was recalled at a 2006 reunion in Trimdon Labour Club.

"I'm glad it's a TMS do," said someone, perhaps unkindly. "If it had been Arriva I wouldn't be here yet."

As well as its regular services, one of TMS's chief responsibilities was getting East Durham miners to their work, a job the company took very seriously and a dedication not always appreciated by the colliers themselves. If the winter snow were so bad that the buses simply couldn't get through, the miners could claim a Bevan Day – payment for no work. Trouble was, TMS was like the Wells Fargo stage: they always got through.

"The early shift drivers would be brought in a couple of hours before their time to help clear the road," it was recalled at the reunion. "The miners weren't too happy. They'd call us worse than clarts and then worse than that."

They were the days of conductors and conductresses and, around the Trimdons, a midwife who'd go about her daily round by bicycle. If a night time delivery were required she'd phone the TMS foreman and they'd send a bus to fetch her. Bob Lewis also started Zebra Holidays, employing 33 people at a call centre in Trimdon Grange and organising around 60,000 trips each year. He sold the business in 1990.

Trimdon Labour Club was perhaps even better known as the venue of many of Tony Blair's victory gatherings – none could work a room better than the former prime minister – though perhaps the most memorable evening I spent there was when skiffle king Lonnie Donegan played in the year 2000. Lonnie was pushing 70, had had two heart attacks and a triple coronary bypass and was further handicapped by a broken toe.

The most approachable of men, he leapt around the stage like a 21-year-old, his Rock Island Line so perfectly timed that he might have been invited to tender for the Northern Rail franchise – but more of that doomed outfit very shortly.

Lonnie died a few months later.

Another sign of changing times, the Labour Club had closed even before the seismic events of December 2019 which turned the Sedgefield constituency blue. Blair Central's a carpet warehouse now.

DO ferries count as public transport? None in the North-East, save that which tootles two minutes across the Tyne between North and South Shields, but indispensable around the Highlands and Islands of Scotland, with which we're greatly familiar – if not frequent flyers then sedulous sailors, anyway. Now nationalised, the fleet carries the flag of Caledonian MacBrayne, recalling familiar doggerel among the highlanders:

> *The earth belongs unto the Lord*
> *And all that it contains,*
> *Except for the kyles and the Western Isles*
> *And they belong to MacBrayne's.*

THEN there are the railways, which might reasonably be supposed a love/hate relationship. None born in Shildon, none who spent most evenings and every Saturday morning train spotting, could fail to have affection for Britain's railways. None with many miles on the clock could be blind to rail's failings, or insensitive to a whiff of steam.

After thousands of journeys, I still relish the little branch line from Bishop Auckland to Darlington – might they finally get regular steam in time for the Stockton and Darlington bicentenary in 2025? – though the iron road extension through Middlesbrough to Saltburn may not be quite so greatly loved, not even by its own mother. Much has been written and broadcast about Teesside Airport railway station – one train a week westwards, none in the opposite direction – though its position as the country's least-used station was usurped in 2018 by Redcar British Steel.

RBS, on no account to be confused with the Royal Bank

of Scotland, had just 40 recorded passenger movements all year – though many of them may have alighted and never been seen again. The timetable listed two stopping trains a day in each direction, though my ticket one late December day in 2018 was the first the guy in the breakfast time booking office had sold to that station for years.

British Steel's fires had been dampened in 2015, but the perilous site remained like something from a film set for *Quatermass*. Prominently headed 'Keep out: risk of death', notices at the exit from both station platforms warned of high voltage electricity, dangerous chemicals, hazardous gases, unsafe structures and HGV and train movements. It said nothing, though it might have done, about dying from lack of nourishment. What's a guy to do when leaving the wooden platform might mean a short trip to kingdom come and the next train back is eight-and-a-half hours away?

Eventually I climbed a fence, found a road and was intercepted by an incredulous security guard who said that those trains which stopped at British Steel should never have been in the timetable. He was right, of course – and after December 2019 no trains did stop there, though the station remained, unloved and unvisited, in the timetable. I like to think that the column which exposed that potentially lethal nonsense, and which an hour's walk later also survived a greasy spoon breakfast in South Bank, had something to do with the decision.

LONGER and less life-threatening journeys are still eagerly anticipated. These days Sharon and I frequently travel first class, such the vagaries of the ticketing system that it can often be almost as cheap if booked on-line and with buckshee food and drink agreeably served en route. The glorious run up the coast to Edinburgh often offers particular bargains in the posh end.

A big perk was that the company reimbursed the cost of my tickets, almost always without question. If the fancy took, and the column justified, I'd just go. Another obvious benefit was that the column could be written on the way back – something not recommended at the wheel of a company car – though it was easier to sleep, and to oversleep, on the train.

Sometimes the railways themselves would pay, as with the 40th birthday trip from Wick to Penzance, the system's extremities, including a sleeper westwards from Paddington. Rest unassured, sleepers are overrated.

We're particularly lucky in the North-East to have the delightful Esk Valley line from Middlesbrough to Whitby – served in the 1970s by a 5am milk train on which rail roving photographer Rodney Wildsmith and I were for much of the way the only passengers – and the little-less attractive line through the Tyne Valley from Newcastle to Carlisle.

It was with Rodney, come to think, that – not long after starting the *John North* column – I wandered into one of Middlesbrough's more notorious pubs and noticed a lady with '£1 10s' chalked on the sole of her shoe. Rod, more worldly-wise, was able to explain that it represented – how might this be put? – her going rate.

In any case the lass was out of date. Britain had gone decimal months earlier.

LARGELY volunteer run, the restored Tanfield Railway near Stanley in County Durham is also a lovely experience – summer-time cream tea specials especially recommended. Causey Arch, the world's oldest railway bridge, is nearby.

The Weardale Railway, recently bought by the Auckland Project – the company set up by millionaire philanthropist Jonathan Ruffer to revitalise Bishop and its environs – may also be set for more adventurous times. The charismatic Mr Ruffer talks of direct services from Darlington up the dale; maybe it's they who will once again fill Shildon tunnel with smoke.

The privately owned Wensleydale Railway, a few miles down the road from us, runs from Leeming Bar to Redmire –

almost in the shadow of Bolton Castle, where Mary Queen of Scots spent several unwilling months appreciating both the scenery and her plight – is also delightful, with some very good walks around Redmire and an excellent pub, the Kings Arms, not half a mile from the station.

Among Redmire's more curious claims to memory is that in the 1970s I was invited officially to open the village hall. When it had been completely refurbished 25 years later they asked me to do the honours again. I look forward to completing a hat-trick.

Like any railway, of course, the Wensleydale is better when it has steam – and best of all when steam traction is provided by 69023 *Joem,* a little green giant of a tank engine which in British Rail days worked as station pilot at Newcastle. There's probably a railway by-law against proposing holy matrimony to a steam engine, otherwise we might long since have been coupled. Last I heard, alas, *Joem* was still in bits on the floor of the North Eastern Locomotive Preservation Group's workshop in Darlington and with melancholy mut-

LITTLE GREEN GIANT: *Joem*

terings about its prospects of emerging intact. A little model stands, expectantly, on our dresser.

There seems little point in banging on about the railways' shortcomings. Northern has had a deservedly dreadful press and lost the franchise early in 2020, TransPennine was until recently even worse and threatened with Northern's fate. Imagine the anguish after a few beers in Manchester upon discovering that the train back to the North-East doesn't even have a working toilet. It's happened several times. Like a lovelorn battered husband, I always come back for more.

40 : UP THE JUNCTION

OTHER than home, and there really is no place like home, my favourite location on earth may be Garsdale railway station – railway stations, come to think, would make up most of the top ten – and the surprising thing about Garsdale is that it's not strictly in North-East England at all. By a couple of hundred yards it's in Cumbria.

Cumbria's curious. In happier times the *Echo* would sell to very many of the homes all the way along the Durham and North Yorkshire dales but – save for an occasional incursion into Kirkby Stephen – seem abruptly to run out of puff at the county border. As dear old Lonnie might have sung, there appeared to be a Cumberland gap.

Nor were our journalists (and the erstwhile news editor) much inclined to venture into uncharted areas – an annual ride up to the Appleby horse fair, maybe, a check with the fell rescue boys to see which side of the county line the latest casualty might have fallen, a gently raised eyebrow if things cut up rough in Brough. Magnetic west, Garsdale station proved nonetheless irresistible.

Opened in 1876, known formerly as Hawes Junction, it's on the glorious Settle and Carlisle line about six miles beyond Hawes at yon end of Wensleydale. The branch from Garsdale eastwards was worked as far as Hawes by an anonymous tank engine known locally as Bonnyface – presumably no relation to Saint Boniface, the patron of lost causes, but an interesting example of what they say about beauty and the eye of the beholder.

STATION IN LIFE: *Garsdale*

The branch closed in 1959, Garsdale station 20 years later. It was reopened in 1986 when the Settle and Carlisle's potential was at last realised. On one visit I'd bumped into that great Dalesman Bill Mitchell, author and editor, who talked about getting back into his pyjamas at 3pm each day – "I've a strange belief that it helps keep all those dreadful nervous diseases at bay".

He was in his mid-80s, thought that one day he might be found dead slumped over a keyboard – there may be worse ways to go – believed that Garsdale station looked out of place up there, but in its improbability lies it glory. Whoever would have supposed it possible?

Barely half a mile away and only a little more probable, is the tiny Hawes Junction Methodist chapel, known on high days as Mount Zion, opened in the same year as the station and, like the station, still joyously serving. The chapel, of which more shortly, has one advantage over its neighbour, however: Mount Zion's in North Yorkshire – and make that two plus points if the heating's on. Garsdale station was itself the venue for Church of England services between the wars. The faithful gathered in the waiting room, their singing accompanied by an elderly harmonium known (it's said) as the ill wind, because it blew nobody any good. Dances were held in the little room beneath the 80,000-gallon water tower.

The *Daily Express*, then Britain's biggest-selling paper, came up to chronicle it all in 1937 and was followed 13 years later by *John Bull* magazine – remember that? – beneath the headline 'Alight here for the back of beyond.'

"They were reet good do's, we had't piano ower three times," someone recalled of the water tank terpsichorea, though whether that was also a load of John Bull it's now impossible to say.

The station's south of the main road towards Sedbergh and the M6. Beyond the two platforms the black-blasted Coal Road rises 1,750ft to Lea Yeat and then drops slightly to Dent station, five miles from the village from which larcenously it took its name and the highest railway station in England. Dent's not bad, either.

IN the early hours of Christmas Eve 1910 a signalman's error – "I think I've wrecked the Scotch Express," he presciently told Garsdale's station master – led to the death of 12 passengers when the midnight train from St Pancras to Glasgow ploughed into the back of light engines heading north to Carlisle.

POLES APART:
Author and wife at Garsdale station

The bodies were taken to the Moorcock Inn, just down the hill from the station, the inquest held there three days later.

The station turntable was stockaded, such

the ferocity of the Helm wind, Bonnyface valiantly turning to confront whatever the storms might throw at it.

The station's long been unstaffed, save for the signal box, but has well-kept waiting room and toilets and, near them, an £8,000 bronze statue of a collie called Ruswarp, faithful companion of Graham Nuttall who was secretary of the Friends of the Settle and Carlisle at a time when the threatened line needed all the friends it could get. On the basis that he was a regular user, just like his master, Ruswarp had even been allowed to sign the petition against the line's closure. The paw print was impressive, perhaps decisive.

Not long after the campaign's great triumph, Graham suffered a fatal heart attack while walking in the Welsh hills, his body found 11 weeks later with Ruswarp still by his side. The dog attended his master's funeral but itself died soon afterwards.

These days the Settle and Carlisle has a much improved service, though hopes of reopening the branch line back to Hawes appear as wild as the terrain. An example of integrated transport which might be copied elsewhere, most trains are now met at Garsdale by a Little White Bus, the volunteer-led service instigated by inspirational local councillor John Blackie, who died in 2019.

It's not necessary to take a bus, or even a train, of course. Just go to Garsdale, look round, and marvel.

HUMBLE and homely, Hawes Junction Methodist chapel is no less wonderful, though services these days are generally limited to major festivals like Easter, Christmas and, of course, harvest. Safely they gather in, thronged like the glory days and fed like the five thousand.

The Methodists always have done the best church teas – I write from replete experience – the example set by John Wesley, the founder, as he rode eastwards and viewed Weardale's richness spread below. One of his companions recorded his anticipation:

The promised land from Killhope top
I now rejoice to see.
My hope is full – my glorious hope –
Of good spice cake and tea.

Early arrivals at Hawes Junction chapel sit knowingly near the great spread, the repast temptingly shrouded on long trestle tables, the Ten Commandments amended to include the additional requirement that thou shalt not snitch a sandwich until the last Amen. Latecomers may have to stand, so small the chapel, the record for most people in the pulpit – eight? ten? – debated as vigorously as that for a Guinness telephone box. Hawes Silver Band is oft in attendance, too, a sausage roll from salvation.

Old faithfuls recall, or recall being told, when the Sunday School had 70 pupils and nine teachers, when the annual trip to Morecambe – "once even to Blackpool" – was augmented by half a crown apiece from chapel funds and a further 2/6d from a shopkeeper up in Sedbergh. Some of the hymn books

HIS AND HAWES: *The chapel at the junction*

are dated 1933, some further indicating that they were a prize from Heptonstall Methodist Sunday School, which sounds like it should be in Lancashire.

"Value of marks gained, one shilling," the inscription adds. "Value of prize 2/3d. Amount to pay, 1/3d." Yorkshire, then.

Though Cumbria cockstrides nearby, preachers like to remind their congregation that they remain in the White Rose county, and thus God's own. One time we were up there, the appropriate reading recounted the parable of the lost sheep, prompting the minister to tell of the Yorkshire Sunday School teacher who asked his charges why, even with ninety-and-nine enfolded, the good shepherd was so keen to find the 100th.

A young arm shot up. "Please sir, perhaps it were't tup."

Another preacher offered a Yorkshire definition of conscience. "Summat that meks yer tell yer mother before yer sister tells her fust."

The most memorable service of all, however, may have been on Easter Sunday 2016 when proceedings were led by Andrew Fagg, a Methodist local preacher.

Faggy, great guy, was a good dalesman who lived in Hawes, possessed an accent as broad as a prize bull's buttocks but worked for the BBC in London – coincidentally alongside my younger son, Owen. When the BBC had no need of his weekend soul, he played football for Hawes United. The day before Easter he'd finished night shift at 8am, dashed to Kings Cross, was seriously delayed on the journey north, alighted at Northallerton, drove home, kissed the kids, picked up his boots and turned out in the Wensleydale League match against the Buck Inn, from Richmond.

Hawes were 3-0 down when the fightback began, Faggy heading the equaliser but taking a boot in the face in the process. He lay briefly unconscious in the mud, unable as the Good Book enjoins even to turn the other cheek – or any

EASTER RISING: *Andrew Fagg (left) at the chapel*

other part of his anatomy – but United, inspired, won 4-3. "We were absolutely finished; almost dead and gone," he told the Easter gathering, his battered face bearing witness to his suffering.

"When things look dead and buried, as they did for our team yesterday," he added, "remember the Easter story – victory snatched from the jaws of defeat, just like Hawes United."

It's noted elsewhere in *Trifles* that, hitherto, the most memorable sermon had been that which compared the Kingdom of Heaven to the cyclists' café at Gargrave. On Easter Sunday 2016, Hawes United's star striker rose head and shoulders higher.

FROM Garsdale, the next station north is Kirkby Stephen, once in Westmoreland but now a little more securely in Cumbria. Formerly Kirkby Stephen West, that station would also feature in the top ten places on earth, particularly if something steam hauled happened to be passing.

Kirkby Stephen East was nearer the village, on the dramatic and oft snow-blocked Stainmore line which until closure in January 1962 ran from Darlington and Bishop Auckland across the Pennines to Penrith and Tebay. Today the line would be called challenging, or at least it would if it ever these days it snowed, though railway firemen probably called it much worse. KSE is now headquarters of the Stainmore Railway Company, committed to restoring the station to 1950s operational days and with steam services up towards Warcop camp. They do a terrific job, as *Echo* photographer Stuart Bolton once discovered.

Photographers are an inky trade sub-species, of late much endangered, almost always in a rush and usually protesting that they needed to be ten miles away 20 minutes previously. Stuart was so taken by all that was going on at KSE, and by the station cats, that he stayed for 75 minutes and recorded 726 images. If every picture tells a story, what's to be said of 726?

The Stainmore's chief movers are Mike Thompson, a North Tees hospital consultant who retired at 50 in order to devote more time to the railway, and his wife Sue Jones. They live in Sedgefield. When they married in 2010 they chiefly asked for SRC donations in lieu of presents but mentioned that what they might really like was a cement mixer.

It duly arrived. "Just what we've always wanted, a real boon," said Sue, or words to that effect. A solid foundation to marriage, anyway.

KSW, a wilder location where a plaque records a visit by the Prince of Wales, a few years back had a little café and railway memorabilia shop in which Sharon – a dab hand at surprise birthday presents – spotted the best ever. Thereby, very nearly, hung a tale.

On the line between Manchester and Glossop there's a station called Broadbottom, which as kids our boys thought hilarious, and another – in an unremarkable suburb – called Flowery Field. One day, I told myself, I'd write a book chronicling journeys to some of Britain's most graphically named but ultimately prosaic railway stations – places like Rose Grove (Burnley), Gypsy Lane (Middlesbrough), Carshalton Beeches (suburban Surrey) and Ash Vale. Dust to dust.

Echoing one of the Beatles' greatest hits, the book – and how many more never get beyond a clever title? – would be called *Flowery Field For Ever*. As serendipity would have it, the shop on Kirkby Stephen West offered for £75 a large Manchester Passenger Transport Executive station sign – one careful owner – from Flowery Field. Goodness knows how she smuggled it home, but on birthday morning she bore it triumphantly.

The sign still hangs in our hall, the book hangs in semipermanent abeyance – but if any of the train operating companies wants to sponsor a jolly read by a budding author, then they need look no further.

41 : THE ITALIAN JOB

I'VE never been much of a foreign correspondent, though there was once a flight from Blackpool to the Isle of Man. Wing spreading might otherwise have meant the Spanish City at Whitley Bay or distance learning at a weekend school near Ripon, travel's attraction further dimmed by a lifelong preference for my own bed.

Mind, they did once propose to send me to New York to write a series of features on the anniversary of 9/11, the only problem that Peter Barron, the well-intentioned editor, mentioned it to the GP we had in common before ever mentioning it to me. The great and good Dr Bagshaw at once rang home, where Sharon answered.

"Mike must on no account fly to New York or anywhere else," he said. That was a legacy of the deep vein thrombosis and pulmonary embolism back in the year 2000, an unforeseen consequence of a "routine" varicose vein operation. I'd been grounded.

There'd earlier been a few jollies, as press trips are usually known, once on a slow boat to Rotterdam, on another long-gone occasion by air to the Prix de la Arc d'Triomphe and several times with British Rail, as then they were, across the Channel to France. What larks.

Then there was Guernsey. Are the Channel Islands abroad? I suppose they must be. Back in the 1970s, when smoking was considered rather less noxious than now it is, cigarette companies like Rothman's and John Player were major sponsors of sport, presumably in an attempt to persuade ever more folk to hammer another nail into their coffin.

Rothman's, who employed many hundreds at factories in Darlington and Spennymoor, for several years very generously sponsored the Northern League, and other leagues like it across the UK – and in the Channel Islands. If anyone thought the tie-up inappropriate, they never coughed. The Rothman's Cup was contested by invited teams from all those leagues, the big prize a trip to Guernsey or Jersey.

Was the draw weighted so that a disproportionate number of teams got to head across the Channel? Goodness only knows, but it was a thrill when Shildon were paired with Vale Rec in Guernsey and better yet when the firm agreed – for they were very different days – that photographer Ken Ferguson and I might join the chartered flight from Teesside Airport. The headline said 'Shildon for Europe.'

The aircraft might have come straight from the pages of a Biggles novel – the author Captain W E Johns had been based not far away at Marske-by-the-Sea airfield, where he pranged planes regularly – the Guernsey folk were wonderful hosts. Each player was given a female escort, many of them nurses, and, since it was a much more innocent age, it should be stressed that the escorts simply escorted. We won, king size.

Much the most unforgettable overseas expedition, however, was that in the summer of 2009 which took us to Turin for the centenary of West Auckland FC's first 'World Cup' win and which proved pretty much calamitous.

The original story's locally legendary, nationally well known. Sir Thomas Lipton, a millionaire businessman and philanthropist with interests in Britain and Italy, launched a four nations football tournament, to be played in Turin and with a solid silver 32-inch trophy for the winners.

The inaugural participants in 1909 were Stuttgart from Germany, FC Winterhour from Switzerland, the local champions Juventus – and West, third bottom of the Northern League. None really knows why they were invited, various theories suggesting that they were mistaken for a very different WAFC – Woolwich Arsenal, the Gunners – or that one of Lipton's employees was a Northern League referee. Sir Thomas might even have intended the English representatives to be Bishop Auckland, better known then as now, instead.

West's team were mostly miners, obliged to beg time off from the pit and then to travel third class to Italy. They'd not even booked a hotel, spending their nights on a Turin church floor. Improbably victorious, West were invited to defend their trophy two years later, hammered Juventus 6-1 in the final and were allowed to keep the precious silverware – at least until someone stole it from the village workmen's club in 1994.

Books have been written about those long-gone heroics, films made – the best remembered starring Dennis Waterman and Tim Healy.

The centenary match with Juventus was West's idea, took a year to plan and seemed a very good idea at the time. The English FA put up £10,000 towards costs, Unilever – a Lipton successor company – contributed another £5,000. Most of the party made the 1,100 mile 28-hour journey by coach, Sharon and I travelled by train, spending a couple of agreeable days in Milan before heading back north to Turin.

It was in a Milanese park on a 35-degree morning that I heard of the death of Sir Bobby Robson, one of football's all-time greats. Of some men it's said that they'd give you their last £10; Sir Bobby would not only have given you his last £10 but, if he could have done, his last ten minutes as well.

On a table outside a bar, someone had left a copy of *La Gazette Dello Sport*. There appeared to be a great deal about Juventus, not a word on West.

WE arrive at the South Turin Holiday Inn, soon to be known

as the Holiday Inncompetent and to compare unfavourably with a church hall floor, just 30 minutes before the team bus. Problems at once become apparent. Both bar and restaurant are closed for the month of August, the promised swimming pool doesn't exist, the receptionist can't even run to a few sandwiches. Some people take a siesta until 3pm, the Italians take one until September. The Holiday Inn gives every impression of not expecting visitors.

As the weekend wears on, it's to resemble nothing more closely than an episode of *Juve Been Framed*, though none from West Auckland is laughing.

The Juventus first team had beaten Real Madrid on the Friday evening. The collection of youngsters assembled to face West Auckland the following tea time gathers at a Juventus training ground in the hills 40 miles from our base. You can tell the West lads: they're the ones with socks under their flip-flops. No one's there to welcome the visitors, not even with a communal tea bag and a packet of ginger biscuits; Anne Palfreyman, the West chairman's wife, is obliged to pay 10 euros to get in and has her way blocked until she does so. "At least they haven't confiscated my passport," she says.

Several words come to mind, none of them entente or cordiale. It isn't what you'd call a red carpet, or even a proggy mat. Stuart Alderson, general manager and trip organiser, has already been on the phone to the travel agent back in Bishop. "Just wait till I get home," he says, in the manner of a harassed mother threatening a recalcitrant bairn with the belt from its dad.

West have not only brought the silver replica of the original cup, guarded like vestal virginity, but a selection of mementoes for their hosts. The Italians ask for the exchange to be delayed until half-time, find a blank plaque at the back of a cupboard and add a couple of books on Italian wild flowers, probably unwanted Christmas presents.

"What am I supposed to do with these?" asks Stuart.

"Look at the pictures like you always do," says Jim Palfreyman. West are wearing new club ties, best bib and tucker. Juventus don't even wear their best jeans. Things will only get worse.

West team manager Brian Honour, shortly afterwards to be named Hartlepool United's player of the century – "I'll get where watter cannot," he says – admits in his pre-match team talk to uncertainty about the age and quality of the opposition.

CUP-TRIED:
Stuart Alderson

"You just don't know whether to get rove into them," he says, adding a little extravagantly that the eyes of the world are upon them.

It's Juventus who prove the wild rovers, a goal up in four minutes and four ahead in 26. "Gerrimwhacked," shouts a travelling fan, an instruction probably akin to roving into them. Veteran supporters Frankie Patrick and Les Nevison stand sentry yet more closely over the Sir Thomas Lipton trophy. "They're not getting this off us," says Frankie. At half-time it's 6-0, at the end 7-1. In time-honoured tradition, two West supporters have long since left for the pub. "Great toasties," they report, improbably.

The Italians can barely be bothered even to shake hands. "I hate to think what would have happened if we'd won. They'd probably have thrown us in the dyke," says Stuart.

Then things get yet worse. After hanging around for half an hour, the party is advised to walk to a nearby bar where both teams gather at outside tables, either side of the steps.

After much pressure, someone brings the visiting players crisps and pop, like kids on a Sunday School trip. The officials, and the sole representative from Her Britannic Majesty's Press Corps, get nothing at all. After a few more minutes a bell rings and the Italians disappear up the steps for a fresh salmon salad.

A couple of ladies from the British consulate hang around ineffectually, toting union jack carrier bags but showing little of the bulldog spirit. Very far from home, the visitors are left with their crisps, a century of anticipation crumbled in an evening.

We arrive back at the Holiday Inncompetent at 9.45pm, the players intent on a night on the town. "What else can go wrong now?" asks Jim Palfreyman, and is shortly to find out. It's around 6.30am on the Sunday morning when fire alarms wail throughout the hotel. We stumble to the door, the air in the corridor acrid. It smells serious; all are evacuated in various stages of undress.

Twenty minutes later the fire brigade arrives at about 10mph – "I could have passed them on me bike," someone says – accompanied by gun-toting carabinieri, similarly unhappy at the dawn chorus. The West lads, returning from touring Turin, have set off the powder-based fire extinguishers. Club officials, hotel management and an overnight wedding party are jointly (and understandably) furious. Eventually the players' passports are returned in exchange for a 2,000 euro payment to make good the damage.

They face a 28-hour return journey. Next time they'll take their holidays in Redcar.

42 : SERVICE WITH A SMILE

FROM the early days at Sunday School, where a coloured stamp might be had simply for not playing hookey down the Rec, I've clung precariously to the Church. The Church, in turn, has never quite been able to shake me off (though once or twice it tried.)

In the mid-60s, when I was chairman (what else?) of the St John's Shildon branch of the Anglican Young People's Association, we conducted a somewhat spurious survey which purported to show that 50 per cent of young people were drinking alcohol under age. It didn't apply to St John's AYPA, of course. Most of us had just turned legitimacy, though we'd been on the beer since the days of the fifth form dance.

The subsequent headlines attracted the BBC, though so long ago that it was still the North Home Service. They sent well-remembered reporter George Lambelle – who seemed ancient and must have been at least 35 – to interview me. It took place, of course, in a pub and with a tape recorder the size of a suitcase.

It was the first of very many broadcast interviews over the next 50-odd years. A media tart was born over a BBC brown ale.

By the age of 23 I was churchwarden, church council secretary and parish newspaper editor at St John's. By 24 I was senior churchwarden – in terms of service, not age – and that's when things got really interesting.

Stephen, a smashing young curate with what seemed to

me a marked lack of self-belief, was due to lead 6pm Evensong in the absence of the vicar. At 5.30 there was no sign of him. By 5.45 we were starting to worry. Since the Book of Common Prayer enjoined that, in the absence of a minister, the service should be led by the senior layman present, I asked the other churchwarden to get in his car and try to find our missing curate.

What if he couldn't? Would I be required to preach an off-the-cuff sermon? Could I rebuke the backsliders, those who (as the service book still had it) had erred and strayed like lost sheep and in whom there was no health?

Truth to tell – and you'd expect nothing else from a senior churchwarden – it was probably a slight disappointment when, on the stroke of six, Stephen rushed apologetically into church. The curate had slept in for Evensong. Think of the story, think of the headlines. Think of the money when I flogged the tale to the nationals.

Stephen begged me to say nowt. Maybe it was the couple of pints he stood in the Red Lion afterwards which influenced integrity, but nothing made the papers. It was an improbable clash of God v Mammon and, just for once, God won.

Other curates like Vincent Ashwin and Tom Thubron, both subsequently to serve as overseas missionaries, became good friends. Stephen left the ministry soon afterwards to run a convenience store. It was the priesthood's loss.

THERE were church posts elsewhere, even a place on the Durham diocesan stewardship committee, the ear of the great and (presumably) good. Then things changed.

Asked to become church council secretary in the North Yorkshire village where still we live, I attempted to wield a slightly new broom. It swept dirty. They appeared to regard me as a moderniser – great heaven forfend! – and thus as something akin to the devil incarnate. A kangaroo court was called one Saturday morning with the ultimatum to support the status quo or to go. There were sleepless nights; I went.

After several years following the Children of Israel on a grand tour of the ecclesiastical wilderness, I finally found salvation.

The Times each Saturday carried a column called *At Your Service*, written by Ruth Gledhill – an attractive-looking blonde who was also a ballroom dancing champion. Probably a better writer than I was, she would undoubtedly have been a better waltzer.

Her column involved attendance at a different church service most weeks of the year. Maybe I could do the same thing for the *Echo*, maybe even keep the same inspired title? Show me the bit in the Ten Commandments where it says anything about not plagiarising thy neighbour's bright idea. *AYS* became my sixth column each week, and the Sabbath no longer a day of rest.

It started in 1994, was to run for more than 17 years until my retirement from full-time journalism and unlike the *Eating Owt* column, which operated unannounced, always sought permission to attend. It was only three times refused, on each occasion a Methodist church, each one of which was closed within a few years. Just saying.

It was also at a Methodist church – in the former pit village of Ramshaw, near Evenwood – that I persuaded the lady minister to include *O For a Thousand Tongues* among the evening's hymns in exchange for a post-service curry in the Indian restaurant improbably across the road. I forget how the expenses explained it.

The first column, perhaps inevitably, was back at St John's, Shildon, where the vicar was Father Raymond Cuthbertson. The new column, he told his flock perceptively, was to be a sort of church person's *Down Your Way*.

Father Raymond, it might digressively be added, had also won the *Backtrack* column's quote of the year award – no prize – in 1992. We'd sat together at Wembley, the stadium having recently undergone one of its periodic makeovers.

Raymond was unimpressed. "Fifty million quid," he said, "and you still have to pee against a wall."

Though chiefly Christian, and chiefly Church of England, *AYS* also visited Muslims and Sikhs – great hospitality, great curry – Jews and JWs, Latter Day Saints and one or two who might never have achieved canonisation had they lived to be as old as Methuselah.

Churches were changing, adapting, and very largely for the better. Preachers even essayed a little levity, like the bishop who told of a fellow bishop's wife, criticised for turning up in a fur coat. "What poor creature had to die for you to wear that?" demanded her accuser.

"My mother-in-law actually," she said.

FEW services were more memorable than that in Les Barrass's garden shed, a spiritual Tardis. Les had been a mounted police officer with the Met – "stoned and spat at for a living" – became a travelling chiropodist, shifted to Darlington and in 1991 survived multiple injuries in a car crash.

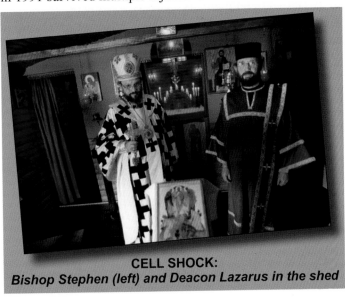

CELL SHOCK:
Bishop Stephen (left) and Deacon Lazarus in the shed

Perhaps it was for that reason that he became known as Deacon Lazarus – he who rose from the dead – when setting up a cell of the Celtic Orthodox Church in that windowless but incense-scented and truly fabulous shed.

It was divided into areas symbolising 'earth' and 'heaven', only the priesthood – and certainly not jobbing journalists – allowed through the royal doors and into heaven. If earth were opulent, heaven – seen from somewhere this side of the Pearly Gates – was positively refulgent in its splendour.

If Deacon Lazarus were magnificently attired, then Bishop Stephen – up from York for a communion service – was more lustrous yet (and should on no account be confused with Stephen, the sleepy head of St John's.) The day after the column and accompanying pictures appeared it was pinched by the *Daily Mail.* Isn't there a commandment against that, too?

Though the *AYS* column seldom strayed far beyond the North-East, there was a trip to Shetland and the UK's most northerly church – the minister, we discovered, came from County Durham, more of that elsewhere – another to Dublin and an 8.30am Mass at Notre Dame, interrupted by the 21st century equivalent of the money changers and them that sold doves in the temple.

The headline was 'Dame disgrace.'

Closer to home, I attended a Remembrance Day parade at Stockton when, on the very stroke of the 11th hour of the 11th day of the 11th month, an elderly veteran fell forward from the front line, instantly dead. Incredibly poignant, that one – unsurprisingly – made the front page.

A challenge which was nonetheless never properly addressed was to convince the readership that *At Your Service* was an entertaining and fairly offbeat read in its own right, and not some glorified Saturday Sermon. An ambition was to win the *UK Press Gazette*'s specialist writer of the year award for the column. Though it made a shortlist of three, it was a real disappointment only to come second.

249

AMONG the Church of England's glories – its characteristics, anyway – have long been its eccentric priests. Doubtless the Romans have a few, too.

Appointed as curate to St Mary's in Barnard Castle, the Rev Paul Walker swore that his first sermon began with the text about woe unto hypocrites and sinners – "Who hath warned ye of the wrath to come" – at which point he sat down again. He later won the *Times* preacher of the year award.

Archdeacon Granville Gibson, visiting the same church, bemoaned in the vestry beforehand that no one had told him that that blooming Mike Amos was coming but forgot that his pectoral microphone was switched on and that he could be heard throughout the building. Granville, in truth, didn't really need a pectoral microphone to be heard throughout the building, or probably as far off as Middleton-in-Teesdale.

Few may have been more improbable, however, than the Rev Arthur White Officer, vicar of Rookhope, in Weardale, from 1919 until his death, half-blind and aged 91, in 1973.

In 1955, when he was 74 and the average congregation about 70 fewer, he wrote to villagers explaining why he wouldn't contribute to the parish magazine.

"It wouldn't be printable," he said. "The least said, the better."

Arthur Officer lived in a ten-bedroom vicarage with his housekeeper, a transistor radio and from time to time a few hens. Said to be a good visitor – he'd take a pound of tea to new babies, presumably for parental consumption – he didn't much care for being visited, particularly not by Phyllis Carter, the diocesan secretary, up from Auckland Castle in her Morris Minor.

Since he'd seldom answer correspondence, the diocesan secretary thought an annual visit essential. Somehow the vicar would get wind of it. He was always out or, if not quite out, then definitely not in.

In those 54 years he took just three days off sick, sold

strawbs for a shilling a pound, walked down the middle of the road with his white stick but seemed somehow to be borne in the arms of St Christopher, at least as far as hospital visiting in Stanhope.

The Rev Edward le Grice Hill and the Rev Edward Underhill may have been cut from the same cloth. The former was at Hawes in Wensleydale for more than 50 years, having said he was coming for three. He was also 91 when he died in 1981, the year after finally agreeing to the bishop's suggestion that it might be time he retired – though on condition that he continued as organist and choirmaster.

He'd won the MC, swore that he couldn't remember why, was a bit of a film buff – Hedy Lamarr the world's most beautiful woman, he thought – complained that his binman earned more than he did, grumbled that all the Church of England appeared to be interested in was stunts. "I wouldn't care if they filled the pews," he added.

His funeral was on Maundy Thursday. I took several buses to Hawes, wearing a suitably sober three-piece tweed suit, shoving a couple of cream eggs in the waistcoat pockets as Easter offerings when I got home. By journey's end the waistcoat was ruined and the cream eggs were a bit curdled, too. It's funny how you remember things, isn't it?

Edward Underhill was 85 when, in 2009, he finally retired after half a century as Vicar of St George's in Low Fell, Gateshead. "If the Lord wanted us to move he'd have moved us," he said. I'd attended in 1997, part of the centenary celebrations, the elderly congregation fewer than 30 and a computer redundant in the vestry because none knew how to use it. It was one of few churches still always to use the Book of Common Prayer.

The centenary brochure acknowledged their faithful priest. "It has been said by someone close to him that he can do two things well – dig a kitchen garden and write a letter."

Michael Ball, then the Bishop of Jarrow, was less circumspect in his centenary message: "Some things don't change, and I'm glad that you are one of them."

THE churches' tapestry was rich, their diversity extraordinary. Though there were many closure services, especially involving small Methodist chapels that had declined to let me attend, it became clear that North-East church folk remained both dedicated and undefeated. Most were inspiring people; it was great to see.

There were men like Clarrie Beedle, a long-time Methodist local preacher and farmer on Teesdale's wildest extremities, who liked to quote the advice once given him that all he needed to survive up there was a good wife and a good muffler. "I'm lucky," he said. "I've had both."

The Methodists of New Brancepeth, west of Durham, even forgave – indeed greatly enjoyed – the classic mishearing when the *AYS* column reported that *Love Divine All Loves Excelling* had been sung to the tune of Blindworm, and wondered how it came by that curious name. In truth it was *Blaenwern*, Welsh apparently, a rare example of the blind leading the blindworm.

THERE were just two occasions on which the column failed to live up to its name, the first at Bearpark parish church – also west of Durham – where a misunderstanding over timings meant that we arrived just as the service was finishing. Sharon swore that I wrote the subsequent 1,000 words from the contents of the churchyard notice board. "Nothing new there, then," she added.

The second came when County Durham's adopted warship tied up on the Tyne, the Bishop of Durham there to lead an on-board service.

The problem was the gangplank, or whatever these days they're called, rising about 60ft and with only the Quayside beneath. It was about 58ft higher than my infamous head for heights allowed. You forget how huge those ships are.

Serendipitously, or perhaps just further evidence of God's mysterious ways, there was a pub about 20 yards away. I was on about the fourth pint when joined by Tom Wright, the bishop – mentioned earlier – who in exchange for a pint of his own happily did some card marking.

Tom was among senior churchmen with whom I became well acquainted. Michael Sadgrove, the 6ft 5in Dean of Durham at much the same time, was so media-friendly that he once rang to ask if I could include a paragraph wondering if anyone knew where he could buy a pair of size 12 blue suede shoes. It wasn't that he fancied an alternative career as an Elvis impersonator, just that he was a bit fed up of clerical black. He got his shoes.

None was more engaging than the Rt Rev Kevin Dunn, the late Roman Catholic bishop of Hexham and Newcastle, though he still declined publicly to address one of the great mysteries of faith.

It was St Patrick's Day, a Friday morning, hundreds with Irish ancestry thronging the church of St Michael in Elswick, Newcastle and many, so it seemed, with a certain gleam in their eye. No matter which way Easter was shifted, and it's a truly moveable feast, St Patrick's Day always fell within the 40 days of Lent.

The Rt Rev George Snow, then the Anglican Bishop of Whitby, had told me many years previously that what he gave up for Lent was picking his nose. What many of St Michael's congregation still tried to give up was the booze – but did feast days like St Patrick's count, especially as the Tyneside Irish Centre, opposite St James' Park, promised a long day of emerald extravagance? Remembering all that's said about abstinence making the heart grow fonder, might they be allowed a day off?

Bishop Kevin – "his smile as broad as the Liffey" – remained otherwise tight-lipped. Fr Joe Travers didn't.

In Ireland, he said, Lent had 39 days, not 40. "Today eve-

HAPPY NEW YEAR: *Carmelite and Poor Clare abbesses, December 31 1999*

ryone is Irish. We return to Lent on Monday."

THE convents of the Poor Clares and of the nuns of the Carmelite order in Darlington were separated by a high wall and by silence. Both were contemplative, enclosed orders. For 142 years until New Year's Eve 1999 the two communities – good neighbours in every other sense – had never once met.

To mark the millennium it was decided that they should, a joint service in the Poor Clares' chapel. Of the 800-or-so *At Your Service* columns, none was more memorable.

By road the journey from heavy wooden gate to heavy wooden gate was 200 yards. More practically, whispered one of the sisters, they might have been put in a cannon barrel and fired over the wall. Fourteen of them travelled those 200 yards in a bus from Enterprise Travel, though the occasion transcended mere enterprise. It was historic, epochal, properly and unequivocally unique.

Members of other Darlington churches were there, too. "You are terrifically welcome to this extraordinary occasion," said Sister Frances, the Poor Clare abbess, and for once in its hyperbolic history the word "extraordinary" became an understatement.

Elderly nuns carried chairs two at a time, their physical strength perhaps underlying a spiritual fibre, too. Even the photographer was offered a seat and stayed for the whole service. Truly there's a first time for everything.

Since it was still Christmas, a small procession included 'Mary and Joseph'. There being a certain physical difficulty in recruiting a Joseph from two convents, the carpenter of Nazareth was portrayed by the most surprising bearded lady in the annals of central casting.

The Archangel Gabriel was there, too. "You can tell she's an archangel because there's tinsel in her hair," someone whispered.

The two orders faced one another in the choir stalls, joyously sang carols like *O Come All Ye Faithful* and *Of the Father's Love Begotten*, said the order for Vespers, adjourned for tea and mince pies. There was something of rapture about it. Outside, as darkness fell on the last day of the second millennium, it was snowing – and it was simply perfect.

The Poor Clares left Darlington for Hereford in 2007 after 150 years in the town; the Carmelities are no longer in the convent they had in 1999 but retain a house elsewhere in the town.

THOSE 'church' columns offered many other memorable moments. I really wish that more could have been persuaded to read them or that the thing had been better and more imaginatively promoted in the paper. Better late, perhaps, here are ten further highlights.

✠ We'd two or three times attended the annual cyclists' service at Coxwold, in North Yorkshire. Someone even told the only known joke about vicars and bicycles but since it involved the seventh commandment, perhaps best not repeat it. (Oh, you know, "so that's where I left my bike.")

NEW DAWN: *Sunrise Easter service in upper Weardale*

On one occasion the preacher was Dr David Hope, the retired Archbishop of York. "The Kingdom of Heaven is like unto the cyclists' café in Gargrave," he began, for a long time the most memorable start to a sermon I ever heard – and a subsequent visit to Gargrave in the company of Kit Pearson suggested that Dr Hope probably had a point.

✚ It became a custom to attend Easter Day 'sunrise' services, often atop a perishing Weardale moor, accessible by road, or at the peak of Penhill, in Wensleydale, which involved an invigorating dawn climb.

The most vivid of all was on Redcar beach, the photographer – bless them, they also rose – Easter ecstatic because the sun peeped precisely to time above the grey North Sea.

On the promenade at 5.30am, a No 29 bus went past. "Like Easter," observed the column, "the No 29 bus cannot easily be explained."

✚ Long redundant, the former St Hilda's parish church in Darlington had become the Light and Life church, chiefly serving the area's travelling community. Many members had repented former ways by full-immersion baptism. Over 100 were present, few sober suited. The sermon was on the Beatitudes. "If a man sticks the nut on you, you don't stick the nut back," translated Gary Nixon, the pastor. "You say 'That's all right, mate, here's a tenner'."

✠ Kate Alderson was a hugely bright young thing from Sedgefield whom I tried to help into journalism. Entirely on her own shining merits, refusing to take any answer save "You start on Monday", she got a job on the *Times* and was driving to an assignment when, while on the phone, she was in collision with another vehicle and was killed. She was 28.

Kate's memorial service was at St Bride's on Fleet Street, historically the journalists' church. "The inky emporia have gone, disseminated, sold the front page," said the column. The choir sang *The Girl From Ipanema* – "tall and tan and young and lovely." What a star she would have been.

When young father and *Echo* photographer Ian Weir died from a heart attack – inspiring a vigorous coronary care campaign by Pete Barron,the editor– the congregation sang *That's Amore*. You remember these things.

✠ Quaker meetings were the only 'services' which Sharon would regularly attend. Usually she just went for a walk,or listened to the *Archers* omnibus if it rained. Sometimes the meetings were almost completely silent, on one occasion accompanied by the gentle sound of snoring – neither hers nor mine.

The most tranquil was at Countersett, an idyllic hamlet above Semerwater, in Wensleydale, a meeting house since 1710. "It just seems to me," someone said, "that whether you sing joyously or are silent, it's equally valid."

✠ Wind Mill Methodist chapel, half-hidden near the A68 in west Durham, celebrated its 150th anniversary in November 2019 – a remarkable example of survival and of spirit in a village with fewer than 50 residents.

The column rarely needed an excuse to attend services there, particularly at harvest time. "An old-fashioned sort of chapel where mint imperials are passed surreptitiously before the service," I wrote. The post-service spread was fit for an emperor, too.

✠ Dr David Jenkins, that most unforgettable of Durham's bishops, had retired when he preached at the International Workers' Memorial Day service at St Thomas's on Stanley hill top – aka Mount Pleasant, otherwise Woolley Terrace – above Crook in County Durham.

Woolley was pronounced almost as in "poorly", not as in "bully". Woolley Terrace Methodist chapel, next to the village's wonderful little football ground and like the football ground now abandoned, was a glorious little place, too – not least at harvest festival.

Bishop David was in fiery form. "Today the most obvious and chief reason for not believing in God," he said in his sermon, "is the words and actions of those who say they do."

✠ Weeks before his consecration as Archbishop of Canterbury, Dr Rowan Williams – a small man for such a big beard – was at St Mary's in Thirsk, North Yorkshire. "Seats for the press over there," said the Rev Jonathan Jennings, his press officer, indicating the nearby cattle market.

The press had largely welcomed the appointment, though not the Rev Dr Peter Mullen, a prolific columnist on the *Echo* and elsewhere. "The new archbishop," he wrote, "is in danger of bringing down the church faster than anyone since the blinded Samson in the temple."

✠ Michael Turnbull, another of Durham's bishops, was the best preacher I ever heard. Twice we crossed paths at 'closure' services, one at Denton in west Durham – goodness knows how it survived as long as it did – and the other at All Saints, Shildon.

The most memorable final service may have been at the Methodist chapel in Wearhead, its back wall patched like a Women's Institute quilt. Once there'd been two Sunday services, more than 50 at each. By the end there was one service, sometimes fewer than five in attendance. Les Hann, the minister, warned of what clever folk call trip hazards – "if I'm not careful I'll break my neck, which would enliven reports in certain newspapers." He didn't.

✠ Blaydon Methodist church, south bank of the Tyne, hosted an evening of West Gallery music – the sort that accompanied services before, as someone put it, the Victorians came along with their great big organs and threw us out.

The musicians dressed the period part, one bearing a credible though not necessarily intentional resemblance to Johann Sebastian Bach, another a cross between the Fat Controller and that snooty fox which promotes Old Speckled Hen beer.

It was glorious, not least a rendition of Charles Wesley's hymn *And Can It Be* which persuaded me that it should be one of the three (minimum) at my funeral. The others will be *O For a Thousand Tongues*, Wesley again, and *Thine be the Glory* – but, please, not for many years yet.

43 : FINAL THOUGHTS

THAT'S the trouble with getting old and knowing quite a lot of people – far too many funerals and no sign of cessation. Fast falls the eventide, as Henry Francis Lyte immortally observed. The most memorable funeral was Bert Trussler's.

Bert was a traditional and much-valued workmen's club entertainer, usually accompanied on piano by his old mate Charlie Raine. They were Shildon lads, both customers for four years on my pre-school milk round – Bert and family two pints of TT, Charlie and Connie a pint of pasteurised.

Charlie, a delightful man, was a former LNER boxing champion whose nephew, Craig Raine, became a poetry professor at Oxford. Not too many of those from Shildon – more of Craig shortly. Uncle Charlie and Auntie Connie lived in a former Stockton and Darlington Railway cottage, company plate still on the wall, where I once found him exultant – like so many more – after appreciating the benefits of cataract removal.

Charlie, one of those men who talked with his hands – "if I lost a finger I'd have a speech impediment," he once observed – was reading the paper. "Good to see you enjoying my stuff again," I said, optimistically.

"Bugger your stuff, I'm studying the horses," said Charlie, and toddled off to the bookies, conveniently next to the King Willie, to place his shilling each way.

Bert, his pal, died from cancer. At the start of his funeral in

St John's, where all those years previously I'd been church-warden, it was announced that they hoped it to be a happy occasion, in keeping with his lifestyle. Some hope.

At the end of their shows, Bert and Charlie would always sing the old Gracie Fields number *Goodnight, Good Luck, God Bless You*. Knowing that his days were numbered, Bert sang it one last time into a tape recorder, his voice tremulous, Charlie tinkling away on the joanna. The recorder was behind the coffin, switched on towards the end of the service. At the 'happy' funeral, there wasn't a dry eye in the house.

Those 'happy' funerals are these days called celebrations of life, though it doesn't always seem that way. One that worked was for Geoff Hill, the former Bishop Auckland Grammar School English teacher mentioned in the book's first breath. Whatever the weather, recalled his eulogist, Geoff would drive them scatty in the staff room by singing *Oh I do like to be beside the seaside*.

All crowding the crematorium were then invited not just to join in the words but to essay the trombone-sliding actions. Very sadly, I wasn't there, because it must have been a wonderful way to go.

CHICKEN and egg, or the end-of-life equivalent, I also seem to write an awful lot of obituaries. Tellingly, they're almost always of men and I only write them about those I've known. It's always intended to be kind, a real privilege to be able to offer comfort in that way, though on two occasions the supposed deceased was able, while on this earth, to decide for himself. The most posthumously unforgettable was Tom Spencer OBE.

Tom was a test match cricket umpire and former professional footballer, a man of Kent who'd moved to Seaton Delaval, north of Whitley Bay, where his wife's family had long had the fish shop.

The first two of his 17 tests were 15 years apart, his debut the occasion on which Zaheer Abbas of Pakistan had hit an unbeaten 279, each successive 50 marked by joyous spectators encroaching onto the pitch and shoving money for the batsman into Tom's white coat pocket. When Zaheer asked about his windfall in the bar, Tom realised that it was still in his pocket in the locked dressing room. "I had to lend him £15," he said.

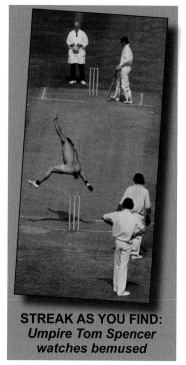

The match for which he is best remembered, however, was the 1975 Lord's test in which a gentleman named Michael Angelow, wearing only shoes and socks, leapt the stumps at the striker's end with Tom – possessed, as *Wisden* put it, of a gummy

STREAK AS YOU FIND: *Umpire Tom Spencer watches bemused*

smile – standing bemused at the other. Later, it may be recalled, Mr Angelow wore a policeman's helmet, though not upon his head.

I'd interviewed Tom in 1990, in the village workmen's club. He still carried a photograph of the athletic Mr Angelow – "Gives the lads a laugh, they never get tired of seeing it," he said. He died on November 1 1995, aged 81, an affectionate obituary appearing in the *Backtrack* column six days later.

In January 2003, a number of calls began arriving from magazines like *Wisden* and the *Cricketer*. Was I sure that Tom was dead? Sure I was sure. Inexplicably everyone, even the near-infallible Association of Cricket Statisticians, had missed it.

Better late than never, the rest of Tom's obituaries appeared more than seven years after his death – rather the opposite of a long gestation period. The story made the *Times*. "Mark Twain's death may have been what he described as greatly exaggerated," it began, "but the demise of one of the leading cricket umpires in England since the second world war was hardly reported at all." *Wisden* was almost apologetic: "His death was not widely noticed at the time," it said.

I've myself delivered several eulogies, most memorably for Harry Dobbinson – notional Mayor of Hunwick, though that village near Willington never did have a formal first citizen – and himself, coincidentally, a cricket umpire. Wasn't it Harry, the tribute recalled, who'd strode to the middle at Etherley, called "Play", and then realised the ball was still in his other coat pocket in the pavilion? He'd lived in the same house all his life – "mind," someone else had recalled, "if they'd changed the curtains he'd still nivver have found his way yem."

I also much appreciated the chance to pay formal tribute to my true friend Mike Armitage, perhaps the only man to be slagged off at his own funeral for his execrable taste in beer. He loved his Smith's Smooth, did Mike.

By way of what might be supposed funeral planning – thinking out of the box, as it were – several still living have already asked me to provide their valediction. A melancholy thought, but I still hope that I get the chance – circa 2050 – to oblige.

44 : OUT WITH THE OWT CROWD

EATING Owt sounded great, at least one meal on expenses every week for 27 years. It wasn't so cushy a number. Chiefly the problem was that perhaps ten per cent of those meals were outstanding of their kind, perhaps five per cent terrible on any argument and the rest piggies in a porridge-predictable middle.

How do you write 1,000 vibrant words about one more packaged pate, a B-minus burger and yet another offering from Brakes Bros' pregnant pudding club?

Sharon found it a particular chew. At least I had the challenge of turning sow's ear – or some other part of the porcine anatomy, latterly belly – into pearls after swine. All she had to look forward to was driving home in the dark and without even the consolation of a large gin and tonic. She'd never drink and drive.

Elder son Adam, when about five, got a bit fed up, too. "Can we just eat this?" he plaintively asked of yet another pub meal, "or do we have to talk about it as well?"

The foot of each column was leavened by what were claimed to be the bairns' 'food' jokes, whiskered chestnuts like "What's yellow and white and travels at 125mph?" – a train driver's egg sandwich – or "What's purple and cries for help from a castle tower?" A damson in distress. What's a Frenchman's favourite breakfast? Huit-heures-bix. Particularly I liked the one about what you get if you cross a panda and a harp: a bear-faced lyre.

Always we'd dine incognito – though inevitably sometimes recognised – and always insist upon paying. Sometimes, like the country pub lunch when a chunk of wood was discovered in a trifle, a howking – remember howkings? – was unavoidable. More often we were charitable.

On two or three occasions the owner of a criticised establishment would ring with threats of grievous bodily harm, always receiving the perhaps unwise riposte to come and have a go if they thought they were hard enough. Happily, none did.

The column also seriously angered Sir John Hall, the former Newcastle United chairman and the man behind the MetroCentre – with whom hitherto I'd got on well enough – after some criticism of a dining experience at Wynyard Hall, near Billingham, which he also owned. It underlined a classic provincial newspapers' dilemma – Wynyard was a major advertiser.

Though the paper's senior men sought earnestly to appease Sir John, none conceded the critic's right to be critical. It was much to their credit.

VORACIOUS:
The Rev Nick Beddow

Sharon might occasionally have a week off, and be glad of it, her place at table often taken by the Rev Nick Beddow – known to *Eating Owt* readers as the Voracious Vicar – the much-loved incumbent of Escomb and Witton Park, mentioned earlier, and a former chaplain to the Bishop of Durham.

Nick, a lovely man of

strong views and prodigious appetite, would swiftly clear his own three courses before essaying a passable impression of the devil thy adversary, prowling around seeking whatsoever else he might devour. If conversation lapsed, which rarely it did, he'd hold forth on how journalists – all journalists – were not to be trusted. It seemed a bit like biting the hand that feeds you, though there was nothing in the Good Book about that.

Eating Owt never laid claim to epicurean expertise, only to knowing what we liked, though owner/chef James Close had only been a few weeks at the Raby Hunt in Summerhouse, a few miles west of Darlington, when we visited, forecast great things but railed (again) against the aberrant apostrophe. Toilet's, indeed!

The Raby Hunt now has two Michelin stars, probably the highest-rated English restaurant outside London, and can successfully offer better-heeled North-East folk a tasting menu for £150 a head. Whether they've sorted out the aberrant apostrophes, I'm afraid I've no idea.

The column lasted until my retirement from full-time journalism in 2011 – by then well sated. Food reviews were taken over by a rota, its members advised in a memo from the deputy editor not to try to be like Mike Amos, because they couldn't. I never quite knew what to make of that.

It invites allegation of small town favouritism to observe that Savino's, just about the most memorable restaurant in which ever we plonked feet beneath the table, was back home in Shildon. Andrea Savino was from Sorrento, met and eventually married a good Shildon lass while on holiday – she, not he – settled in south Durham and no matter how often urged to come back to Sorrento, concluded that Shildon had more to offer.

To say that Andrea was colourful was akin to suggesting that Joseph's technicolour dream coat was a bit on the bright side. He was as warm as a Sorrento summer evening, as memorable as a Florence nightingale and, just occasionally, as volatile as Vesuvius. Hospitality included a seemingly bottomless supply of complimentary limoncello, like he'd found a well of the stuff out the back. The food was great, too.

One evening we were seated a couple of tables from a Crown Court judge, entertaining – mock trialling, indeed – a party of fellow legal luminaries. Wonderfully funny, it gave new clarity to the phrase about being as drunk as a judge. Andrea, much mourned, died in 2007.

In all those 27 years of *Eating Owt*, I'd only once been professionally consulted. It was when Darlington businessman Ralph Wilkinson was thinking of opening a real ale bar on the edge of the town centre. Was it a good idea, he wondered?

I advised against – just a bit too far off the circuit – and so Ralph, of course, went ahead. Thirty years later Number 22 still thrives, has won numerous awards and no doubt made the old Yorkshireman a lot of money. Ralph has even moved to our village, though on a level both physically and socially higher than we are, all the better to smile down and to say "I told you so."

45 : PUBLIC OPINION

IT'S mistaken to suppose that journalists spend half their working hours in pubs. These days they haven't the time nor, very likely, the money. A lot of us used to be pretty regular – though, of course, always alert to anything that arose.

In my time as news editor, the newsdesk and most of the head office reporters had passed a rainy evening sheltering from the storm in the Britannia in Darlington when a great cacophony of two-tone sirens suggested even to us that something in the town was amiss.

A quick call established that serious flash flooding had left several streets under water. I led – of course – from the front, wading knee-deep up a poor chap's garden path and trying somehow to suggest seniority, not to say sobriety.

Given the circumstances, the guy was remarkably accommodating. "Come in and sit down before you fall down," he said – and then opened another bottle.

The novelist George Orwell wrote in 1946 a celebrated essay in the *Evening Standard* listing the ten qualities which would constitute his perfect pub. Almost appropriately, it would be called The Moon Under Water. The Wetherspoons chain alone is now said to have 14 pubs of that name, including one in Manchester that's reckoned the UK's biggest boozer.

Unlike my sons, especially the younger lad, I'm not much of a Wetherspoons fan –and not just because they omit the errant apostrophe – though that's unlikely much to concern them.

Summarised, Orwell's criteria were that the pub's architecture and fittings would be uncompromisingly Victorian; that games such as darts should only be played in the public bar; that the place should be quiet enough for conversation and with no radio or piano; that the barmaid knew everyone by name and took an interest in them all; that the pub sold tobacco and cigarettes, aspirins and postage stamps and was obliging about using the phone; that there was a snack counter where things like liver sausage sandwiches and mussels might be obtained; that a good lunch could be had upstairs for around three shillings; that it offered a creamy sort of draught stout served in a pewter pot; that there'd be no glasses without handles; and that there'd be a fairly large garden in which women and children – not just the blokes – might agreeably foregather.

The Brit ticked very many of those boxes – for liver sausage sandwiches read ham and pease pudding – during the 25-year tenure of Pat and Amy Kilfeather. It also embraced a rich chapter in literary history.

In 1849, ten years before it first sold ale, the house was

LOCAL KNOWLEDGE: *The Britannia in Darlington*

WELL READ: *J M Dent – he posed for his advert, too*

the birthplace of Joseph Malaby Dent, tenth child of a house painter, who left school at 13 and became an apprentice printer before turning to bookbinding and heading for London with half a crown in his pocket and, who knows, Dick Whittington on his mind.

A biographer described him as small, lame, tight-fisted and apt to weep under pressure, adding that he was given to paroxysms and had a scream that could pierce a man's soul – a condition, it's said, for which Dent sought advice from an eminent Belgian consultant. Put your head in a bucket of cold water, said the doc.

It was also supposed that J M Dent couldn't spell for toffee, but in 1906 he launched Everyman's Library with the vision of making the great works of literature open to all.

Fifty were immediately available, a shilling apiece, hundreds more followed. "For a few shillings a man may have a whole bookshelf of the immortals," wrote Dent. "For £5 he may be intellectually rich for life."

Probably the Brit's only reading matter back then was that morning's *Echo*, but it sold a superb pint of Cameron's Strongarm, brewed in Hartlepool since 1955 and promoted at its launch as "beer for men who work hard." They'd heard about me and Steve Hobman, then.

The Brit had neither dart board, piano or radio – save perhaps very quietly during an Ashes test match – and while there mightn't have been garden or restaurant, it possessed in Pat and Amy immaculately attired licensees who'd greet all, or almost all, like old friends.

The exceptions, as we've mentioned earlier, were those whom Pat formally didn't wish to serve. Though the law didn't require him to give a reason – and he never would – suspicions centred on chewing gum, wearing grimy clothing and visiting the betting shop on the other side of the ring road. Their loss.

The Brit was a haven, an oasis, which is precisely what a pub should be. Though women were greatly welcome, it almost resembled a gentleman's club – and before the blessed smoking ban, a purple-hued one. Countless thousands of words these past 50-odd years have been written in a quiet-corner over a heady Strongarm and a five-bob butty. It continues agreeably, though there have been numerous suggestions as to where the juke box might most appropriately be relocated. None has been polite.

ANOTHER great pub – then as now, despite all that the Arkle Beck could hurl at it in the summer of 2019 – is the Red Lion at Langthwaite, in Arkengarthdale, North Yorkshire. Relations didn't get off to the best of starts, however.

Just as she is today, Rowena Hutchinson was licensee back in the 1970s when someone let me know that a rather surprising notice had appeared on the pub door. Gentlemen would not be served, it said, unless removing their caps before setting foot in the bar.

There were dales farmers almost surgically attached to their caps, who'd probably only remove the things when exchanging workday worst for Sunday best, who'd feel as naked without their caps as they would without their trousers and whatever it was they wore underneath. Rowena was adamant, the story went nationwide. Until the summer of 2019, when flood water wrecked the Red Lion during the worst deluge in history, the caps-off order and everything else about that glorious little pub remained unchanged.

No posh dinners, maybe, no family garden out the back, but Orwell would have loved it – and Rowena, bless her, had long since forgiven the cap capitals. Happily, she was able to reopen by Christmas 2019 (though coronavirus soon compelled further closure). Not least because there's no cooked food, there's not a more pleasant country pub anywhere.

Chief among my pub pet hates is extraneous noise – juke box, piped music, wall-to-wall televisions and, worst of all, asinine commercial radio. Surely it's counter-productive?

It's therefore greatly ironic that this part of the book should have been drafted in the coronary day ward at Darlington Memorial Hospital while spending several stressful hours awaiting an angiogram. Finally in the laboratory where such do-or-dye\procedures are executed, I was at once greeted by the cardiac-arresting sound of Radio Gaga.

The doc perhaps didn't fully understand the impatient protest. "It's the only station we can get," he said. Now fully over the shock, I can offer a list of ten other North-East pubs – past and present – of which old Orwell might enthusiastically have approved.

THE COLPITTS, Durham. Samuel Smith's is a brewery beyond compare, Yorkshire based and Yorkshire minded. Among its more recent contributions to licensed relaxation is a total ban on electronic accompaniment – no bandits, television or music machines. Some report that mobile phones are now also frowned upon and that, yet more happily, Sam's have introduced a zero-tolerance policy on swearing.

What, though, of jingle bells? When a thirsty morris dancing side tintinnabulated into the Swan and Three Cygnets, a Sam's pub near the Wear in Durham, the manager refused to serve them on the grounds that music was forbidden.

Protests fell upon deaf, if not deafened, ears. Clearly the manager knew the old rhyme about rings on their fingers and bells on their toes, and having music wherever they go. The story, sadly not mine, went global. Sam's, as always, declined to comment.

The Colpitts, a classic street corner Sam's pub, is on the other side of the city centre and almost beneath that magnificent railway viaduct. It's unspoiled, unchanged, has several little rooms and a greatly welcoming atmosphere in which all ages feel comfortable.

Back in 1981, Sharon genuinely believed that our first born was about to arrive on the tap room floor, causing considerable consternation. It would have emphasised his good taste and much pleased his father. Northallerton maternity hospital wasn't the same; nor was it licensed, though in the early hours of the morning the nurses made a surprisingly good salad sandwich.

Like almost all Sam's pubs, the Colpitts sells a perfectly decent pint for £2. Even the crisps are own-brand, and much cheaper than elsewhere – and yet it's only the second-best pub in Durham.

THE VICTORIA, Hallgarth Street, Durham. What was it that George Orwell said about being uncompromisingly Victorian? The Vic has hardly changed since it opened in 1899, a rich treasure house cherished and curated by the urbane Michael Webster, himself landlord for almost fifty years. A Campaign for Real Ale multiple award winner, it has three connecting rooms – parlours, then as now – wonderful coal fires in winter, little in the way of food though it's reckoned that the bed and breakfast letting rooms upstairs are as classy as is the pub. Convenient for HM Prison, too.

THE NORTH BRITON, Aycliffe Village, County Durham. If ever a pub were made by its landlord, it was the North Brit. Sadly, both the pub and the ebullient Allan Edgar are no longer with us.

Big Allan had been a policeman in Jarrow, was an extremely good wicket keeper for Bishop Auckland and others but not a noted runner between the wickets. "I've seen milk turn faster," Durham County scorer Brian Hunt once observed.

As Orwell would have hoped, Allan and his barmaids welcomed all – though it probably helped if customers knew their way around a cricket field. Many international cricketers drank and stayed there, none more memorably than the great Colin Milburn – the Burnopfield Basher – who, in desperate circumstances, died in the pub.

A consortium of regulars also owned a half-decent racehorse, officially saddled with some semi-formal Jockey Club name but known in the North Brit as Tuppence. Allan also staged memorable sportsmen's dinners, himself a gifted raconteur. I wish I could remember his joke about the crow. The beer was OK, the food was OK but the sum of the parts was simply magnificent.

THE GREY HORSE, Consett. Camra's North-East pub of the year in 2019, augmented from a brewery out the back with superb ales like Red Dust and White Hot recalling the town's steel-making past. In winter, and on oft-parky days in the summer, blazing fires add to the ambience. No formal menu but the toasties are recommended (or were until the machine blew up.)

The great thing about the Grey Horse, however, is its sociability, the inescapable feeling that the chief reason for gathering is companionship and conversation. A very good bet, it works wonderfully.

THE SHIP, High Hesleden, County Durham. A Sunday lunch staple for many years, but best of all is the quality and variety of its real ales – another former Camra North-East pub of the year.

A large pub with views from the car park over the North Sea at Blackhall Rocks, its Sabbath offering is huge and inexpensively priced and with remarkably efficient service. The down side? Peter and Sheila Crosby may have sold it, or shut it, by now. Blackhall, it might be added, also has the region's best name for a Chinese takeaway. It's called the Blackhall Wok.

On one occasion at the Ship, the young barman at once recognised our kidder and insisted upon buying him a pint. Dave hadn't clocked him, was told that he'd taught the lad English at Hartlepool Sixth Form College – "the best and most caring teacher I had," said the barman. It was a good moment.

THE GEORGE AND DRAGON, Hudswell, North Yorkshire. Camra's national pub of the year three or four years back, a re-born community pub near Richmond which serves impeccably kept ale and a wide choice of home-made pies. Beer garden with lovely views across the Swale, though the fox got the chickens.

Last time we were in there, we bumped into local MP Rishi Sunak who'd just officially opened the new lavvies and by all accounts with great aplomb. A few months later he was made Chancellor of the Exchequer and in difficult times seemed pretty good at that, too.

CROWN POSADA, Newcastle upon Tyne. On a hill leading down to the Quayside, the second oldest and ar-

275

guably the best of the city centre's many pubs and for those who thirst after righteousness, just a short walk – downhill all the way – from the Anglican cathedral. Renowned for the range and quality of its beer, its stained glass, its 1941 gramophone – records of similar vintage – and its cartoons of former customers. The snug at the front is lovely, the bar likely to be thronged. Try also to fit in an hour in the wonderfully bohemian Cumberland Arms on the Ouseburn, a mile or two east.

THE DRUNKEN DUCK, Close House. I'm walking home late one night in the 1970s – it often happened – when a car pulls up and the driver starts telling me a story. He lived in Close House – not the posh people's golf course in the Tyne Valley, the former pit community near Bishop Auckland – and liked a drink at home. His wife liked neither the drink nor the sight or smell of it (and maybe, who knows, of him.)

That's why he transformed the shed at the bottom of the yard into the Drunken Duck, Britain's first micro-pub and better yet because, unlicensed, he wasn't allowed to charge. It proved a glorious little place, complete in every detail – he could even get his pipe down there – and it made for a great column.

Sometimes the serendipitous almost fall over stories. About 11.30pm that Friday evening, that was one of the occasions.

THE RAT RACE, Hartlepool railway station: Any pub on a railway station has a head start – that at Stalybridge is incomparable, the Left Luggage Room at Monkseaton Metro hugely well done, a new place at Hexham yet to be visited – and Pete Morgan's shoebox-sized micro-pub at Hartlepool beats the hell out of the average waiting room, too.

Once the W H Smith's newsagency, it has no bar. Pete, Trimdon lad who must have been there ten years, emerges from a corner cupboard so small that the barrels are suspended from the ceiling because there's no other room at the inn. Usually four immaculately kept real ales and a cider, lots of reading matter, pub games, limited opening and – a slight inconvenience – keys to the station toilets along the platform.

The best thing of all about getting into the Rat Race, however, is that people talk to one another – even strangers, even journalists – and it's one of the few places on earth where you hope that the train might be late.

PIT LADDIE, Spennymoor. Not so much a pub as a day in the life, the Pit – Vaux house, and like the Sunderland brewery long gone – was across the road from Spennymoor magistrates court, where every Tuesday morning in the 1960s the usual suspects would be summoned. The court sat at 10am, the pub opened at 12.

It was from the pub call box that the day's peccadillos would be reported to the *Despatch*, followed by a couple of pints of Gold Tankard and a game of shove ha'penny with the chap from the *Gazette*. Does anyone still play shove ha'penny, or did it die with decimal coinage?

Lunch thereafter was at Oliver Smith's house. Oliver ran a fish and chip shop but was also the paper's Spennymoor correspondent, one of a small battalion of penny-a-line men known as stringers, an etymology I could never work out.

The *Despatch* had weekly correspondents' columns from every town in south Durham. Most were written by the guys themselves; Oliver simply provided the ideas, the transport and a sumptuous Sunday dinner every Tuesday. Then we'd head off round the town in his VW camper van, the acclaimed artist Norman Cornish and gyrocopter pioneer Ernie Brooks among regular subjects.

Tuesday's proceedings might well end with a couple of long-winded evening hours at the urban district council's housing and highways committee, such the demands – and the very real pleasures – of life as a junior journalist. After

277

that we were ready to sink another in the Pit and head back to work with a fishcake from Berriman's van.

46 : TOUR OF BRITAIN

A MONG the job's many joys has been the chance to travel the length of Britain, almost always pursuing a North-East connection and almost always by train.

Save for a few self-flagellating football forays, it's hard to remember many really long journeys by bus, though for those with strong bladders and plenty of time the four-hour coastal run between Newcastle and Berwick – service bus every hour, usually a double decker – is greatly recommended. As with the school bus all those years earlier, there's a rush for the front seats upstairs.

Trains generally offer greater comfort, save on the erstwhile Northern Rail, though also the opportunity to oversleep. Sharon tells the story of a late night call from the lost property office at Leeds station, reporting that they had found her husband's briefcase.

"Good," she said, "but can you tell me where my husband is?"

London, by virtue of size and stature, has probably been most visited – everyone from Sir Bobby to the Beverley Sisters and from the House of Commons to living like a lord. Other destinations have ranged from Leicester to Llandudno, Norwich to Northampton, Cornwall to Caerphilly and almost always there and back in a day. I do like my own bed.

An exception was for a January 1999 football match at St Blazey – he a Christian martyr said to have been killed by excoriation with wool combs – against Dunston. St Blazey's at yon end of Cornwall, Dunston on Tyneside, the team sponsored at the time by the now lost Federation Brewery. It was the longest journey made by a visiting team in a national cup competition – Morpeth Town may since have overtaken them – a two-night stay required at an out-of-season hotel in Newquay.

Self-disciplined on the Friday evening, 5-0 winners the following afternoon, the Dunston lads let their collective hair down that night. Sunday morning dawned bright and sunny, the Dunston FC manager phoned home in Middlesbrough. "There's six inches of snow here," said his wife.

Back at the breakfast table, several complained of feeling unwell – "it's mebbe that bit fish I ate" – while another rather regretted the bright red bruising on his neck. "D'you think our lass'll believe that I got brayed by the ball?" he asked. The consensus was that probably she wouldn't.

For its final decade or more, the *Backtrack* column also ran a Railroad to Wembley feature, following Northern League clubs all over the land in the FA Vase and usually with some agreeable travelling companions. Things often went awry; on one occasion they didn't. "You'll have nothing to write about," observed Kit Pearson, sagely.

Dunston also featured in a trip to Formby, on the Mersey estuary, there early enough to explore the sand dunes where Ginger McCain had trained Red Rum. They were also the home, apparently, of great legions of natterjack toads, the amphibians' racket in the mating season known thereabouts as the Bootle Organ.

Kit Pearson's the son of the late and much lamented Arnold Pearson DSO DFC, recalled in an earlier chapter from his time in the *Darlington & Stockton Times* office in Northallerton. Kit has inherited many of his dad's admirable qualities but not, emphatically not, his ability to navigate. Kit is truly a lost cause. Ask him one day about Wisbech.

With or without his assistance, I've found my way to some

memorable places and met some unforgettable people. Ten forays follow – and then Scotland has a section of its own.

THE man who made the Queen's eyes water was a Shildon lad who dreamed of being an engine driver and instead became one of the world's leading pyrotechnicians, a bright fizzer among firework men.

Invited in 2002 to mastermind the 14-minute display to mark Her Majesty's golden jubilee, Wilf Scott worked on it for months, spent six weeks clambering round the roof of Buckingham Palace, persuaded the monarch to launch a huge rocket from The Mall towards her home.

A few weeks later we were in his local in Cambridge, a city in which many years earlier I'd had lunch with the great George Armstrong, a Hebburn lad who'd starred in Arsenal's 1970-71 double winning team. "It was extraordinarily brave of the royal household to allow it to go ahead, and us with tons of explosives around the back," said Wilf. "The one thing you never do in this industry is stand a living monarch on top of a pile of explosives and ask her to press the button."

It worked wonderfully, what might be supposed his

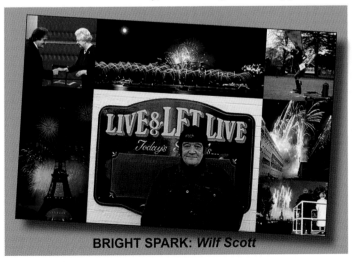

BRIGHT SPARK: *Wilf Scott*

crowning glory, and though he swore that the next time he wanted to be in charge of the concessionary toilets – "it was all just too stressful" – in fireworks' fantastical firmament, Wilf was the local lad made god.

His dad ran a bakery overlooking the approaches to Shildon wagon works. Remembered as somewhat Bohemian – the perfect word – Wilf failed the 11-plus and was sent by his parents to the fee-paying Scorton Grammar School, near Richmond, which meant leaving home at 6.20am. "I loved it," he said, "it was trains."

On Saturday mornings, he and his brother – who became a squadron leader – would have to light the coke fires in the bakery. "I'd pretend that it was a Gresley A4 Pacific and that I was in Darlington shed lighting the boiler," he said.

When the wagon works closed in 1984 he tried to get financial backing – "I came very close to it" – for a display involving a pyrotechnic steam engine and a 10ft inflatable Margaret Thatcher. The Prime Minister, it's reasonable to suppose, might have come off second best.

He'd studied art, gained two degrees, turned to fireworks after deciding that he couldn't paint a barn door from 50 paces. He worked for the Russian government and the Saudi royal family, for Wet WetWet and for the World Wrestling Federation, received a personal message from the elder George Bush after illuminating the G7 convention, lit up the Edinburgh Festival and the Lord Mayor's Show and amid global competition won the Monaco International Fireworks Competition.

The Queen appointed him a Member of the Royal Victorian Order and personally invested him. His autobiography, I suggested over the fifth or sixth pint of Elgood's ale, should be called *Famous for Fourteen Minutes*. He called it *From Pits to the Palace* instead.

Wilf retired at 60, eventually moved alone from Cambridge to Richmond, North Yorkshire, where his domestic environment remained Bohemian and his collection of model locomotives incredible and very valuable. When he died there in 2019, aged 72, the death notice in the *Echo* described him as "a supernova of the fireworks industry."

We'd last had a pint together in 2017, shortly before Guy Fawkes night, though the celestial choreographer said that he wouldn't be turning out. What, under the bed like a frightened puppy?

"No," said Wilf, "I don't want to miss *The Archers*."

VIC Wakeling had a pre-school paper round in Low Westwood, near Consett, was reading the *Blaydon Courier* en route when he spotted an advert for a junior reporter. Just a week after O-levels, he jumped on his bike, raced across to Blaydon and was promptly hired at £3 19s 6d a week, an income substantially and fairly immediately supplemented by flogging stuff to the nationals.

"I remember thinking 'Damn, I'd better do something for my own paper'," he recalled.

He moved on to the *Shields Gazette*, went to Fleet Street, and by the time I caught up with him in January 1998 was head of Sky Sport, said – to his serious discomfort – to be the most powerful man in British sport. That day there was a problem, however.

The interview had been arranged for 1pm at his top floor office in Isleworth near Heathrow Airport. At much the same time, Rupert Murdoch decided to look in to see him – in which event it's probably prudent not to mention that the *Northern Echo* man has an appointment and could Murdoch call back later.

Apropos of the previous chapter, incidentally, it's all but impossible for some of us to write 'Murdoch' without thinking of the put-upon polliss in *Oor Wullie*.

They left me alone in Vic's office with coffee, sandwiches and the day's cuttings file, a document so weighty that it might have been stapled with a windy pick. Clocks on the wall proclaimed the time in Sydney, Los Angeles, Hong Kong and other faraway places, a trio of television screens showed what then were all three Sky channels. The cuttings file had much about stock exchange problems for BSkyB, the parent company. The ash tray overflowed.

Wakeling, a man who in turn seemed never to switch off, had been a Newcastle United fan since childhood, recalled like so many more being passed over the heads of the St James' Park crowd to the front, thought Mitchell and Milburn demi-gods, regretted a professional detachment in later life.

"I've changed and it's a shame. I find that much of the time I'm watching a programme as much as I'm watching a game, even Newcastle's. You have to take the detached view, listen for the right sound, see if the colour's up to scratch, think about camera angles. Football's all about emotion, and in that sense the fans are getting more out of it than I am."

Not that he was complaining. "I have the best job in world television. You wouldn't tell Rupert Murdoch but I'd do it for half the money. I get bloody cheesed off when the newspapers talk about Murdoch's millions having done this and that. This place is run by sports fans for sports fans, it's the team that does it.

"I'm from an area that has a passion for sport, where men read the paper from back to front and now the passion for sport has exploded and we were one of the catalysts."

Murdoch had left the building, or at least Vic Wakeling had left the presence, at 2.20pm. The delayed interview lasted until 3.30, at which point his secretary mentioned that Geoffrey Boycott had been on the phone. Vic lit another fag. "It's quite a long way from Consett magistrates court," he said.

The former *Blaydon Courier* cub reporter died in 2017, aged 73. "No other TV executive," said the Royal Television Society, "has been so influential in spearheading the changes in on-screen sport."

CAERPHILLY'S in south Wales, probably best known for its

cheese and its castle, the UK's second biggest after Windsor. For Stan Wilson, fighting Caerphilly for the LibDems at the 1992 general election may have been like storming the ramparts while armed with a twopenny catapult.

The most affable of men, Stan was a retired PE teacher and district councillor in Redcar. Not even on the candidates' list, he'd been persuaded to tackle Caerphilly after stopping for a cup of tea at the Welsh stand – where his wife was a steward – at the party conference.

His only previous experience of Wales had been 45 years earlier, ten weeks basic training ("Private No. 22358318") with the Welsh regiment in Brecon. "There must be a few votes for an old soldier in the British Legion clubs," he said, optimistically.

Sometimes calling himself Big Stan, sometimes Never Say Dai Wilson – was that wise? – he'd paid his own deposit, funded his own expenses, run off his election literature in the back bedroom in Redcar. Someone, he said, had to draw the short straw.

"When Paddy Ashdown parachuted me in, I asked him what happened if I was taken prisoner. He told me that in every war there have to be some casualties."

"For the Liberal Democrats to send an elderly gentleman from the North-East of England shows how seriously they treat the people of South Wales," said Ron Davies, Labour's pugnacious incumbent. The only local issue, added Davies, was "Get the Tories out."

My boys, then ten and seven, came not just for the train ride but to count the election posters in Caerphilly's windows: Labour 138, Plaid Cymru 18, LibDem two, Tory nil. I bought them an orange juice on expenses.

Elias Evans, 82-year-old local historian and Lloyd George enthusiast, offered support. "Stan's just what the doctor ordered, a man with personality and I'm a great believer in personality. He could be from Timbuktu, Redcar's not so very far away now, is it?" he said, rolling his r's like chucking out time in Bedlington.

Stan remained as happy as a Redcar sandboy essaying an impression of King Canute, said what he had to, bought the ice creams. "My morale won't be shattered if we don't win. I suppose we're going for second place. If I get a decent vote I'm going to the *Guinness Book of Records* for the highest number of votes for the smallest expenditure."

The bairns and I caught the homeward train by seconds; Stan yelled after us. "It won't be as close as that on Thursday," he said.

Caerphilly result, 1992 general election: Davies (Lab) 31,719 (58.04 per cent), Philpott (Con) 9041, Whittle (Plaid Cymru) 4,821, Wilson (LibDem) 4,247 (8.4 per cent, down 5.6 per cent on the previous election).

"I enjoyed every minute," said Stan. "It was alphabetical order, wasn't it?"

MARY Holder was born in Meadowfield, a former County Durham pit village, began working life in a draper's shop opposite Durham bus station and then at a holiday camp in Somerset. "It wasn't much like *Hi-de-hi*," she'd recall.

These days she's known professionally as Elizabeth Richard, lives in a rented basement flat in Lambeth in south London, earns a living as a Queen Elizabeth II lookalike. "Guaranteed to bring a touch of class to any event. Meet and greet, mix and mingle," said her agency website at the start of 2020. Prices, it added, started at £500.

I'd gone down to see her in January 2010, arrived five minutes early. She answered the door majestically clad but with her hair in rollers. "You're not supposed to see me like this," she said.

The audience lasted two-and-a-half hours, the woman who would be Queen wholly charming but seriously homesick. "I only work for the money so that one day I might be able to buy a place back in County Durham," she said.

"If imitation really is the sincerest form of flattery, I think the Queen would be quite pleased, but I'd stop tomorrow if I could. Show business is very difficult.

"There's so much jealousy, which is sad, so much envy, so much back stabbing. There aren't many nice people in show business. Playing the Queen can be quite stressful, too. The excitement has gone. I'm not a very happy bunny at all."

Testament to her North-East browtins up,

DOUBLE ACT:
Elizabeth Richard

she spent most of her time in the little kitchen/diner out the back. The front room was for best – at home in Shildon we usually only used it, certainly only ever lit the fire, on Christmas Day. The parlour was where Elizabeth Richard held court, where we ate chocolate digestives and drank 'proper' tea. "It's not that I'm trying to be like the Queen," she said, almost defensively. "I just don't like tea bags."

It seemed wiser not to reprise the old joke about why Marxists don't drink Earl Grey – because all proper tea is theft.

She was nine years younger than the monarch, had decided that she might double her money 19 years earlier when her marriage broke up and she looked in the mirror. "I was in my 50s and thought 'Oh God, I'm never going to exist on the old age pension.' Something had to be done. The likeness was there, same height, everything." She bought a copy of

Stage magazine, found herself an agent, dyed her hair silver – "I was a redhead, they tend to go salt and pepper" – chose Elizabeth Richard because Richards had been her married name and Equity, the actors' union, already had an Elizabeth Holder. Initially it was better, too.

Physically the resemblance was marked, verbally she was almost perfect. "You can only tell where I come from when I get excited," she said.

It was an expensive business, and a pretty competitive one, possible to see doubles all over the place. Her hats were from the Queen's milliner, her specs from the Queen's optician, her outfits from Harrods and Selfridges and her tiaras, crowning glory, cost £1,200 apiece.

"I've a friend who's a Del Boy lookalike," she said. "It's all right for him. He only needs one outfit."

'Royal' engagements had sent her all over the world. Closer to home, she'd appeared – mixing and mingling – at the opening of the Dalton Park shopping centre at Murton in east Durham and at a function organised by Greggs, the Newcastle-based sausage roll supremoes, after the company chairman was knighted. "I told them I liked to look after my new knights," she said.

Perhaps the most improbable assignment was filming a commercial in Poland for a German firm promoting a Spanish paella. "You can see from the photographs that I was frozen," said ER.

She'd never met the Queen, once saw her from a distance in Ealing – "I'm not one to push myself to the front" – had encountered a royal equerry on a cruise. "I told him I'd never do anything untoward, I think that was quite succinct. You get asked to read all sorts of scripts, some of them quite dirty, disgusting really. I just won't do it. The Queen is admirable and I'd never do anything to embarrass her. I've turned down lots of work because of that."

ER talked almost as much about Meadowfield as majesty,

wistfully recalled the Kinema in the main street, running errands to Brandon and Byshottles Co-op, the workmen's club in which as a youngster she was forbidden to set foot. She'd hoped that I could have stayed longer, but there was a seat on the seven o'clock train. As with every one of the many hundreds of journeys I've made on the East Coast main line, I was very glad that the homeward leg was northbound.

SAMUEL Johnson may never have said truer word than his observation that whenever two Englishmen meet, the first topic of conversation is the weather. We love it, happy always to suppose that things can only get worse.

Many may affectionately recall Bill Foggitt, a gentleman of Thirsk, whom once I interviewed in the Three Tuns – his usual haunt – over wee drams of varying sizes and whose folklore-ish, frog-spawned forecasting had made him a national celebrity. Sometimes he even got it right.

Bill's family had kept weather records since 1830, often based on the comings and goings of the birds. His own first log had been when he was 12, in 1925: "Snow showers, king slightly better," it said.

He'd hoped to become a Methodist minister, turned no more successfully to the Church of England when Methodism blew him out, lived alone in a large and slightly Addams-familial house on the outskirts of town. He died, aged 91, in 2004.

Then there was Wincey Willis, a perky pin-up on Tyne Tees Television – real name Winsome, lived at Winston, very fond of animals – and Bob Johnson, a Scot who introduced North-East folk to the weather-word 'dreich.' Bob, nice man, had much cause to employ it.

As part of the Swaledale Festival in 2014, I'd also heard Michael Fish, perhaps best remembered of all, give a talk in Reeth Methodist church. A nod to the BBC, they called it the Reeth Lecture. Fish, then 70, listed 'grumpy old man' among his hobbies and tried quite hard to make the point. "I

CLOUDED: *Jack Scott*

never get tired of presenting the weather or researching the weather," he said. "I just get tired of being blamed for it."

The poor chap might feel yet more greatly under a cloud were he to google himself, as I researched him, and discover that half the entries are for Michael's fish shop, opposite Hampden Park in Glasgow.

Jack Scott – hail fellow, well Met – was among the first television weather men, a County Durham lad retired to Oxfordshire, a man of naturally sunny disposition but who when I visited 20 years ago was living under a slight depression (and that's enough meteorological puns, I think).

He'd been born and raised in East Howle, a now-disappeared pit community near Ferryhill in which folk lived cheek by jowl, would sit on the doorstep nattering, looked out for one another.

"I talk to the lady who lives over the road and I might say how-do to the chap out the back but apart from that I don't know anyone else here at all," he said. "That's what strikes me as the big difference between here and up north; if you stopped to talk to someone in the street down here, they'd think there was something wrong with you."

He'd been one of just two kids in the village school to

pass the 11-plus – the scholarship, they called it. "My parents were very proud, but a bit bothered, too. They didn't want the neighbours to think we were better than anyone else, that suddenly we'd become posh."

The weather hadn't much interested him. "It just came and went. The only interest we had was whether it would stop us playing football out the back. It took a lot to stop that."

The kindly joke in East Howle was that when he became familiar, several forecasts a week, his mum would wear her fur coat whenever Jack was on the telly. "Well, she was very proud, but she thought all mothers were proud of their sons. It was nothing to do with me being on telly."

He'd retired from the Met Office and the BBC at 60, was recruited by Thames Television and became yet more famous down south – personal appearances, after-dinner speaking, all sorts. After retirement, however, none recognised him.

"I wondered if they might have done, but it just never happened. I wouldn't want to be seen as above anyone because I'm not," he said. "You get used to living like this, I don't hold it against anyone. I'm very glad you're the *Northern Echo* and not the *Oxford Mail*."

Meteorology had come quite a long way since Bill Foggitt's forebears surmised that swallows' early arrival presaged a super summer. "The person telling you several times a day what it's going to be like has a whole host of scientists behind him," said Jack. "You just have to accept that occasionally they'll get it wrong."

Delightful man, by then widowed, he died in 2008, the year after we met. He was 81.

WHY do men grow south-hanging moustaches which make them look so thoroughly miserable – or, as Alan Meale allegedly supposed, made him a ringer for Clark Gable?

Sir Alan, as he became, was from Leeholme, County Durham. Though his parents had intended simply to call him Alan, the local Roman Catholic priest insisted that all 'his' babies should have saints' names. He became Joseph Alan – and despite the lugubrious tash, he was a very engaging feller.

At 15 he decided to see the world, joined the Merchant Navy, saw the sea and became the National Union of Seamen's youngest-ever shop steward. "I was no great enlightener, just the only one who'd do the job," he self-effacingly observed.

After the 1966 seamen's strike he became a chef at Durham University and then a student at Ruskin College, Oxford, where Arnold Hadwin – my first editor – had honed his values. By just 56 votes in 1987 he became Labour MP for Mansfield, former colliery country, the plight of horse-racing stable workers– "those poor devils," he was apt to call them – among his many causes.

When in 1993 I dug down to see him – Mansfield in those days about ten miles from the nearest railway station, another ultimately successful cause was that it should be better served – he'd also become vice-president of the National Association for the Protection of Punters and was fretting because the chap who looked after his leeks was in Lincoln Jail for non-payment of poll tax.

The betting man, he said, had a very raw deal – "the least considered person in the high street, all the dice loaded against him. Racing is the fifth or sixth biggest industry in Britain. The punter is the customer and needs to be looked after."

Betting shops, he thought, were also onto a winner. "At least some of them now have clean floors but there are others where you would have to dislike someone very strongly to encourage them to go in."

After the great parliamentary expenses scandal, it was discovered that he'd claimed £13,000 over four years for 'gardening'. Perhaps it had gone to the guy who looked after his leeks.

In 2017 the secondary school boy from County Durham lost the seat to a young Conservative, the first time the Tories ever triumphed in Mansfield. In the December 2019 election they bagged 63.9 per cent of the vote. Sir Alan appears to have gone quietly, though you wouldn't bet on it.

THE formal collective noun for bishops, at least for Church of England bishops, is a house. What might, informally, it be? A blessing? A bother? A beatitude?

I've known quite a lot, got on well with almost all of them. The Rt Rev John Pritchard, when Bishop of Jarrow – he became Bishop of Oxford – even had a cat called Amos, though he insisted it was for scriptural reasons. Have I mentioned that before? Diligent perusal of the Old Testament book of that name reveals nothing about moggies, however.

Michael Turnbull, when Bishop of Durham, shared a love of cricket but could never be persuaded to turn out for the diocesan clergy team. Tom Wright, among his successors, proved an ever-generous host at Auckland Castle. George Carey, Archbishop of Canterbury, shared an affinity with the Arsenal.

Perhaps the best-remembered recent Bishop of Durham may have been Dr David Jenkins, he of the (alleged) conjuring trick with bones, with whom I had a pub lunch in Bishop Auckland even before his consecration. It was only when halfway back to Darlington on the No 1 bus that I realised neither of us had paid the bill.

Interviewed on his 80th birthday, Bishop David remarked that his two octogenarian resolutions were never again to drive more than ten miles and never to undertake a train journey which involved changing at Birmingham New Street. Both were entirely understandable.

It was only for Stephen Conway's consecration, however, that I got as far as the front circle (if not quite the stalls) at St Paul's Cathedral. Stephen was 6ft 6ins tall, what might be called high church. Unable to find suitable off-the-peg vestments when appointed area Bishop of Ramsbury, in Wiltshire, he'd headed ecumenically to the Vatican equivalent of Long Tall Sally and found something suitable, indeed fitting, over there.

He'd been a parish priest in Darlington and then Archdeacon of Durham. Asked who among his contemporaries would next be a bishop, the Rev Nick Beddow – hungrily mentioned earlier – had at once replied that it would be Stephen.

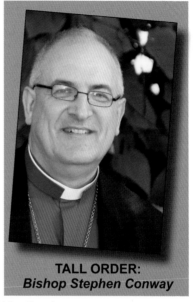

TALL ORDER:
Bishop Stephen Conway

Great crowds of dog-collared clerics seemed to rise from St Paul's underground station, recalling the old escalator advert about 75 per cent of Britain's clergy taking the *Times*. "The other 25 per cent buy it," a graffiti gremlin had scribbled beneath.

Canon Jon Bell, then the Bishop of Durham's chaplain, paced anxiously around the cathedral steps. The new bishop was in a mini-cab and the mini-cab was in a jam.

"Being anxious is part of the job description," said Jon, clutching a card signed by as many Durham folk as might reasonably fit on Clinton's finest. Since not even Clinton's sell 'Welcome to your new diocese' cards, however, it simply said 'Good luck.'

The new man remained anxious to talk up the North-East. "When I met the people in Salisbury diocese, I said how much I admired North-East outspokenness and asked if they were the same. They said they weren't sure," he said.

All went smoothly. Tom Wright talked of how much Durham loved the new man to bits and had bought him cope and mitre as a farewell present. "Since it would take two strong men to carry them, he'll have to have them later," he added.

Tall orders, Stephen became Bishop of Ely in 2010. In Cambridgeshire he remains.

I DON'T know what it is about Blackpool – well I do, but it sounds awfully middle-class and snooty – but I just can't stand the place. Morecambe's much nicer, and the Midland Hotel's terrific.

Mind, the Midland was falling to bits when I visited in 1999, officially to write about Paul Wheater – a country and gospel singer from the Whitby area who, best known for his Jim Reeves numbers, was playing the Empire every Thursday.

Opened as an LMS railhead in 1932, the art deco hotel had been over the road from the station. When the station was relocated, its site turned into a visitor centre selling milk chocolate sardines, the Midland became washed up, too, not so much white elephant as peeling grey mastodon. They'd closed the Winter Gardens, too, shortly after Shirley Bassey publicly complained about the state of the dressing rooms.

The Midland lounge back in 1999 overflowed with elderly floral armchairs down which a few stray sixpences might still have been found. The barman, receptionist and porter proved to be the same person, keys clanking collectively like an extra from *Porridge*. An elderly resident in sandshoes – sandshoes, not trainers – shuffled through, said "Warm" to an otherwise empty room, paused as if to assess the profundity of his remark and wandered onward in search of a milk chocolate sardine.

Subsequently someone spent a great deal of money to restore the Midland to its art deco glory, but with cons so mod that when we stayed ten years later, we couldn't even open the bathroom door. Lovely sea views, though.

Back in 1999 they'd spent £40m on Morecambe itself, including a statue of Eric of that ilk – unveiled by the Queen – an edifice called the Polo Tower which the young 'uns doubtless thought mint and paving slabs into which little jokes had been engraved. Where do sea birds go to see paintings? An art gullery. Which side does a lapwing have most of its feathers? The outside.

Morecambe, certainly, but was it wise?

A few years earlier, Paul Wheater had paid £12,000 to hire the London Palladium for the night – "Paul goes for busk," the *Sun*, reporting the story, had observed. Now he played to 40 or so at the Empire, probably much the same Over 60s crowd as had been at the American wrestling rumble the evening previously. A couple at the back went through salt and vinegar crisps the way that a chainsaw might go through a bit of plywood.

Paul regretted that the big record companies didn't want to know, remained philosophical. "I now know that I'll never be famous, but I have no regrets whatever. I've had some lovely times, wonderful memories, I haven't been a star but if I hadn't taken the opportunity, I'd always have thought that I might have been."

In 2019, by then 75, he was still singing, still taking part in athletic events like throwing the hammer and putting the shot. By then he'd given up on Morecambe, though. By then he was doing summer Thursdays in Filey.

IT was Budget Day 1993. Tom Burlison, Labour Party treasurer and deputy general secretary of the General Municipal and Boilermakers Union, had been up at 4.30am for a meeting in Nottingham, sorted out a strike at a Burton's biscuit factory while on the train, arrived back in London to do a budget bit for the BBC and at 6pm met me in the Princess Louise in Holborn, a splendid pub best known for its magnificent Victorian urinals.

A pint was £1.60 and being supped like Norman Lamont

had announced he was giving it away. "The budget will do bugger-all for industry, though to be honest I don't understand half of it, anyway," he said. Mind, Tom added, he'd been on the telly with a tax expert and the expert knew nee more than he did.

Afterwards we went to a posh restaurant in Chinatown. You could tell it was posh because it didn't have salt on the table (nor, very likely, did it have sweet and sour pork on the menu.) Neither were there forks.

Tom was a miner's son from Edmondsley, County Durham, played professional football for Hartlepool and Darlington, reckoned he might have fared better yet had he not been so shy. "It's a deficiency and it remains. I still have to force myself to do things," he said.

What, a shy trade union leader, initially a GMWU recruitment officer in Newcastle? "There are two ways to be a trades union official, one is to be a table thumper and the other is to be a carer," said Tom. "I was able to fulfil it in the quiet fashion which suited me."

When confined to the capital he was a bit of a Chelsea fan, as others claimed to be. "I've never seen John Major or David Mellor there," he said, sardonically, "but perhaps they don't stand in the same place as me."

He was ennobled in 1997, Baron Burlison of Rowlands Gill in the County of Tyne and Wear. The first ex-professional footballer to become a life peer, he was one of a North-East group who might have lived like the Lords but who never lost the common touch.

I once had the most convivial tea on the terrace with Lord Dormand of Easington, still Jack to all who'd known him, greatly enjoyed the company of Lord (Derek) Foster of Bishop Auckland, the town's late MP, though the columns still teased him rotten about his pin-striped suits. Baroness Armstrong of (Stanley) Hill Top, who followed her father as MP for NW Durham, is another old friend (and must be forgiven the fact that her husband's a West Ham supporter.)

Dame Vera Baird QC, former Northumbria police commissioner and now the Victims' Commissioner, is an acquaintance of nearly 50 years standing – right back to the *John North* column days when she was tending a patch of orchids on a pit heap at Ludworth –and has changed little, either.

Chinatown dinner – Tom insisted on paying – had broken up about 9.30pm, he to go back to polish a speech for the next day and I to catch the last train from Kings Cross. His parting words echoed those of the Queen lookalike and of so many exiles I'd interviewed. "I'll tell you what," said Tom, "I wish I was going home with you."

A truly charismatic man, he died in 2008, aged 71.

THE *New Statesman*, siren songster of the Labour left, was dismissive in the autumn of 2002 of the Countryside Marches, burgeoning bucolically throughout Britain. "A final rally by a tribe that has lorded it over us for centuries but is now doomed," the magazine claimed. They'd probably not taken into account the Shildon Countryside Movement. There were guys among that number who weren't even lord and master in their own house, unless their lass was at the bingo.

The marchers' chief concern was the Blair government's determination to outlaw fox hunting, their watchwords Liberty and Livelihood, though the nearest the Shildon lads might have got to a red jacket was when dressing up as Santa Claus for the grandkids. They were ratters and they were rabbiters, ferret breeders and nature lovers. Sometimes they might even act as beaters for a shoot – if you can't join them, beat for them – always remembering to touch their caps, of course.

I'd joined their bus at Scotch Corner services at 6.30 one September Sunday morning. "Bloody hell, the things you see when you haven't got a gun," said Mike Hardy, the wide-awake Shildon chairman, appropriately.

No less appropriately, they watched en route a film called

The Rat Catchers, centred around a pitta bread dump in Ashington – they have pitta bread dumps in Northumberland? – said to be overrun by the pesky things. "They reckon that wherever you are, you're never more than six feet from a rat," said Paul Kirtley, who presented it, though the stats might demand downward revision in Ashington.

Their nemesis was the working dog, from which not even a rat up a drain pipe might be safe. Most were terriers or lurchers, though one appeared to be a poodle – if not exactly a pussy cat. The technical term, apparently, is that the dogs worry them, though in their position I'd be positively terrified.

There was even talk of a working dog march to Tony Blair's constituency home in Trimdon. "I wouldn't care," said Mike Hardy, "at one point if you wanted a good lurcher you never looked past Trimdon." After that they showed a film in which Jack Charlton, another Ashington lad, talked about deer hunting. He called them stairgs, of course.

The marchers almost overflowed the capital, around half a million they reckoned – not all, of course, from Shildon – friendly folk eyed by friendly pollisses. Someone asked a bobby when he thought they might reach Marble Arch. The bobby surveyed the throng. "About Thursday," he said.

"I've never seen a queue like that since karaoke night at Elm Road club," said one of the Shildon lads.

A pompous placard bore a message about liberty being written in the blood of the forefathers, an Elvis lookalike displayed a hound dog message for Mr Blair – "you aint never caught a rabbit and you aint no friend of mine" – a third advocated keeping the cow shit in the country and the bullshit in the town. The best of all urged eating Cumbrian lamb – "ten thousand foxes can't be wrong."

The ban on hunting with dogs still became law, though goodness only knows if it applies to ferrets – but if you smell a rat in Ashington, then you know full well whom to blame.

47 : BONNIE SCOTLAND

SCOTLAND'S magnetic north, ever attracts. Though the highlands and islands are incomparable, there've been work-related trips to everywhere from John o' Groats in the north – more of that in an earlier chapter – to Gretna, many times, at the opposite extreme.

Bonnie is how they spell it north of the border, not to be confused with the 'bonny' sometimes adopted by old Durham miners – and, more particularly, their wives. "Mind, you came home in a bonny state last night" suggests nothing very pretty at all.

I enjoy a good haggis, love Stornoway black pudding and greasy scotch pies, avoid whisky – devil's water – have consumed *The Broons* and *Oor Wullie* since childhood and, a book at bedtime, still do. How else might it be known that, around Dundee, they call the binmen scaffies or that a Scot must be pretty jiggered to be wabbit?

A few years ago I was even invited by the Durham University Burns Society formally to propose the Immortal Memory at its Burns Night celebration, a grand and doubtless formal affair with the cream kilted at high table. Told that every person in the room would know more about old Rabbie than I did, the woman became quite huffy – the line about seeing ourselves as others see us came to mind.

Much harder to refuse was the invitation to become Chieftain of Newton Aycliffe Pipe Band, a role which involved little more than promoting the band and marching at its head – tartan army – on parade. My old dad, a Queen's Own Cameron Highlander, might have been quite pleased about that one; even my mother-in-law said I had nice legs – the line "Shame about the boat race" may refer. Alas, I was writing six columns a week, chairing the Northern League, producing its magazine and trying very occasionally to be a half-decent husband and father. There just wasn't any more time.

Not everything north of the border is glorious, of course. Possibly the two worst pubs in history were in Inverness and on Lewis with Orkney a close, calamitous, claggy matted, third. The world's most miserable town was Cowdenbeath – home of the Lochgelly tawse – the worst café in Gretna. I wonder if the bloke's washed his string vest yet. The most multifarious midges were on Lewis and Harris – as were the most sedulous Sabbatarians, as Ken and Kathy Smith discovered after their wedding in 2002.

Ken had been a classmate at Timothy Hackworth juniors and was a lifelong Salvation Army member, as was Kathy. Their honeymoon took them for an overnight stop at an hotel on the Scottish mainland and then a flight to Stornoway, Lewis's principal town.

Kathy, who organised the hotel, thought nothing further of it until the receptionist wondered how they were getting onward to Stornoway because there were no flights on the Sabbath. "Yes, there are," said Kathy, "I've just booked one."

Unsuspecting before that point, they had seats on the first ever Sunday flight into Stornoway, such incursions apparently being forbidden in the Old Testament Book of Something or Other. On Lewis and Harris, they don't even hang out their washing on the Sabbath and in some parts still chain up the playground swings, lest the we'ans become sacrilegious.

So it was that the happy couple were greeted at the airport by 50 placard-waving protestors and a great maul of media men – is nothing sacred? The placards warned of the fire and brimstone to come, their bearers – Wee Frees and Wee Wee Frees, the latter yet more hair-shirted – chanted the 46th Psalm, something about the raging heathen and the desolation awaiting the earth.

Not only would Ken have been able to recite Psalm 46 by heart, he could probably have played it on the cornet, an' all. "He was just disappointed he hadn't been interviewed by the television people," said Vincent, his brother and best man. "He'd have told them he was bringing the Gospel to Stornoway. It's quite amusing to think of him and Kathy accused of being wicked sinners."

Reasons to haste back far outnumber those for staying south of the border. How could it be otherwise in a country with the West Highland Railway, the Oxford bar in Edinburgh – where Mr Ian Rankin finds inspiration for his detective stories – and the blessed skirl of the bagpipes? Isn't there something in *The Merchant of Venice* about Scots who, when they hear the pipes, cannot contain their urine for affection?

THE Shetland Islands, approximately the same latitude as southern Greenland and closer to Bergen than to Aberdeen, are as far north as it's possible in the UK to venture without falling, drookit, into the Atlantic. Lerwick, the islands' capital, boasts – yes, boasts – the country's most northerly Chinese takeaway and most northerly bakery; Baltasound has the most northerly pub and Haroldswick, on Unst, the most northerly bus shelter and church.

Even by the utilitarian standards of bus shelter construction, rural Scotland's are bare-bones basic. That at Haroldswick breaks the mould. Differently colour-themed each year – yellow when we visited in 2002 – it had television (though someone in the visitors' book complained that they couldn't get BBC2), radio, microwave, chintzy curtains (yellow), book shelves (their volumes all yellow-backed) and a telephone directory but no telephone. The phone book, of course, was Yellow Pages; another book (honest) was called *Tell Me a Swiss Joke.*

What do you call the Moscow Symphony Orchestra after a visit to Switzerland? A trio. All that the Haroldswick bus shelter seemed to lack was a bus service, and certainly not one with the required connection to North-East England.

Then serendipity struck yet again. The northernmost church is Methodist, an environmentally conscious replacement for a building which blew down in a 107mph wind – little more than a zephyr by Shetland standards – in 1992. While we walked around, the minister wandered in for a chat – and his accent seemed awfully familiar.

Douglas Graham was from Langley Park, a few miles west of Durham. A farmer's son who as a boy had delivered Bobby Robson's milk, he'd taught RE in Washington – the one over here – spent 20 years as co-warden of the Marygate Centre on Holy Island, came to Unst on a three-year contract in 1990. "I just seemed to stay," he said, happily.

On a snowy first day of April in 2006 I'd written an *At Your Service* column from Holy Island. Ten thousand might visit on a mid-summer day; few on April 1 swelled the resident population of 140 – six of whom were priests. The service began at 10.45: Even at 10.30 folk wandered in for a warm, belatedly realised that on a Sunday morning a church on Holy Island might actually be holding a form of worship and not flogging Lindisfarne mead to help fix the central heating, and self-consciously wandered out again.

Canon Kate Tristram, the 75-year-old preacher, had herself been warden of the Marygate Centre. She talked of death. "Some say that men undergo a kind of death on the day they realise that their sons can run faster than them," she said. With me it happened when they were about three.

BACK among the Shetland Islands, I then got luckier yet. Mooching around while awaiting a last day ferry, I saw on a village notice board that John and Betty Bates on Fair Isle – the most remote of Britain's inhabited islands – had won an environmental award. John and Betty, it said, were from Durham.

Both nurses, they'd raised their children on Fair Isle –

population 70, 240 different plant species, eight school pupils and an awful lot more birds – and were delighted when two of their offspring returned. "The biggest drawback is that you need a second mortgage to be able to visit anywhere else," said John when I rang.

Together he and Betty ran the island shop and sub-post office; John was also a marine environmentalist, crofter, builder, artist and Methodist minister – "those few minutes in the pulpit are the only time folk don't contradict me" – his son the island's special constable ("I can't remember when last there was a crime") and his daughter drove the fire engine, for which she'd been on courses at Teesside Airport.

The only disappointment was that we were back home before all that was tied up, or down, but that was a canny column, too. The only worry is that Ms Sturgeon will get her way and there'll be border controls and guards armed with dirks. I no longer hold a passport.

AS the island hopping continued, we discovered the South Uist branch of the Shildon FC Supporters Club – flag proudly displayed though the membership appeared to be one.

Many of the Scottish forays have been for sporting reasons, and may mostly for this purpose be put to the back of the mind, though it was while in Stranraer for the football that I came across a very Scottish paragraph in the *Wigtown Free Press*.

A gentleman down from Glasgow in the expectation of a good swallee – as I believe they say in those parts – had booked into a bed and breakfast and, anticipating that at some late hour he might become unwell, had left his falsers (Granpaw Broon called them wallies) on the table by the bed.

Sure enough, the constabulary found him slumped in a shop doorway at 2am, gave him a cell for the night and then discovered a problem. The chap with the gummy grin couldn't remember where he'd left his top set. The bit in the paper appealed to any guest house owner who'd found a set of dentures...

I'd also ventured north to watch Queen of the South, the Doonhamers, at a time when five or six of the side had been imported from the Northern League in England. Not everyone was impressed. "If we'd wanted a team of Geordies," said a disgruntled Dumfriesian, "we could have signed Jayne Middlemiss."

Ms Middlemiss, as some may remember, was a Bedlington lass once voted the world's 77th sexiest woman. I forget the other 76.

There have been other adventures. It was from Queensferry, some time in the early 70s and when the head for heights was rather more firmly secured, that I sailed on *HMS Wolverton*, a Royal Navy minesweeper of the same class as *HMS Iveston*. It was what press people call a facility trip, supposedly promotional.

Iveston, named after a village near Consett with a very good Chinese restaurant – that bit may be irrelevant – became in 1970 the last Royal Navy ship on which crew members were charged with mutiny, something about singing drunken Irish songs outside the wardroom.

After a couple of nights at sea on Wolverton, it became clearer why the navy was restless. The matelots really weren't jolly jack tars at all. The copy had to be vetted by someone at the Ministry of Defence and they hacked it. I never hacked it again.

Drop in the ocean, ten more Scottish memories follow.

MOIR Lockhead was a raggy-arsed kid from West Cornforth, a working village near Ferryhill in County Durham which usually and not entirely explicably answered to Doggy. "All West Cornforth kids had raggy arses," he said.

Born in 1945, once said by the *Guardian* to look a little fearsome – "thuggish even" – he failed the 11-plus ("first half," he said, "never mind the second"), left West Cornforth secondary modern at 15 and began as a £9-a-week apprentice in the workshops of the United bus company in Darlington.

"They gave me work which required attention to detail, that's always been my strength. In other words, I like to do things properly," he said after I took the train to Aberdeen in 2008, shortly after he'd been knighted.

By 1979, fewer than 20 years after leaving West Cornforth school, he'd become general manager of Glasgow City Council's transport department. In 2008 he was chief executive and deputy chairman of the First Group, based in the Granite City, which at the time had 137,500 employees, a £5bn annual turnover, a 23 per cent share of both bus and rail operations in the UK, ran 60,000 yellow school buses and the legendary Greyhound coach company in the US and had interests worldwide.

"I was delighted to leave school, but I never left learning," he said.

Far from fearsome, I found him wholly engaging and came away with several model buses, but maybe that was because we compared notes, talked not just about global transport but about the animosity between Doggy lads and

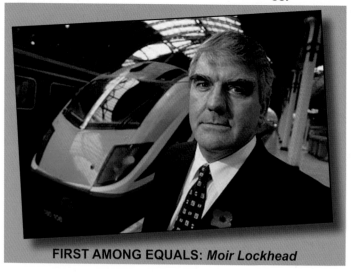

FIRST AMONG EQUALS: *Moir Lockhead*

Ferryhill lads. "It wasn't the sort of stuff you hear about now. It wasn't warfare, but it was still rivalry. Ferryhill lads hated West Cornforth lads," said Sir Moir.

He retired in 2011 to the family's 300-acre farm near Aberdeen where, doubtless successfully, he bred Highland cattle. The Englishman from West Cornforth became chairman of the Scottish Rugby Football Union and of the National Trust for Scotland.

In January 2019, reporting a £50,000 fine from Aberdeen City Council for failing to run an adequate bus service on its doorstep, the Aberdeen *Press and Journal* felt able to describe the First Group as "beleaguered."

THE Highlands appear to have an awful lot of places called Uig – chicken and Uig? – one on the west coast of Skye the terminus of the eight-hour service bus route from Glasgow, unsurprisingly voted Britain's most scenic. Newcastle to Berwick was somewhere up there, too.

The Uig in which Kirsty Wade and her family contentedly settled is yet more greatly on a limb, one of Lewis's extremes, 36 miles from Stornoway Co-op and absolutely nowhere near a bus route. "Even by Hebridean standards," said one of the guidebooks, "Uig is remote."

Kirsty had been Britain's top woman middle distance athlete, won three Commonwealth Games golds when representing Wales, – and Blaydon Harriers – set multiple Olympic records, travelled the world but never smelt the tangle o' the isles. Every which way but Lewis?

"There's never been a morning when I've not been grateful to wake up here. If nothing is perfect, then this comes pretty close," she said when we tracked her down in 2005, and no matter that it gets a bit wet and wild – a bit extreme – up there."You don't come to Lewis for the sunshine, you come for the light," said Kirsty. "The sky is awesome."

She and Tony, her husband and coach, had run a fitness club in Rowlands Gill, the village near Gateshead from which Baron Burlison took his title. "The last two years there our car was broken into six times, they even took all the Christmas presents" she said. "Our house was burgled, our garage broken into. We loved our house in Rowlands Gill but wondered if it was really the best environment in which to be bringing up children."

Out on that Lewis limb, none even realised her international athletics status – nor did she talk about it – until one of the children's friends saw her name in the Guinness Book. "It must have been a pretty old one," said Kirsty.

She still trained – "not

CAST AWAY:
Kirsty Wade

very hard and not very often, usually because I get such pathetic looks off the dogs" – but was taking island life at her own pace. "People might think that this is quite insular but in fact there's a wonderful camaraderie, a sort of self-preservation society against the elements."

Last I heard she was still there. Kirsty Wade had stopped running.

RUDI West and Mike Milligan were North-East comedians. The three weeks they played the Edinburgh Festival Fringe, festal virgins and pretty much drowning in the Liquid Room, proved no laughing matter at all.

Mike – graduate, former tampon salesman and self-described hippy – was by then a primary school teacher in Newcastle. "The school had an Ofsted inspection last year and it wasn't half as dreadful as this lot," he said.

Rudi, named North-East club comedian of the year and married to fellow comedian Lynnie Larkin – they met in summer season at the Cosy Nook in Newquay – had used a free night in the three-week run to play Tindale Crescent workmen's club, near Bishop Auckland. "It was packed to the rafters. I was so excited at getting a crowd again I went berserk and gave them an hour and 35 minutes," he said.

It was 1999, the Edinburgh show called *Up to the Neck in Wit*. The Liquid Room nightclub rather resembled the front of HM prison Slade. Once it may have been a second-hand clothes shop, or a poor house on its uppers. The Fringe programme listed 198 different venues, none of which was the Liquid Room.

I joined them. Half an hour before the start the audience was two, an elderly couple given tickets by a taxi driver who'd been given them by someone else, probably as a tip. By the appointed hour it had increased to six. Mike and Rudi decided that the show must not go on, gave them their money back and adjourned to Deacon Brodie's Bar.

To make things worse, they'd been involved in a car crash on the way over the border, though their agent used the incident for a bit of publicity. "We've made more impact being hit by a knacker than we have in two weeks working our nuts off," said Mike, inadvertently maintaining a testicular metaphor.

"The trouble is that too many people hear there are comedians and still expect to get Tommy Trinder," said Rudi. "At least in the workmen's clubs you know things are going wrong because they start talking to one another. Here it's like they've herded together the worst audience in Scotland. They just don't do anything."

Goodness knows what hour we left Deacon Brodie's

Bar. Mike and Rudi went back to a rented flat somewhere, I grabbed a couple of hours' kip on a Princes Street bench before catching the first train home. There'd be no doubt who slept better.

IAN Nelson, in his last working years *The Northern Echo*'s man in East Cleveland, was one of the best reporters I ever met. He never lost his enthusiasm for community journalism or his satisfaction at turning in a sound nightly news list. Some said that he bore a bearded resemblance to the chap who cooked up Kentucky Fried Chicken, but Ian hadn't any doubles. He was unique.

His finest hour had come on March 3 1960 at Prestwick airport in Ayrshire, when he became the only journalist to interview Elvis Presley on the one occasion the King set foot on British soil. Sgt Presley was being demobbed from the US Army in Frankfurt, leaving behind at the airport a weeping 14-year-old called Priscilla Beaulieu, an officer's daughter with whom he'd been walking out.

Ian was then on the *Scottish Daily Mail*, the only journalist with radar sufficiently attuned to Prestwick to know who'd be on board when the plane stopped to refuel. "Elvis

ALL SHOOK UP: *Ian Nelson interviewing Elvis*

was just like the kid next door. He gave me a good 20 minutes in a little lounge," he recalled of his lifetime scoop.

He was less fortunate, it has to be said, when finding himself in the next chair to Frank Sinatra in a Prestwick barber shop. The interview request was brusquely declined, the two-word response not just Sinatra's way.

On the *Echo* he worked from home in Saltburn, had a second home in the men-only Lune Street Workmen's Club, once told the ladies and gentlemen of Saltburn and Marske Parish Council that if they didn't cease their blethers by 9.30 he was going home. Whether that was his first home or second home can only be imagined.

We'd meet in Lune Street club every January 1 for a Hogmanay livener and a game of dominoes, occasions on which Ian introduced the term firkling, a word unheard in the Darlington and District 5s and 3s League, though they'd sometimes use something similar. I never did work out what it meant.

When he died, aged 89 in 2009, his family asked me to deliver the eulogy – back in the crematorium in Ayr. It seemed to go all right, Elvis recounted once again, and was rewarded with a round of applause and a very good bottle. The second-best story, however, had been emailed earlier by Norman Faulds, the minister. Norman had spotted in the local paper the tale of an unemployed chap in Ayr who'd bought a charity shop T-shirt for £3 and who, in the subsequent act of blowing his nose, had dropped the receipt and a £10 note – an inadvertent action at once rewarded with a £50 fixed penalty fine for littering.

Protests that he was on the dole and hardly likely deliberately to be casting currency to the west coast wind fell, like the £10 note, upon stony ground. At the golf club wake afterwards, Norman declined a drink. "If you can get fined £50 for dropping a tenner," he said, "if the poliss catch me driving after a wee dram, I'll be in jail for life."

AUCHENBLAE, apparently meaning Field of Flowers, is somewhere near Stonehaven in what formerly was Kincardineshire and now, apparently, is just The Grampians. It's an awfully long way for a day trip – and with only one lady driver – to the Drumtochty Highland Games.

For Auchenblae read Tannochbrae, a Dr Finlay's casebook of proud men and rich culture, of Highland fling and highland thing and perhaps a Mistress Niven.

It was June 2006, a chance for the natives to forget that England were in the World Cup finals and Scotland, once again, were not. Though rain threatened, the scene was wonderful, a porridge packet panorama of teuchter tradition. The piper who played for Madonna's wedding accompanied the highland dancing, judges seeking shelter in a little cabin reminiscent of a night watchman's hut in an *Oor Wullie* cartoon.

The North-East connection was Stephen Aitken – son of Auchenblae, manager of Darlington auction mart and a Games champion at several disciplines, particularly tossing the caber. He was 6ft 3ins, weighed 18 stones – built like an ox, as might be supposed of a cattle market manager – but comparatively something of a lightweight.

"I win events despite being quite wee," he said.

The folk were at once friendly, community spirit evident, most in full tartan fig. There are men, most men, who wear the kilt with panache and with pride and there are a few who wear it as a rag man's horse might wear an ex-Army blanket. Steve Aitken was very much the former, stirred by pipes and Drumtochty. Proud Scot? "Och aye," he said, "there's not a Scotsman alive who's no' proud."

The caber was 24ft long, weighed almost 300lbs, cupped as lesser men might nurse a bedtime Ovaltine, rested against the shoulder as a new father might cradle his first-born – run, stop, grunt, heave. The hope is that it lands at 12 o'clock, if not necessarily high noon. "It's seven out of ten strength and ten out of ten technique," said Steve, beaten on the day by his brother Bruce, a man built like the Broughty Ferry.

Six years later Steve died, tragically, in his office at the cattle mart. He was just 45.

LIKE Sir Moir Lockhead, Garry Gibson was a County Durham lad – Wheatley Hill, home of the dog track – though Garry made his money from property development. He lost a lot of it, too.

He stood 6ft 6ins, became chairman of Hartlepool United FC and a member of the Football League management committee, wrote some very readable columns for the *Echo* and in 2005 enjoyed the most opulent wedding – not having been on George Reynolds's guest list at the Castle of Mey – that ever I attended.

It wasn't his first. The first do had been 30 years earlier in the canteen at Whitbread's brewery in Castle Eden. "Ham and pease pudding and a bit tongue," said Garry. Mind, he added, it was a canny bit tongue.

The second wedding was to Gaynor Salisbury, statistically six years his junior, though he'd knocked five off his own age when they met. The ceremony and reception were at the Mansfield Traquair, a glorious former Roman Catholic church described as Edinburgh's Sistine chapel and opposite a legal firm called McSporran's. Entertainment was by a bunch called Four Poofs and a Piano – there was some debate about the pronunciation of "Poofs", in Wheatley Hill it rhymes with scruffs – flown up from London for the occasion.

The gentlemen were flown up, understand. Whether the piano followed on the nine o'clock from Kings Cross I've really no idea.

First, though, we'd to find our hotel. Few others being afoot in Edinburgh's suburbs that Saturday morning, we sought directions from the binmen – those scaffies again. A bit like my old man who said follow the van, they insisted on the dust cart escorting us all the way and up the hotel drive.

Sharon wrote a nice letter to the council.

The wedding was wonderful, though Gaynor was late. One consolation, someone whispered, was that she was unlikely to have run off with the turn. Speeches were replaced by a question and answer session. What's the difference between a camera and a spare sock? One takes photos, the other takes five toes.

We went back to scaffie central, the happy couple off on a month's honeymoon – joined for the final ten days by Garry's 76-year-old mum who'd never hitherto left the country. Sadly, they were divorced and Gaynor subsequently died. Garry survived a quintuple heart bypass – is it a record, he wonders – and is still in Scotland, still seeking to make another fortune.

THE good news for Alan Donnelly was that at the Glasgow Govan by-election in 1988 the Tories had beaten both the Raving Loonies and the Rainbow Zippy Alliance. The bad news was that they hadn't beaten them by much.

Alan was the Conservative candidate in the 1992 general election, among the more improbable of the eternal tribe of windmill tilters, the electoral equivalent of painting the Forth Bridge with a nail varnish brush.

The *Glasgow Herald* offered encouragement – "He's not really an Englishman, he's a Geordie" – then thought better of it. "One of the great entertainments of any general election is watching the Tories trying to win votes in Glasgow," it added. "These men and women who toil in infertile territory deserve special status, almost like a protected species."

Alan was a 37-year-old Jarrow lad, worked on the oil rigs, had joined the party as a 21-year-old merchant seaman and disciple of Margaret Thatcher. Govan was his 11th election, parliamentary and municipal, and he'd yet to win one – not even the Primrose ward in Jarrer.

"A lot of people in Jarrow know and like me, they just don't like my politics," he said, and should presumably not be confused with another Alan Donnelly from Jarrow who became the area's Labour MEP, a big trades union man and friend of Bernie Ecclestone, the former Formula 1 supremo.

Warmed on a bitter Saturday in March by a single bar electric fire, Govan's Conservative Party headquarters was a wooden hut of disreputable shabbiness which once had been the colour of the candidate's jeans. Best jeans, of course. His strategy, he said, was to split the Labour and SNP vote. Not so daft as they might appear, the Loonies weren't standing.

In the 90 minutes I was there the phone never rang and no one looked in. "A chap came in yesterday," said Alan. Beneath a table sat a huge quantity of Andrex toilet rolls. It seemed prudent not to ask.

Then we did the guided tour, a Govan street urchin offering to mind his car – he really did – for 50p. Over at Ibrox Park, the Old Firm were in action. Lots of votes there, Alan supposed. "I'm not a merchant banker, a barrister, an economic analyst or whatever, I'm a down-to-earth working lad who understands people like these," he said.

Glasgow Govan general election 1992: Davidson (Lab) 17,051, Sillars (SNP) 12,926, Donnelly (Con) 3,458. The Rainbow Alliance didn't stand either.

STEWART Regan was chief executive of the Scottish FA, a post for which the words poison and chalice come to mind. Ralph Ord was chief operating officer of the 2014 Commonwealth Games in Glasgow. What they had in common was that both were from Crook in County Durham.

Stewart had been at the helm at the time of Rangers infamous demotion down the leagues, recalled the born again club's first game, at Brechin. "The Rangers fans sang 'If you hate Stewart Regan clap your hands'. There seemed to be an awful lot of people clapping."

He'd also directed a modernisation which meant a much reduced role for the 93-member SFA Council, still privately cherished the headline in the *Scottish Sun*. 'Regan 93, Blazers 0.' The three of us met over a Hampden Park lunch in 2012 – Ralph just two weeks in post – the Crook men as eager to talk of the past as to ponder the future.

They spoke wistfully of the Mile Lonnen and of Queenie's Café, of the old woman at the top of Church Hill who scared the life out of the kids, of Tazzy's sweet shop – "You'd ask for daft things like strawberry potatoes, he'd always look for them" – of the under-age back room at the Mill House-pub and of Dode's, the dear old Cow Tail, above the town at White Lea.

Stewart's father had been sergeant in charge of the police dog training school at Harperley Hall nearby, reckoned they'd look into Dode's for a swift one while the handlers were walking their charges. "The dogs were only allowed a shandy, mind."

Ralph's dad was a renowned local cricketer, twice took all ten, still lived in Langley Park. Ralph himself had bought a coffee farm in Australia but had found the lure of Scotland irresistible. "I feel a real affinity with Glasgow, if I didn't I'd have stayed in Australia. Scotland's too small to host a World Cup or an Olympic Games but this is a massive challenge. The budget's still bigger than the GDP of some small countries."

Crook's tour, they could have reminisced all day. Lunch lasted 90 minutes, the Crook lads lasted a little while longer. Ralph's now back on the Australian Gold Coast, wakes up and smells the coffee.

FOOTBALL forays always sought scotch pies, too, though (whisper it) the best ever were at Berwick Rangers, in England.

No excursion was more memorable than that to Cowden-beath, Christmas 2011, the disappointment that there were no pies at the Oxford Bar – aforesaid – compounded because there were none on the train from Edinburgh to Cowden-beath, either.

316

"Aa can do ye jelly beans," said the trolley molly, but probably not on toast.

Cowdenbeath's about 18 miles north of the capital, a town of around 11,000 people. 'A merry Christmas from Cowdenbeath,' said a sign on the municipal tree, though serving only to illumine the fact that it's a dump. The team which with Scotian sarcasm they call the Blue Brazil were at home to Dumbarton, a poster in the bookie's offering 11-4 the draw. The boys, there with their uncle Dave, fancied a few bob and were told it had come down to 5-4. They suspected a Chinese betting syndicate.

The Central Park ground was antediluvian, atmospheric and sold scotch pies, though in front of the tea hut a puddle in which the Commonwealth Games high-diving event might have been held had first to be negotiated.

Behind one end was Beath High School, alma mater of Sunderland football legend Jim Baxter, of the Oxfordian Ian Rankin and in the early 1980s the school attended by Jane Cosans's we'an, the bairn excluded for declining – not unreasonably, some might suppose – to be belted by a teacher. His mother took the case to the European Court of Human Rights, or wrongs as the case may have been, and won. She was awarded £12,000 and costs. Belting bairns in Scotland was outlawed soon afterwards.

For years the ground was also home to speedway, then stock car racing, perhaps the only such venue in the world at which the safety barrier was a brick wall. It was second home to Donald Findlay QC, a former Rangers vice-chairman said by the *Scotsman* once to have been in trouble with the legal hierarchy for telling a vulgar joke about a nun.

A poster promoted 'Crowd control in sport.' If that seemed a bit optimistic, so did a second poster stating that gates would be open at 1.30pm, 90 minutes before kick-off. The crowd was 271, including a quartet from Tunbridge Wells. "We do it because we're idiots," one said. Admission was £14.

The weather was what Bob Johnson on the television liked to call dreich. Barely ten minutes had passed before the wind blew an advertising hoarding cartwheeling the length of the pitch. The players scurried to safety, the ref watched-dispassionately, as if observing a stray jelly beans wrapper.

"It's offside," someone shouted. The ref ignored it. It re-called an incident in 1983 when the cover – what football folk call a cow shed – at the Chapel Street end simply blew away. It moved Cowdenbeath to verse of which Burns him-self, or perhaps his compatriot William Topaz McGonagall, might have been proud.

> *There was a coo on yonder hill*
> *There was a coo on yonder hill,*
> *It's gone, it must have shifted*
> *There was a coo on yonder hill.*

Another song began "When the sun shines on the cow shed", to the tune of *Una Paloma Blanca*, but though there's nothing about nuns the words can't possibly be repeated here. To little surprise, the game ended goalless. The boys and their uncle Dave wished they'd put money on it. They blamed the Chinese betting syndicate.

IAN Porterfield was one of Wearside's all-time heroes, the man who scored the only goal when Sunderland beat Leeds United at Wembley in the 1973 FA Cup final. We met on a bleak Friday afternoon in January in one of Edinburgh's poshest hotels, a chap in the bar simultaneously cradling a pint of heavy with one hand and scratching his expansive belly with the other. Like bell ringing, I suppose. Not least because the delightful Glenda Porterfield was also there, we moved into the lounge. A pianist played *Bonnie Bonnie Banks of Loch Lomond*.

The man known to all Sunderland simply as Porter was a pitman's son from Fife, played junior football for Loch-gelly Welfare. Lochgelly, memory suggests, promoted itself as "home of the tawse", the tawse being a fearful cat o' nine

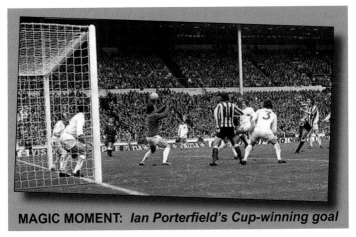

MAGIC MOMENT: *Ian Porterfield's Cup-winning goal*

tails device with which Scottish school teachers, not least those in Cowdenbeath, would remind the we'ans of the error of their ways.

Glenda was from Trinidad, 12 years her husband's junior and named after the actress Glenda Jackson. "My mother named all her children after movie stars," she said. They'd been back north visiting Ian's mum.

Glenda had known nothing about football – once having been taken to a match and asking whose side the linesmen were on – and not much more about Scotland. "I love the Scottish people but every time I come here it rains," she said, not unreasonably. Ian, conversely, had become a wing-heeled Whicker in management jobs all over the world.

"It's a trade off," said Glenda. "I still don't understand football but I have a fantastic lifestyle and a wonderful husband. Maybe one day we'll return to the Caribbean. Most Trinidadian girls are quite keen to leave, I'm the one who wasn't."

In turn she'd tried to teach Ian chess, but it didn't work. Probably he wanted to know whose side the linesmen were on.

A few weeks earlier, on Christmas Day, he'd guided his

319

team Busan I'Cons to victory in the South Korean cup final, so convinced they'd never reach it that he'd booked a festive family holiday in America. "Mr Chong, the chairman, was quite pleased," he said. "Obviously 1973 was very important to us, a major occasion, but this was a different kind of emotion.

"It was the biggest thing that ever happened to Busan I'Cons, a dream just like Sunderland. It was certainly a different way to spend Christmas Day."

We chatted for two-and-a-half hours, they a truly lovely couple with whom I kept in touch. Ian was 59 at the time. Two years later colon cancer killed him.

48 : CHESTNUT PURÉE

IT seemed to me that *Northern Echo* columns should not just chiefly be about North-East people and places but intrinsically embrace the region's passions, traditions, language and culture. Unnurtured, they perish.

How many readers might otherwise have known that their dinner was kizzened, or that dottle should not be dropped on the proggy mat, or that they were scumfished when simply they thought it was a bit warm? How else would they learn the purpose for which a windy pick might be used or what it meant to get a good howking? That one, of course, has been explained already.

How many might know that bullets came in a glass jar, about sixpence a quarter, or understand the joke – told many times – about Geordie inviting his mate to name a card game?

"Ice hockey," says his mate.

"Ice hockey's not a card game," says Geordie.

"Why," ripostes his mate, "it's the cardest game aa knaa."

The younger generation should not be blamed. Many perfectly able North-East journalists were brought up or educated elsewhere, have probably never read the late Scott Dobson's invaluable *Larn Yersel Geordie* and associated volumes and simply don't understand, not even the ice hockey joke.

The North-East's working class culture – the phrase is used trepidantly – may best be preserved among pigeon flyers and leek growers, though I've had surprisingly little to do with leek shows. I did once or twice help judge the annual

321

ugly vegetable show at Wheatley Hill Old Scouts' Hut – surprising how often the word "ugly" seemed synonymous with "phallic" – a licensed social club round the back of the dog track. Half the lads were retained firemen, on one occasion turned out half way through proceedings.

They guessed at once that it would be to flooding in Wingate. "If it rains in Wheatley Hill, it floods in Wingate," they said.

Though esteemed for all sorts of good reasons, John Burton – Tony Blair's long serving constituency agent in Sedgefield and another MBE recipient – was rarely more proud than when he won the award for the tallest thistle, all eight-and-a-half feet of it, in Trimdon Village. Quite recently I also covered the annual giant nettle competition at Castleton, in the Esk Valley near Whitby.

There's a wonderful musical tradition, too, and not just among brass bands. On Good Friday 2008 at Hetton-le-Hole Methodist chapel we attended the 138th successive annual performance of Handel's *Messiah*, the dinner-suited choir including 75-year-old Doug Weatherall, for 50 years a familiar sports writer on the *Daily Herald* and the *Daily Mail*.

The Victorian miners had built the huge chapel themselves, hard labour at the end of a long shift, and no matter that the seats might have given the hobs of hell a bad name. After a three-foot seam, they were luxury. At much the same time, though for reasons more greatly to do with mammon, the Commercial pub had been built across the road, prompting one of Hetton's little legends.

The second part of *Messiah* has a glorious piece called *The Trumpet Shall Sound*, just about the only reason for anyone to blow his own. One year the trumpeter decided to nip across to the Commercial until his big moment came and was, shall we say, unavoidably detained.

Whatever else sounded thereafter, it certainly wasn't the trumpet.

Let's for the moment return to the Trimdons, and tangentially with the Blairs. Guarded round the clock by armed police, the former Prime Minister's constituency home was in Trimdon Colliery, about a quarter of a mile from The Royal – the pub where the world conker championships annually went head to head.

Rumours abounded, or at any rate were propounded, that Cherie and little Leo (as then he was) might be seen around the local lanes every October foraging for the big one, the all-conkering. That they never actually fulfilled that Royal engagement – the PM neither – must have been because the lads had beaten them to it.

Truth to tell, there was another conkers world championship in Northamptonshire – truth to tell, it was held on the same Sunday afternoon – but talk of a north-south showdown never materialised. Something else along the lines of come and have a go if you think you're hard enough. Southern softies, see.

Like everything else of a fiercely competitive nature the contest had strict rules, by no means invalidated by the fact they were signed by "the commity." Near enough, someone said. Nor did it much worry them that the *Guardian* had had a piece on the Northamptonshire nuts, which quoted Newton's third law of motion.

Trimdon quoted Gavin Mercer, three times champion. "They just stole our idea. They don't have proper conkers down them places, anyway." The *Guardian* probably only had one reader in the Trimdons in any case, and only then when he hadn't stopped the papers and decamped to Downing Street.

There was a rule about ropesey, another about stamping on an opponent's conker ("instant disqualification"), a third about random drug testing – the conkers, not the contestants – and a fourth about not switching conkers during the game. Chiefly it was insisted that conkers must be "virgin", not drilled before the big event. That was Phil the Drill's job, and you could tell he was important because he wore a yellow fluorescent jacket with his name on, like a gaffer on the road works.

Mad Frankie Fraser, another mentioned earlier, was also frequently to be found in possession of a Black and Decker drill, though not necessarily for piercing conkers.

"In the event of £20 not being added," said another rule, "the venue may change."

The original trophy was a bit of skirting board from someone's grandma's, winners' names – "the legends" – written in ballpoint on a bit of sticky yellow card. "Cokers' trophy," it said. Spelling clearly wasn't their strong point.

It had also been the custom to stick the champion conker to the trophy until the time that someone, identified only as Chunky – "something to do with pineapples" – was found guilty of trying to pinch it and banned indefinitely. Sin died, as mortally may be supposed.

The contest lasted four hours, the conkers bright burnished with all manner of mysterious substances, shining like an outhouse door knob. Watson's No 6 came to mind. The ale flowed, the pub heaved like New Year's Eve half struck, barely room to swing a cat much less a world beating conker.

The *Echo* photographer was struck by a piece of flying chestnut shrapnel. "I thought ice hockey was the most dangerous sport we had to cover," he said, and may have been told a very old joke to add insult to injury. Others, more predictably, suffered hand injuries. Conkers, they agreed, was a blood sport. Goodness only knows who won but it's as the Bible says, by their fruits ye shall know them.

THEN there's egg jarping, a sort of ovaform point-to-point, the world championships held these past 38 years in Peterlee, County Durham, and probably not dissimilar in intent to conkers.

Last time I attended, 2009, a chap – a southerner, perhaps self-evidently – was a bit surprised to see HM Press in attendance and wondered if I did serious journalism, too."What do you think this is?" I said.

As with old chestnuts, the word "world" may be a little far-fetched, not universally acknowledged. In Sedgefield every year they staged the world spoons playing championship, usually won by a delightful old miner called Bert Draycott for whom the world really was his lobster. "Contestants come from Newton Aycliffe and all over," he insisted.

The conkers once had a chap from South Africa, but he was staying with Roy Simpson, the organiser. Roy was also keen to point out that another guy had come all the way from Easington; dependent on whether he meant Easington Village or Easington Colliery, it could be getting on three miles away.

Roy, chairman of the World Egg Jarping Association, or WEJA to its friends, is a retired ICI executive and a JP, sworn to uphold fair play. There are 23 rules, divided – lest anyone suppose his eggs all to be in one basket – into "administrative" and "competitive." The first group includes the stipulation that the eggs are boiled together on the night before the event – unlike conkers, contestants don't bring their own – and then stored securely in the club cellar.

The eggs are then stamped and numbered. "We used to have one of those stamps that were used when you got twopence back off a bottle of pop but we lost it," said Roy.

Each entrant picks an egg, one the jarper and the other the holder though both hope to be a dunsher. There's also a rule that every contestant gets a free supper – that is to say the chance to eat his own eggs. Salt and pepper are also free.

Contestants must keep both feet on the ground, physically at least, and face instant disqualification if caught tampering with the egg. Nail varnish is a favourite, though some swear by John Smith's Smooth (which has to be good for something.) Perhaps better at getting a grip, women tend to win.

Given the arcane nature of the proceedings, Roy even

found himself invited onto the *Richard and Judy* show, debating the finer points – the broader ones, too – with the footballer Ian Wright and with Meatloaf, the singer. "It's a daft little tradition, it does no one any harm and it raises a few bob for charity," he said.

A couple of years ago he was appointed MBE. The citation said that it was for services to cricket and the community in Peterlee, but insiders knew differently. It was for doing folks' ends in every Easter.

FIRST foot forward, the North-East traditionally knew how to see in the New Year, too. Perhaps not quite as boisterously as the Scots, perhaps not Trafalgar squared, but a right good knees-up, nonetheless.

Back in Shildon – happy New Year bottles of stir – there'd be post-midnight processing from door to door, the requested first footer expected to carry a bit coal and a stick for the fire and, above all, to be tall, dark and handsome. It explains the demand I was in. The reward was a glass of sickly sweet sherry, an inch of fruit cake with three inches of icing atop and, with luck, a palm crossed with silver.

Where we live now, and pretty much everywhere else except Allendale, nothing stirs at all. The old year goes to bed early, the new one sleeps through it all.

Allendale's about 30 miles west of Newcastle, close to where Durham, Cumbria and Northumberland fall over one another in wild abandon but administratively claimed by the last of that triumvirate. There's a very good brewery, a legend about a wolf – doubtless big and bad – and every December 31 a celebration so special, so spectacular and so utterly inebriating (though strong drink is by no means obligatory) that attendance should be made compulsory before another year is out.

Up there it's called the Tar Bar'l Festival, its origins said to be Viking and, unsurprisingly, pagan. My debut came on the Saturday night that 2012 was ushered in. Though a whole

HAPPY NEW YEAR: *Allendale has a bar'l*

new bar'l game to Sharon and me, to the good folk of Allendale it's a custom with origins lost in the pitchy mists of centuries. There'd even been a paragraph about it in that morning's *Times*, readers invited to find further information from allendalefiredepartment.com which turned out to be a small town emergency crew in New Jersey.

Save for a call to an over-sensitive fire alarm, the guys over there appeared not to have been overstretched – a bit like Reeth fire brigade in an earlier chapter. Nor did the false alert greatly tax them – the wonky fire alarm had itself been at the fire station.

We'd headed up to Allendale along the length of Weardale, then northwards past Cowshill, through former lead mining villages like Sinderhope and Sparty Lea, arriving at 9pm and finding the normally tranquil village thronged with three or four times its total population. "It's like a time warp," someone said, "a New Year's Eve when people speak to one another."

Many wore fancy dress: a plethora of Presleys – "I've

lost me chest wig," someone said – an Ali Baba sans thieves, someone from the end-of-the-pierrot show, a group of nuns seemingly intent on getting out of the habit. "Don't look now but Orville the Duck's just walked in," said Sharon after finally we'd shoehorned into one of the village's three pubs.

Awaiting its fate, the huge bonfire had been built barely 50 yards from the village Co-op, founded in 1874. Though the Co-op was closed, the food and drink shop across the road – which also offered mulled wine – queued into January.

At 11.45pm, 45 face-painted guisers – all male, Allendale doesn't do guise and dolls – appeared with flaming barrels carried on their heads, each barrel filled with wood shavings, paraffin and tar and each guiser passing within inches of the multitude. A chap in a high-viz waistcoat appeared to be in charge –"they'll have to take notice, I'm wearing me yeller jacket," he said, affably – a chap with a Santa Claus hat jumped up and down on it, the festive millinery having been set alight by a spark.

They were led by Allen Smith, resplendent in presidential robes. Allen was 100, still twinkled like a century of fairy lights, still jigged for the cameras. His brother carried a tar barrel, but he was just a bairn of 92.

The impression perhaps misleading, one of the other why-spoil-the-ship surprises was that there seemed so little formal regard to health and safety. Nor could they have expected a full strength turnout from Northumberland fire brigade in the event of many more Santa hats catching light. Half the village crew were walking round with tar barrels on their heads.

The band played *Daisy, Daisy, Give Me Your Answer Do* and, remembering its place, gave us *Keep Your Feet Still Geordie Hinny*. As the bells approached, the guisers threw their tar barrels onto the bonfire. The crowd shouted "Be damned he who throws last" but, of course, they didn't mean a word of it. A ha'porth of tar but not a ha'porth of bother. The pyrotechnics were extraordinary. The band played *Auld Lang Syne*, the subsequent column was headed 'Having a ba'rl." It was an acquaintance never to be forgot, and the Co-op lived to tell the tale, too.

49 : MEETING POINTS

THE Durham Miners' Gala, or Big Meeting as in these parts it is still widely known, remains for many North-East folk one of the highlights of the social year. By way of summary at the start, here's what I wrote after the 2015 event: "As a deep-rooted community celebration the Big Meeting is wholly without equal; as a remembrance of lives lived and lives lost it's impressive, oft awesome. As a political statement, usurped by the extreme left, it's as relevant to the 21st century as the Tolpuddle Martyrs."

In recent times I've usually gone with some of the Spennymoor lads, buckshee bacon butties in the Voltigeur – named after the 1850 Derby and St Leger winner, owned by Lord Zetland – followed by a short 8am service in the nearby park and by the lugubrious playing of *Gresford*, the miners' hymn. In 2015 they'd followed the Tudhoe Colliery banner into Durham city centre, "in" – as Gala parlance has it – by ten o'clock and in the Dun Cow by five past.

Posters urged those attending to read the *Morning Star* – "Durham miners do" – which said little for the circulation department's knowledge of the long-spent coalfield. A quote from Arthur Scargill was emblazoned across the side of a tent: "What you need is not marches, demonstrations or rallies. What you need is direct action."

It could have been thought for the day and, like the *Morning Star* placard, it all seemed a bit of an anachronism. One speaker even disinterred the old Margaret Thatcher joke about setting the alarm clock an hour earlier so he could hate

MEETING OF MINDS: *The Miners' Gala*

her an hour longer.

Two years later, with Jeremy Corbyn the Labour Party leader and the election a few weeks behind them, the Big Meeting seemed reinvigorated. The mood was euphoric, vibrant, unashamedly triumphant. Was ever there such a reception for the side which came second?

The day boiled, T-shirts the fevered fashion, Jeremy Corbyn's face across many a sternum and Messrs Blair and Miliband across none. As the day progressed, indeed, it became clear that many believed there'd been a Conservative government every day since 1979. Goodness knows what they'll make of Boris.

A warm-up act sang about moleskin trousers and miners' pay – it's always moleskin trousers and miners' pay – but none, mad dogs and Englishmen, needed warming up on so perfect a summer day. The Racecourse thronged. I stood 75 yards from the platform, 75 yards to the left of Len McCluskey – politically improbable, physically unavoidable. Even then there was all the room for manoeuvre of a pit pony on a punishment shift.

Speakers started at 12.50pm, all enthusiastically received but simply preaching to the converted. It may be harder to hook a duck at the fairground out the back than it is successfully to preach Socialism at Durham Big Meeting. Not so much pushing at an open door as leading a herd of deer through it.

Neither shaded nor nuanced, many in the noonday sun turned the colour of the People's Flag (which, it may be recalled, is deepest red.)

McCluskey, the Unite general secretary, said he hadn't had a smile off his face since June 8 – when Labour lost, for heaven's sake – Fire Brigades' Union secretary Matt Wrack recalled Durham Miners' Association official Davey Hopper, who'd died a few days after the 2016 Gala. "Davey Hopper was a complete master of the English language, especially those parts which originated in old Anglo-Saxon," he said.

Left-wing film maker Ken Loach spoke, too. You could tell he was a thespian by the contemptuous way it took him five seconds to enunciate Iain Duncan Smith, though goodness knows what that gentleman had to do with anything.

The deer leader rose to his feet at 2.28pm, announced that he was wearing a Keir Hardie badge, though it was a bit hard to see it from the general vicinity of the Mr Whippy van. Already the speakers had taken as long as a football match and without the saving grace of a pie and a Bovril at halftime, The reception was rapturous, nonetheless. "Oh Jeremy Corbyn," they chanted, endlessly. The sentiment might have been fine, but the lyrics were a bit threadbare and the tune awful.

"The Tories went into the election thinking it would be a walk in the park and it turned into a walk in the dark, a nightmare," he said. He sat down at ten past three, another Cathedral service missed, another duck hooked.

50 : THE OLD HOME TOWN

S HILDON is probably little different from many another post-war County Durham town and (of course) none the worse for that. Though born at Hardwick Hall in Sedgefield, then a maternity home and now a smart hotel, the Amos twins were raised in Albert Street, just down from the beer swilling King Willie and from the bookie's where dear old Aunty Betty would lay her surreptitious sixpence each way.

Eighty-odd years earlier, in 1860, Albert Street had also been home to John Harrison, described as a mason's son, though whether 'mason' should have a capital M is unclear. Several of my maternal uncles held masterful office in Shildon's masonic lodges – one a school caretaker, another a bus mechanic. It said much for the craft's egalitarianism, though I clung always to Groucho Marx's dictum of never wanting to belong to any organisation which would accept me as a member.

Harrison was educated at the Church of England National School and then "privately" in Bishop Auckland, was apprenticed as an engineer and in 1885 emigrated with his parents to Australia, where his father founded John C Harrison and Sons, master builders. Biographies describe the younger Harrison as "a man of considerable height and bulk." Must have been something in the Albert Street air.

He was said also to be particularly fond of cigars, bridge, bowls and billiards and to be possessed of "idiosyncrasies" – aren't we all? – including a campaign against wax matches, which he considered dangerous. Didn't Arnold the barber

RIGHT UP MY STREET: *Shildon*

use those, for purposes I never quite understood?

At any rate, Harrison prospered, was behind the creation of a 75-acre suburb near Sydney as a home for disabled World War I servicemen and war widows and masterminded many of Canberra's major buildings, including Parliament House, Hotel Canberra and the Prime Minister's Lodge. He was appointed KBE in 1923.

Sir John died in 1944, leaving around £89,000 – a fair few bob back then – including a £2,000 bequest to establish a scholarship at the old Church school in Shildon. Though his obituary in the *Canberra Times* shamelessly supposed Shildon to be in Surrey, the money went to the right place.

Oz clearly had an attraction for Shildon lads. The musically gifted Thomas Bulch, who at 17 had become bandmaster of the New Shildon Temperance Band, set sail for the brave new world in 1878. Shortly afterwards he wrote a jolly little number called *Waltzing Matilda*, which seemed to catch on.

Dickie Downs, who played football for Barnsley either side of World War 1 and won his sole England caps when 34, also lived in Albert Street – we delivered milk, pint of red top, to his widow. Barnsley's mascot in Dickie's time was a donkey called Amos, though this must be supposed coincidental. None of us has a blue plaque on the street, not even the donkey.

CELEBRATED Shildon lads like George Romaine and Gordon Peters, who in his youth played the organ both at the Wesley Methodists and at the Rex cinema, have been mentioned earlier. Who else made good? Laurie Brown, who played football for both Spurs and Arsenal, was Shildon born and proud of it – "even the baths at Arsenal had marble floors with heating underneath," he once recalled, "in Shildon we didn't even have a bathroom" – as was John Hope, a wonderful character who was Newcastle United's reserve goalkeeper in the 1969 Fairs Cup campaign, the last time the Magpies won anything.

John, aged 67 when he died in 2016, attended what we called the Council School but was banned by headmaster Keith Newby from the football team until (inexplicably) he could recite *The Miller of the Dee* by heart. Grist to the miller, it worked. After Newcastle, Hopey signed for Sheffield United, where he was on the wrong end – "I went down like a bloody whale" – of a George Best goal subsequently voted the 18th best in world football history. Up in the press box, legendary *Daily Mirror* man Frank McGhee saw a colleague looking at his watch. "Never mind the time, remember the date. You've just seen history," he said.

Lol Brown's funeral was the only service I've ever attended at Shildon Spiritualist church, opposite the Masonic Hall. The music machine played *Welcome to My World*.

Jeffrey Allison left his major claim to fame a little later in life. A fellow Tin Tacks boy – he'd also briefly attended junior school in Butterknowle, west Durham, where they still had a cat o' nine tails – Jeff recalled a carefree wartime childhood in Shildon. "You'd go off for the day with a bottle of water and a sugar sandwich. Your mother had no idea where you were because there wasn't anything to worry about."

He became a Queen's Scout in Spennymoor, was a successful mining and quarrying engineer and had a visionary hand in the opulently successful Middleton Lodge Hotel, near where we now live.

In 2011, when 73, Jeff became the first sailor in the world to circumnavigate the Arctic Circle clockwise – 10,335 nautical miles Hartlepool to Hartlepool including 40 days without setting foot on land. Sadly, he died two years later, his memoir published posthumously.

The town even raised an MP – Dr Keith Hampson, incredibly enough a Tory – and who, like Sir Timothy Kitson, became parliamentary private secretary to Ted Heath.

Craig Raine, born in 1944 and once said by fellow poet Philip Larkin to be a "bearded looney" – whether affectionately or not I've no idea – grew up in a "bookless" prefab in Shildon, describing the town after he'd become an Oxford professor as "typical, ugly and small" and its pride as "faintly ridiculous." He probably isn't a Tory.

Norman, his dad, was a pre-war amateur boxing champion who, after developing epilepsy, became a physiotherapist and, it's said, something of a faith healer. The boy won a scholarship to the otherwise fee-paying Barnard Castle School where there were books aplenty and an inspirational teacher called Arnold Snodgrass.

John Hunter was a barber's son who grew up on the other side of our back street, worked as a lather boy for his dad, become a celebrated hair stylist – "John Hunter of the North" – travel agent, racehorse owner, raconteur and vice-chairman of Darlington FC. He was a truly delightful man. When John and his lovely wife Mary bought a villa in Magaluf they were interviewed by the local press. "It's lovely here," he told them, "but it's not as nice as Shildon."

However prosaic, I prefer Mr Hunter's view to Professor Raine's.

WHILE we were growing up in the 50s, a bit more aware in the 60s, there were around 20 pubs (now six, and struggling), about a dozen churches (now four), four cinemas – all long since galloped into the sunset – and three or four bank branches. They've all closed their accounts, too, as Pete Sixsmith regularly lamented in his notes in the football club programme, though the old place – as Pete also liked to point out – does now have a Costa Coffee.

Class mates at Timothy Hackworth juniors included the late John Robinson, a little lad reckoned both the best fighter and the best marbles player in the class – both badges of honour, but the latter paramount. John not only became a high-grade black belt in several martial arts disciplines but, barefoot, would undertake long and mountainous walks for charity. He was a lovely lad.

The North-East actually has another Shildon, a former lead-mining village north of Blanchland in Northumberland which once had about 170 residents, a little chapel and an engine house which is now a listed ancient monument. Since the region wasn't big enough for both of us, however, it's dwindled to about three houses.

It's also the larger Shildon which is reckoned, somewhere down by the railway embankment on the line out to Middridge, to be a redoubt of the dingy skipper – *erynnis tages* to its lepidopteral friends – a butterfly species said seriously to be endangered on these shores and to like perching on dead flower heads. That's all very well, of course, but how much better had the old place been home to the great and glorious many-splendored skipper? It could be worse, it could be a haven for the grizzled skipper, the dingy's poor relation.

AMONG the other things which made our Shildon unique was that it had a church youth club which in 1963 marked the end of our O-levels with a holiday in Biarritz, playground of the world's rich and famous and for ten days of the spotty-faced adolescents (and their female counterparts) from St

John's. It was organised by Geoff Clarkson, the curate.

Halfway to Kings Cross, Barry Dixon realised he'd left his passport at home, half way to Paris someone nearly got thrown off the train for lighting up in a no-smoking carriage and half way to Biarritz we realised we were sitting in a compartment reserved for pregnant women and disabled servicemen. None of us qualified, not at the time.

We stayed in a school dormitory, spent sunny days on the beach – a bloke kept coming round flogging apricot doughnuts – and balmy evenings in a little bar at the end of the street, drinking Ricard and smoking French fags. I've never had a cigarette since, and precious little Ricard, either.

Geoff Clarkson became chaplain of the notorious Feltham young offenders' institute in Middlesex. After ten days with us lot in Biarritz, it probably seemed like a doddle.

SHILDON'S pits had long gone, though in formative years bands and banners heading for Durham Big Meeting still disturbed our slumbers on the second Saturday of July. The wagon works still went hammer and tongs, employment for 2,500, the town's day punctuated by the starting hooter about twenty past seven and the knocking off hooter about five o'clock.

I don't recall there being a night shift hooter. Probably they didn't want to wake the workforce.

These days the population of the Shildon district– including nearby villages like Eldon, Middridge and Brusselton – is around 11,000 and falling. Back then it had a population of around 14,000, many living in what can only be termed slums, infested with blackclocks and other vermin. A blackclock was first cousin to a cockroach – some might even tell them apart – and there were houses which when the light was switched on were shown to be wick with them.

Directly across our cobbled back street, old Joe Austin would from time to time keep a very large pig in the yard. At the end of the street, Geordie Ellis had a rather forlorn horse.

Since he was a rag and bone man, it was capable of Herculean effort, nonetheless.

Day and night the back street would resound with the cacophony of kids playing football and cricket and with neighbours' protests as we bunked over their locked back yard gates in a semi-permanent endeavour to get the ball back. Old Joe was among the more reluctant to return it; probably the pig didn't help nor the fact that kids from all the streets around seemed to want to play out our back. It was the Wembley Stadium of cobbled back alleys, the single street lamp at the end further flooding the imagination.

Me and our kidder – the solecism must be forgiven – also had that seven days a week milk round from 1961-65, though on those 6.15am starts Dave (as belatedly he happily admits) was very much the sleeping partner. Though we were innocents abroad, as in Biarritz, tales of milk rounds and amorous females can very largely be discounted. They were just too lazy to get dressed.

Up to nine crates, 180 pints, would precariously be balanced on a wooden cart of flimsy construction and with a single, feeble, battery-operated red light dimly to warn other road users of our pre-dawn progression. The round grew apace with the burgeoning Jubilee Fields council housing estate, the pay remained 2/6d a day with an additional half-a-crown for the Friday evening money collection.

Sometimes we'd meet the paper boys, surreptitiously swap half a pint of milk for a *Daily Mirror*. You had to have your perks. Sometimes we'd wear knitted balaclavas, in the fearsome winter of 1962-63 two or three. Save for bank robbers, does anyone still wear them?

If the milk and the morning papers were delivered to the door, everything else seemed to be available from the extraordinary number of corner shops. Shoals of fish and chip shops, too. Within 400 yards of our happy home in Albert Street there must have been a dozen little general dealers' shops, some tiny, and at least four fish shops. I still remember the belt-tightening outrage when a fish and three became a fish and four.

A trap for the unwary, the main street was Church Street and the secondary shopping street was Main Street. There were chain stores like Walter Willson's, which smelt always of fresh coffee and of yeast, and like Home and Colonial, Gallons and the London and Newcastle Tea Company. Hay's wasn't a travel agency but a bakery which sold wonderful plate pies for a shilling and sixpence, a Saturday dinnertime treat.

Folk didn't talk of shopping, they said they were going up the street – still do – or else running messages. The street's much changed. Where once it bustled – and if you thought that Shildon bustled, you should have seen Bishop on market days – now it dawdles, near deserted.

Where once there were six or seven butchers – ah, the enduring aroma of Jack Robinson's pork pies – now there are countless hot food takeaways, two or three tattoo parlours and nail bars, a couple of bookies, doubtless one or two charity shops and, appropriately, a funeral director's. We do have that Costa Coffee, though.

AFTER the Durham Miners' Gala and the wagon works' holiday fortnight, the social highlight of Shildon's year was probably the scouts' carnival, every float preceded by one of the numerous juvenile jazz bands which formed a kazoo's who across North-East communities.

Its predecessor was Shildon Show, not dissimilar to rural shows save for the absence of sheep and other critturs. Shildon Show's highlight was the baking classes, very often a self-raising showdown – bake-offs hadn't been invented – between me mam and me Aunty Betty.

A "float" was a tableau on the back of a lorry, from which none ever fell. I recall on one occasion being dressed as a jolly Jack – riding along on the crest of a wave – and on another as a Church of England bishop, irreverently confirming all that's supposed. Floats these days are flat impossible, health and safety rules those waves.

THE police station (telephone Shildon 6) had a sergeant, six or seven constables and (get this) a detective. Most feared amongst them, at least by kids playing football in the street, was PC 721 Trebilcock, who parents would cite as a sort of bogeyman. "If you don't behave, I'm sending for Trebil-cock."

Tommy Trebilcock was a red-faced West Countryman, came north believing his surname to be pronounced Treb-il-co, emphasis on the second syllable, but eventually gave up the unequal struggle. Trebil-cock he became. In junior journalism, patrolling the cosmopolitan corridors of Bishop Auckland magistrates court, I got to know Tommy quite well. You couldn't have met a nicer feller or, come to that, a better community polliss – though, goodness knows, there wasn't much headline crime.

Then as now, the police didn't tell us much, anyway. The difference these days is that the constabulary employs a small force of public relations people – no budget cuts there – similarly to tell us next to nothing, but in a 500-word statement about a week after the event.

Before 25 I'd become district councillor, churchwarden, church council secretary and goodness knows what else, almost all those activities followed in the Red Lion by a couple of pints of Vaux Gold Tankard and on feast days a pickled egg.

Were she home from university, we might persuade the lovely Jennifer – only the station master's daughter but some thought her just the ticket – to stand on a back room table and give us a bit of Joan Baez. Usually there wasn't food, but on Friday evenings a chap in a once-white jacket would come round with a big basket on his arm, selling shellfish. I swear the same chap's still doing the same job, and wearing the same jacket, too.

By 26 I was gone. One day, still many years hence it's to be hoped, I'll be back. *And Can It Be*, Sharon knows the hymn numbers already.

THE once-in-a-lifetime highlight was the great Cavalcade of Steam, gathered gleaming in the wagon works sidings, which on Sunday September 27 1975 marked to the day the 150th anniversary of the inaugural passenger journey on the Stockton and Darlington Railway – the world's first – flagged off pretty much from that spot.

The planning had been meticulous, the execution magnificent, the crowds global. Though there can't be the same number of locomotives in steam, much is also mooted to mark the 200th anniversary in 2025 – and there's a bonny old battle between Shildon and Darlington over where Locomotion, the inaugural engine, might rest.

I greatly hope to be around for it – make that twice in a lifetime – though it's unlikely that I'll be asked to write anything. In 1975 the *Echo* got me to compile a substantial front-page piece for what then was a broadsheet newspaper. My only real memory is that I didn't in any sense do the occasion justice.

THE football team's nicknamed The Railwaymen, too, fervently and oft fruitlessly followed from childhood. The local match reporter, officially on the *Auckland Chronicle* but a penny-a-line man for the *Despatch* and the *Echo*, was Dennis Robinson, a chap with the build and timbre of Alan Ball but probably not as good an inside right.

It wasn't so much the thought of being paid to watch football which ever more loudly whispered "journalism", however, as the reality that, rabbit in a cornfield again, I had precious few options. The dole office was in a wooden hut in Main Street. Never previously having been stalked by an aspirant inky tradesman, they wondered – perhaps having ridden the crest of too many boy scouts' carnivals – if I might fancy the Merchant Navy instead. After that it really was sink or swim.

51 : A LEAGUE OF OUR OWN

THE Northern Football League was founded in 1889, chiefly through the efforts of Charles Samuel Craven, secretary of Darlington FC, and is officially the world's second oldest after the Football League itself.

Mainly it may be remembered for the pre-eminence of clubs like Bishop Auckland, Crook Town and Stockton, particularly in the FA Amateur Cup in the 1950s and early 1960s though 'amateur', it should be explained, was a term more honoured in the breach than in the observance.

Even an average player would find a lot more than a leather tongue in his boot. The better amateurs might earn more from an afternoon playing football than they could from a week down the pit – shamateurs, they were called, the spurious distinction between "amateur" and "professional" not officially ended until 1974. Now they're all players, and almost all the clubs are payers.

Bishop Auckland won the Amateur Cup in three

CRAVEN IMAGE:
Cover of the Northern
League Magazine

successive seasons, 1955-57, Crook Town four times between 1954-64 – the first of those victories against the Bishops. Each year the victors would arrive back with the cup
at Darlington railway station on a Sunday afternoon, climb
aboard an open-top bus and head triumphantly homeward.
Each year they'd pass through Shildon, crowds loyally gathered on the Hippodrome corner dreaming that next time it
would be the Railwaymen on the top deck. We wait yet.

Towards the end of the 20th century the league's national
profile had dipped markedly, partly because of some poor
decision making and partly because leagues elsewhere in
the country had caught up, then overtaken. In 1987, league
chairman Arthur Clark asked me to edit the centenary history, painstakingly and with wonderful meticulousness being
put together by Brian Hunt, a Durham County Council joiner
who was also Durham County Cricket Club's much-treas-
ured scorer and stats man.

Hunty, known to Sir Ian Botham by a soubriquet which
cannot here be repeated, was a superb historian and research-
er and had also, to his enduring pride, won the Eldon Lane
and District bonny baby competition in 1948. The number

BONNY LAD:
Brian Hunt

of entrants is not recorded.
Whilst he could undoubt-
edly build a better matchbox
holder, however, he'd be the
first to admit that he'd never
have passed GCE English
language. Like Jack Spratt
and his missus, we rubbed
along fine, becoming good
friends.

His script was typed and
double-spaced, the hard
copy then checked and dou-
ble-checked by me. Every
morning between six and

345

eight o'clock I'd pore over it with an editor's pencil, pre-breakfast telephone calls frequently passing between us. One morning the phone caught me with my trousers down.

Certain it would be Brian, I answered abruptly: "Can't a man have a shite in peace?"

"I beg your pardon?" said the lady who'd called to complain about something in that morning's column.

The centenary history, *Northern Goalfields*, was a masterwork, the credit all Brian's. Though he sought nothing, the league gave him and his wife Ann a package tour to the Caribbean, which included a couple of West Indies v England test matches. One morning they'd arrived at the Kingston Oval in Jamaica before realising that all their tickets and credentials were still in the hotel room 25 miles away.

All that Brian had in his wallet was his laminated Northern League all-grounds pass, similar in size to a bank card and every bit as valuable. The gateman glanced at it in the manner of Alan Whicker in an American Express ad. "Ah," he said, "that'll do nicely."

When the book was finally finished, Arthur Clark persuaded me to launch, edit and almost single-handedly write a league magazine. In 1992 I was successful among four candidates in winning a place on the league management committee after Bob Scaife, a huge former North Riding police officer from Whitby, had stood down. Bob remains the only man in history to gain three stones on a sponsored slim. It put him up to 25-and-a-half.

Between 1992-96, a period during which the stamped addressed envelope withdrew in the face of technological advance, I also organised football's first ground hopping weekends, which may need a little explanation. The ground hoppers were football fanatics, men – almost never women – who'd go anywhere for a match, particularly if it were a first-time visit, a tick.

David Bauckham, a senior airline official who photographed, wrote and published a book on football dugouts, also wrote a master's degree dissertation on ground hoppers. "They're all slightly mad," he concluded, neither academically nor unreasonably.

The weekends weren't my idea. Begging for letters to help fill the league magazine, I'd asked Pete Sixsmith – Shildon lad, ardent Sunderland fan, off-beat writer, Costa Coffee enthusiast and a bit of a hopper himself – if he'd contribute a couple of hundred original words. His the inspiration, his the procreation, but me once again left holding the baby. The weekends embraced around eight games over Easter, visitor numbers growing every year. Usually it poured down, frequently it was freezing, once over Easter it snowed. We had to offer the authentic North-East experience.

They were a disparate and sometimes a desperate group, by year five about 300-strong, with nicknames like Veggie Burger and the Blackpool Tram and idiosyncrasies like having to touch the ball, or both crossbars or all four corner flags. Some would even insist that the game didn't count if it had been goalless.

We accommodated them in one of the Durham University colleges, transported them in clapped out and querulous OK double deck buses, fed them with pies, burgers (though probably not veggie burgers) and on Easter Sunday morning at Horden with a cream egg apiece. One or two still twisted; most were very grateful. Men like Gary Brand – among the most generous, big-hearted and convivial men I know, and he a Spurs supporter – remain good friends.

From the first we were also joined by Henk van der Sluis and his mate Johannes de Boer from Holland, lovely lads who wore clogs, at least until the footwear dissolved in an Esh Winning downpour. Like most Dutch folk they spoke almost perfect English, though clearly needing a copy of *Larn Yersel Geordie* by way of a book at bedtime.

Henk was diabetic. One weekend he became so ill that he ended up in hospital in Durham, a kindly aged miner from

Bearpark in the next bed. I visited after Easter Sunday's final match, found Henk in an unusual state of agitation after the old pitman several times told him that he was sorry that he was bad.

"Mike," said Henk, "will you please tell this gentleman that I am not a bad person." It still lost a little bit in the translation.

Now organised commercially, ground hoppers' weekends remain enthusiastically and nationally supported several times a season. I rarely attend – wouldn't have a leg to stand on.

THE league management committee met in a pub back room in Murton, an overgrown pit village near the Durham coast where they'd certainly have known what "bad" meant. There was little room to swing a cat but a stuffed bulldog gazed balefully, almost salivating, from atop a filing cabinet. It was called Nic, after Gordon Nicholson, a former league secretary who himself was known to bark a bit when aroused.

Arthur Clark, also a senior Football Association council member, retired in 1996 after 21 years in the league chair and eventually asked me to succeed him. I wasn't first choice.

First choice was Mike Armitage, mentioned earlier, an accountant who'd been my lifelong best mate since our first day together at Timothy Hackworth infants, and who was longtime secretary of Shildon FC.

We'd even played together for the church youth club – me in goal, Mike in defence – he becoming the first team mate I'd ever seen sent off after too forcibly reminding the referee of the error of his ways. Mike in turn became a superb administrator and succeeded Arthur on the FA Council, the ref became Archdeacon of Carlisle.

So the buck stopped here, Arthur – a former Coal Board surveyor who lived in Whitley Bay – keen to take me under his retiring wing. Once I attended a club appeal against a league decision, heard by an FA panel of three, and was astonished to hear Arthur, the most upright of men, claim something that I knew not wholly to be true.

Angela, his wife, had joined us by the time that I had chance to raise it. "Oh yes," she said, "he'll even tell fibs for the Northern League."

The 1996 annual meeting, at which I took over, was held in a marquee at the Witton-le-Wear home of the Rt Hon Ernest Armstrong, the former North-West Durham MP who'd been everything from deputy Speaker of the House of Commons to vice-president of the Methodist Conference, the highest office open to a layperson. As a young man he'd also been a Northern League footballer, for Stanley United, a defender most kindly described as combative but more tellingly nicknamed Sikey. The spelling may have been different.

Ernest was a true Christian gentleman, though probably more at home holding forth from the pulpit, or the Speaker's chair, than to a football gathering with a few beers inside them. His favourite joke, repeated whatever the occasion, was of the chap getting thoroughly soaked on the exposed terrace at Roker Park, Sunderland's former ground. His cap's shoved firmly in his pocket, prompting a fellow spectator to ask why on earth he didn't wear it.

"What," says the chap, "ye don't think I'm going to get my best cap wet, do ye?"

Ernest died not long after that meeting, his gentle guidance much missed, though league management committee meetings were usually pretty amicable affairs. Were things to become tricky, the atmosphere could always be lightened by long-serving member Peter Lax, a stalwart of Billingham Synthonia FC and a delightful man.

Peter's distinctive characteristic was that he and his native tongue existed in parallel universes. He was a man who made Mrs Malaprop seem coherent, to spoken English what Jack the Ripper was to moral rearmament. His old, old jokes – "we're having the mother-in-law for Christmas dinner, eve-

349

ryone else has turkey" – were excruciating, too.

Peter, bless him, once observed that Synthonia were seeking funds for ground development and had put up the clubhouse as cholesterol. He was the man who asked the canteen lady at another club what brand their tea was– "Rington's? We always use Typhoid" – and who observed that filling in forms was perjury. It's possible he meant purgatory.

After a heart problem, he was pleased to report that all was well again after the doctors put in a stench. I was to have personal experience of stenches during the course of writing this book, though I could have sworn that the doc called them stents.

Peter died in 2012, aged 76, after a battle with Alzheimer's. "Our greatest ambassador, the diamond of our club, the best of men," said the death notice in the Teesside paper. Never was truer word written.

CHAIRMANSHIP of the world's second oldest football league should not suggest any great understanding of the game. Just about the closest I came to insight had come in 1979, shortly after we were married and in that extended honeymoon period when you still do things together. I'd even joined Sharon at the ultra-posh Glyndebourne opera, down south, rather compromising the gesture by falling asleep halfway through.

On this occasion, goodness only knows why, we were watching Carlisle United, who seemed to have a particularly inventive youngster up front. Peter Beardsley had already been rejected by several other clubs. "If that lad doesn't play for England," I said to Sharon – who, happily, remembers the prescient observation – "I'll eat hay with a cuddy."

The man they called Pedro won 59 caps; the cuddy dined alone. In almost every other respect, achievement has been down to good fortune.

North Shields had been the Northern League's last Wembley winners, way back in 1969. Whitby Town got there, winning the FA Vase – it could no longer be called an Amateur Cup – at the end of my first season in the chair. It started a remarkable run of success for which vigorously but vainly I tried to claim credit.

Amid the euphoria came a bombshell. Just days before the Whitby final, the Dunston-based Federation Brewery announced without warning that it was ceasing spon-

TRAVELLING LITE:
Brooks Mileson

sorship of the league. Colleagues made it clear that it was the league chairman's job to find a replacement. Early approaches proved unsuccessful. Then, once again, I got lucky.

Whitby's principal sponsor was Brooks Mileson, once a raggy-arsed urchin from Sunderland – the Pennywell estate, like Ernest Armstrong – who'd broken his back in a childhood accident while playing in a sand quarry, won England cross-country vests in defiance of doctors who told him he'd never walk again, built a hugely successful insurance and construction business and lived almost exclusively on a diet of Lucozade and Marlboro Lite (especially, incessantly, the latter.)

Apprehensively at half-time, I approached him in the Wembley banqueting suite. Brooks, scumfished in pony tail and heavy-duty top coat, asked that I come three days later to see him in his office near Houghton-le-Spring.

Negotiations were the bartering equivalent of a Don Evans job interview. Brooks asked how much we'd like, was given an inflated figure and wrote what passed for a contract on the inside flap of a Marlboro Lite packet, that being the

351

nearest – perhaps the only – bit of paper to hand.

It was signed Charlie Bear, picnic director, and – like the signatory – was worth its weight in gold. We became friends, Brooks a familiar figure in my local in Darlington where he'd lunch on Lucozade and cheese and onion sandwiches, 25p apiece. I knew how to treat our sponsors.

Wonderfully generous, he also sponsored everything from Romanian orphanages to animal charities and the University of Central Lancashire, which in appreciation made him a Fellow. The Northern League, he decided, would be sponsored in perpetuity, throughout his own lifetime and that of his sons.

He lived between Carlisle and the Scottish border, had an animal sanctuary on his land – there was an ostrich called Amos, a handsome creature though with funny knees – was said personally to be worth £75m, raggy arse to riches. In 2003 he became owner of Gretna Football Club, then in the Scottish third division and formerly, improbably, twice Northern League champions. The romance flamed, burned bright but was tragically to die.

Brooks became big news, a Marlboro Lite heavyweight loved by the world's media. An improbable *Sunday Times* poll in 2007 named him fifth in a list of Britain's top sporting smokers. I forget the top four, but sixth was the Wimbledon champion Anna Kournikova. Half the country still thought his name was Miles Brookson, so incorrigibly that he simply signed autographs "Brooks." It saved time, he said.

Within four years Gretna were in the Scottish first division – the second tier – and, amazingly, reached the Scottish FA Cup final at Hampden Park. Though the attention was global, Brooks spent the morning of the final at home, changed into his best jeans – he'd been mucking out the pigs in the others, he said – ate fish and chips from the *Glasgow Herald* with the fans and, foregoing the executive boxes, sat on the terraces with me.

Though Gretna lost on penalties, they qualified for Europe. By then Brooks was clearly unwell, his Midas touch – and much of his fortune – dissipated in pursuit of that great and oddly requited love affair. He died in November 2008, apparently after collapsing and falling into his pond, and perpetuity died with him.

Though there never was a fag packet for that one, he was one of the greatest guys I ever knew. The Northern League Cup is still named in his memory.

WHITBY Town's triumph in 1997 became the first of many Wembley visits, the most memorable Tow Law Town's final the very next season. Tow Law was hardly a town at all, a community of little more than 2,000 people atop a windy ridge in west Durham. Thirty years previously they'd famously thrashed Mansfield Town 5-1 in an FA Cup first round tie, notwithstanding that the visitors had first consulted an Arctic survival expert. Nothing could be as Siberian as a late-November afternoon on the Ironworks Road ground at Tow Law.

Peter Davis, the vicar, was an Australian bachelor and monk who swore that all that kept him from perishing was a cupboard stocked floor to ceiling with Campbell's lobster bisque. He later became a buffet car attendant on the main West Coast railway line, though whether they sold lobster bisque is probably a matter of doubt.

The Vase semi-final had been a two-leg affair against Taunton Town, the first ending 4-4 in Somerset and the Lawyers edging the second 1-0. When the defeated supporters left about 6pm, it was noticeable that someone in the back seat of the bus was waving a toilet brush – its handle inscribed TLTFC – cheerfully over his head.

It transpired that he'd asked if he might have it – a souvenir of a memorable day. Goodness only knows what he'd have sought had Taunton won, but it was – and remains – typical of the spirit of the game at that level.

If that one made few printable inches beyond my *North-*

ern Echo sports column – hobby and job wondrously symbiotic – Sam Gordon's story went much bigger.

SAM was Tow Law's mascot, a skinny little ten-year-old who'd hardly missed a match all season. The Football Association, however, ruled that mascots had never been allowed at Wembley – they'd apparently forgotten about that chap who used to parade around the pitch perimeter in top hat and Union Jack waistcoat – and insisted there could be no exceptions. So much for play it again, Sam.

The crestfallen lad and his parents appeared in newspapers and on television nationwide. That the mascot finally got lucky, however, was because both I and Tow Law chairman John Flynn had become friendly with FA chief executive Graham Kelly, the most traduced man in sport.

His image was of a misery chops, on one occasion observed during a game at Billingham Town with a smile on his face. "It's mebbe a bit wind," someone said.

Graham, who particularly loved grass roots football, had been at the annual Northern League dinner one May Friday in 1997 and was staying with his then partner's family in Middlesbrough. As ever, his boots were in the back of the car. Any chance, he wondered, that I might find him a game the following morning?

TRADUCED:
Graham Kelly

John Flynn played for Durham Buffs – at 70 he still does – a faintly geriatric side whose home games were usually on the Cow Field at Ushaw Moor, a few miles west of the city. Next morning Graham was the first player there, single-handedly put up the nets, all but begged for a game and ran around joyously (if not wholly effectively) when he got one.

After the final whistle, the top man in English football again helped take down the nets, mixed effortlessly as one of the lads, laughed a great deal – it was mebbe a bit more wind – and then joined everyone else in the pub. The drinks, of course, were on Graham.

His image was lugubrious, London-oriented, perhaps a little effeminate. A few months later he turned up at Flynny's fancy dress 50th birthday party as the Queen of the South.

John and I already had Graham's direct line, his home number and his mobile. He at once agreed that the mascot ban was barmy and unilaterally overturned it. There've been mascots on big Wembley occasions ever since.

Graham left the FA a couple of years later – "fired with enthusiasm," he liked to say. Though I was to have another 18 years as Northern League chairman, I never so much as spoke to an FA chief executive ever again.

IN November 1999 I'd joined Graham and Romayne – by then his wife – on a 26-mile leg of their 184-mile walk from Peterborough to Middlesbrough, in aid of mental health charities. Boro had signed the Brazilian player Juninho, Graham had said on the radio that he'd walk a long way to watch him. Someone held him to it.

That fifth leg was also joined by BBC sportsman Ray Stubbs, who noted on air that Inter Milan had just signed Ronaldo and wondered how far R H G Kelly – he always signed his name like that – would go to watch him. "He's not fit for the Hambleton Combination," said Graham.

The funny thing was that it was I who was a Master of Misery, a title given to those who've several times completed the 42-mile Lyke Wake Walk across the North Yorkshire moors – a Doctor of Dolefulness is something yet more extreme – but it was R H G Kelly who cheerfully walked the legs off me.

He was 53, set a formidable pace, all but danced up the sort of slope where normally you'd expect to see a funicular railway at the bottom. "I'm the Mary Poppins of football administration," he said, though I didn't quite understand that one.

Our leg was from the Humber Bridge to somewhere near Malton. The night previously he'd been so jiggered that he'd fallen asleep in the bath, his newspaper dropping in at the moment that he dropped off. "There was a big black mark all the way round the tub," he said.

They were due into Middlesbrough in time for the Saturday afternoon match, though that wasn't the end of the chief exec's exertions. The following day he'd blagged another game for Durham Buffs.

GORDON Nicholson, the bulldog atop the Murton filing cabinet, had been succeeded as league secretary by Tony Golightly, who'd retired at 50 as chief executive of Chester-le-Street district council in County Durham. Usually, almost always, we got on fine.

Another of our teams, Bedlington Terriers, had reached the Vase final in 1999 – half of Northumberland barking "Woof, Woof Terriers", the other half singing *Who Let the Dogs Out* – while Whitley Bay's win in 2002 was to be the first of four in a decade, a unique club achievement which included a hat-trick of wins between 2009-11.

All the time there was copy for the column, all the time the boulder was being rolled towards the top of that perfidious hill, every event grist to the inexorable mill. Even the silly little paragraphs were welcomed – people liked the silly little paragraphs – like the tea hut customer at Northallerton Town, probably a southerner, who wondered why he'd been handed Izal toilet tissue.

The tea hut lady told him he'd asked if they'd had any bog roll. "No I didn't," he replied "I asked if you had any Bovril."

More tales from the tea hut, there was also the infamous

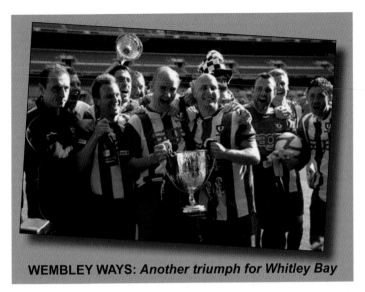

WEMBLEY WAYS: *Another triumph for Whitley Bay*

occasion on which gun-carrying police wailed up to a match at Norton and Stockton Ancients, a well-meaning but seriously myopic spectator having mistaken someone's giant hotdog for a sidearm.

At Evenwood Town's canteen queue, a little kid had simply demanded crisps and Wots-its. The kindly lady demanded to know the magic word, to which the child responded at once. "Pop," he said.

Then managed by Dr Graeme Forster, a vividly colourful character whose PhD was in metallurgy not medicine, Evenwood were also involved in a match at Bedlington when a goalbound Terriers effort was stopped on the line by a black cat. Lucky for some, no doubt.

That one had legs, too, ended up in *The Times* – which wondered if the whole of the cat had crossed the line. Sadly they didn't have VAR.

WHITLEY Bay's first final was at Villa Park, since Wembley was being rebuilt. As usual, a group of league management committee members gathered on the station, the chairman customarily rebuked for singing *Thine be the Glory Risen Conquering Son*, and no matter that it was a Sunday. At Leeds we were joined by a young stowaway.

He was eight or nine, strolled into first class – we did things in style on Vase final day – announced that he'd run away from home. That's how he came under George Courtney's wing. Following in Ernest Armstrong's shoes – remember Sikey? – I'd persuaded George to become league president in 1997. He'd twice been a referee at the World Cup finals, was appointed MBE for services to the game, may even – as he liked to claim – have given to the nation the phrase about being as fit as a butcher's dog.

Most relevantly on this Sabbath morning, he'd been a highly-regarded primary school headmaster. He knew what to do when eight-year-olds proved problematical, if not necessarily ran away from home. George was brilliant, clearly knew his child care, involved the guard and had the little lad met by the police at Birmingham. They rang later to say he was home safe and sound. George probably gave him an autograph, too.

That was also the day, homeward in the buffet on Birmingham New Street station, that George was approached by a lady of the early evening. She got a red card.

It will be recalled that Dr David Jenkins, the former Bishop of Durham, had told me on his 80th birthday that one of his resolutions was never again to make a train journey which involved changing at Birmingham New Street, though it probably wasn't for fear of being propositioned by ladies of the night.

It has to be said that, on all these big occasions, the FA were outstanding hosts – not least in 2012 when the dream of an all-Northern League final, Dunston UTS v West Auckland, finally came true. The governing body even allowed us to organise a half-time photograph on the Wembley turf of representatives of all 44 clubs wearing their team shirts.

We'd almost become season ticket holders in the royal box though not, it should be stressed, its inner circles. These were the one-and-sixpennies, the Princess Michael of Kent seats, not the half-crowns. They were great days, nonetheless.

AT other times, and for many years, relations between the Northern League chairman and the governing body were nowhere near as harmonious. We needn't go into it all. Suffice that the FA wanted to "restructure" the game at what football folk confusingly call non-league level and that the proposals seemed to me both to marginalise the North-East – already out on a geographical limb – and to threaten the standing of the Northern League and its clubs.

The FA's stated chief aims had been to reduce cost and travel for clubs. Their proposals meant the exact opposite. Arguments went on for almost 20 years. Though both sides tried to be civil, things sometimes became acrimonious – not least with the paid FA official charged with seeing the wretched exercise to a conclusion.

It was therefore a very considerable surprise to receive, in 2013, an emailed invitation to the Association's 150th anniversary banquet – a super-posh do in central London in the company of Prince William, FIFA president Sepp Blatter and many others considered great and goodish. A pack of paparazzi preyed in the street outside; had they heard I was coming?

The invitation was yet more surprising upon discovering that I was the only league official to be invited from our level of the game. Incredulously, I'd returned the email. Was I being invited in the capacity of Northern League chairman or as a fairly well known journalist with some knowledge of the game at that level? The former, they insisted.

Some time later I made an interesting discovery. Stonewall FC, based in London, was said to be the country's biggest football club representing the gay and transgender communities. Its chairman was Michael Amos. Stonewall probably ticked an awful lot more FA boxes at that time than did the Northern League and its cantankerous head lad. Had the invitation been sent in error? They again insisted not, though real doubts remained.

I never met my namesake, don't know if he finally was invited as well – if he wasn't, he missed a very good night.

AMONG the other things for which the league became known during my tenure was a perpetual and generally losing battle against what the laws of the game call offensive, insulting or abusive language. Swearing, in other words. The sanction is dismissal – hardly anyone was ever dismissed. Players swore ceaselessly, referees ignored it, the FA proved institutionally stone deaf.

I couldn't stand it, believed that if the perpetrators so persistently and vocally used such language on a Saturday night out they'd probably be locked up. So why should football be different, especially when we were trying so hard to attract youngsters and families?

The best remembered initiative, and probably the most resented, was Secret Shopper – the brainchild of league sponsor John Elliott. Once again, it was I who was surrogate father, left to nurse someone else's love child.

John ran – still runs – Ebac, a Newton Aycliffe-based firm making dehumidifiers and washing machines. Renowned community philanthropist, wonderful character, owner of oft-unsuccessful racehorses, he was born in the west Durham village of Lands, left school at 15 and claims ever since to have regretted it.

"I should have left at 12," he insists.

When many years ago he received the MBE – upgrade long overdue – he swears that the Queen asked where he was from. "Is that High Lands or Low Lands?" she, in turn, responded.

Secret Shopper involved a panel of anonymous league

representatives, working unpaid and often foregoing the offered expenses, visiting grounds to report on the level of offensive language and other misdemeanours – surprising how often it included players peeing behind the dugout.

Clubs didn't like it, broadcasters did. I did dozens of pre-watershed interviews– bit tricky, that – including the Radio 4 *Today* programme on Budget Day. Clearly there was nothing much on the news agenda – and as folk were keen to remind me, I had a face for radio.

The FA was so impressed they gave us a gold award, John and I invited to the FA Cup final and to the banquet which preceded it. The prize also included the services of a speaker at the annual league dinner, but the least spoken about that gentleman the better.

Most footballers who hawk themselves round the sportsmen's dinner circuit are dreadful, recycling rubbish and seeming to believe that a bad story becomes a good one with the addition of yet more gratuitous obscenity. These days very few charge less than £1,000 for half an hour on their hind legs, many receive very much more. Incredibly they like to claim they're there because they want to give something back to the game when all they're doing is screwing something else out of it.

At a dinner in 2019 a few of us round the table had a little sweep on how many times former Sunderland manager Peter Reid would use the f-word and its derivatives – never mind all the other everyday obscenities. In 31 miserable minutes the total was 75. Not even I had been so pessimistic. I paid up morosely.

Among the best was the late Alan Ball, an England World Cup winner in 1966, who had a very high-pitched voice and introduced himself as the after-dinner squeaker. Bally only swore once all evening, and that mildly, when recalling his time as manager of Blackpool and his friendship with the heavyweight boxer Brian London, originally from Hartlepool.

Though he was British champion and had fought the young Cassius Clay, London wasn't particularly good. "He was the only boxer," said his mate, "who had a cauliflower arse."

I also much enjoyed the great George Best, invited to a charity evening at the Barnes Hotel in Sunderland – managed by the urbane Brian Murphy – to raise funds for a little lad seriously injured in a road accident. The first boost was from a pre-dinner book on whether the Irishman would even turn up and, if he did, how belatedly.

George made it, and on time. No one had wagered on that. "I bet that surprised you," he said. After his talk, inevitably embracing the "Where did it all go wrong?" story, a few of us gathered in the bar. George said that he wanted to visit the little lad's special school, near Durham, the following day – or, by that time, the same day. His minder reminded him that he was meant to be doing something in London and was at once rebuffed. George was going back to school.

He also agreed that I could attend with a photographer, on condition that the nationals weren't informed. It was a great story, and terms I was very happy to accept.

The most engaging speaker of all was former England manager Sir Bobby Robson, a Langley Park lad who never forgot his roots. Usually he'd hold forth for a good couple of hours, enchanted all, never sought a penny so long as the cause was worthy (and wouldn't have turned up in the first place had it not been).

Somewhat dubiously, Bob also claimed provenance for the story of his time as manager of Ipswich Town when he encountered one or other of the patrician Cobbold family – the club owners – in the gent's in the Great Eastern Hotel on Liverpool Street railway station.

Bob had finished what he had to do and was heading for the door. "Where I come from," said Mr Patrick – for it was probably he – "we wash our hands after using the toilet."

"Where I come from," replied the Langley Park lad, "we don't pee on them in the first place."

On one occasion he was speaking to raise funds for Tow Law Town, sought nothing for his services more than a plate of pie and peas, cautiously asked before he started if there were any will o' the wisps – he meant journalists – in the room. Only Mike Amos they said.

"That's all right, Mike doesn't count," said Sir Bobby. It was one of the biggest compliments I've ever been paid. I hoped it was, anyway.

The last time I saw the great man was at a dinner in Newcastle. Clearly he was very unwell, nearing the end of a protracted battle with multiple cancers, but he'd said he'd attend and so, of course, he did. Sensing Sir Bobby's frailty, the MC asked guests not to bother him. What to do? By then we were quite friendly and it seemed sadly certain that it would be the last time I'd see him alive. Apprehensively, I went over.

Sir Bobby rose – rose! – with great effort. "Mike," he said, "I'm so pleased that you came across." He really was a great and a gracious man, the finest ambassador for the professional game that ever I encountered.

THE Northern League officially marked the 125th anniversary of its formation on May 25 2014. Chiefly in the belief that few of us would be around to celebrate the 150th, we planned a season of celebration leading up to it.

Thanks to a combination of old friends and new technology we found and laid wreaths upon Charles Samuel Craven's grave in a quiet churchyard on the Surrey/Sussex border and tracked Bob Rogers, his grandson, to Hong Kong.

We had an exhibition at the National Football Museum in Manchester, produced with Jon Smith's expert and invaluable assistance a splendid 125th anniversary history – I may still have a copy or two for sale – and a special magazine. Through retired senior police officer Harvey Harris, we also organised another series of ground hops. We staged a match with an FA X1 and held an imaginative and well-supported church service before the 125th anniversary lunch in Durham, both attended by Bob Rogers and his wife.

The service was led by Canon Leo Osborn, a recent former President of the Methodist Conference who'd long been the league chaplain. Other church services end with tea and biscuits; ours ended with pies and Bovril.

Leo had also been chairman of the Newcastle upon Tyne district of the Methodist church, the shelves in his study heavy with gold-tooled books of ecclesiastical appearance. It was chicanery: inside those handsome binders was every Aston Villa programme, home and away, since the Villa was little more than a shack.

As always, the aim of the 125th anniversary season was to raise the league's profile, to persuade more people to give it a go. It remained the ambition in 2015-16, my final season as chairman, which I decided should be marked with a season-long series of sponsored walks – the Last Legs Challenge – to all 44 grounds.

Last Legs totalled 512 miles. The third or fourth walk was along the glorious Northumberland coast and then inland to Alnwick Town on a lovely Tuesday in August. About halfway, fellow walker Julian Tyley and I sat in the sun outside a pub overlooking the sea and with views of Dunstanburgh Castle, agreed that it was wise to make the most of days like that because you never knew what was around the corner.

Half a mile later, almost literally around the corner – and while stone cold sober – I failed to spot a kerb, instinctively threw an arm forward to break the fall and broke the arm instead. Another walk had been planned for the following day and was duly completed. One more step.

Clubs, almost all of them, were greatly supportive. Last Legs raised £28,000, half for the Sir Bobby Robson Foundation in memory of a truly magnificent man and half in £1,000 chunks to causes nominated by the clubs and drawn from a hat.

The final leg of the 44 had been, by design, to a game at Shildon. By wondrous happenstance, it was the occasion on which they were to be presented with the league championship trophy for the first time since 1939 – one of my last jobs as chairman. A photograph of Adam and me, one hand apiece on the trophy and beaming blissfully, still stands on the mantelpiece. It mightn't have been the FA Amateur Cup, but it was a pretty good way to go.

The league left me to find my own successor, but had secretly formed a sub-committee to mark my departure. Explaining my lifelong allegiance, they even invited Arsenal manager Arsene Wenger to the valedictory annual dinner. Arsenal didn't reply.

At the annual meeting in June 2016, 20 years to the day since assuming the Northern League chair and with things in pretty good fettle, I contentedly vacated it.

52 : HACKED OFF

THIS memoir has been compiled spasmodically, some might say chaotically, the chapters written in no obvious order and then stuck together with a cut-and-paste brush. All which seemed obvious from the first sentence – written in July 2019 – was that the final chapter, this one, really would be written last. In difficult days for the provincial newspaper industry, would I still be employed, perhaps constrained by loyalty, or free to use what might be termed ex-journalistic licence?

The *Northern Echo* marked on January 1 2020 the 150th anniversary of its first publication. Save for an 88-page supplement and other articles masterminded by Chris Lloyd – as admirable, as readable and as inspired as ever – the celebration seemed greatly low-key for so significant an event. The centenary had been marked by a big black tie bash at Billingham Forum. If there were a corporate knees-up this time, or even prosecco and peanuts, I wasn't invited – but by then I myself was history.

Around the start of 2019 there'd been a round robin inviting ideas with which to engrave the milestone. I suggested either that they publish this book – and keep any profits – or, alternatively, carry in the paper a series of shorter pieces reflecting on the past 55 years. My email was never so much as acknowledged.

Precisely five weeks before the anniversary, however, a convivial lunchtime pint with two fairly senior retired colleagues – inevitably lamenting the way of the journalistic world, as old hands do – had been interrupted by a phone call. It was the editor, obliged by some specious sub-section of employment law to read a statement that my part-time post was "at risk of redundancy." That, of course, was euphemistic. Even with my fabled myopia, it was easy to see the writing on the wall.

It was a great disappointment – I was almost certainly the longest-serving staff member in the paper's history and had been quite looking forward to sharing a sesquicentennial shandy – and, in truth, it was a surprise. Though survival had for some time been like that cornfield rabbit run, the bloke on reality's harvester encroaching inexorably and his mate with the shotgun waiting to pick off a few more hapless bunnies, I still hoped that I was valued. The rabbit was duly picked off.

Among the ironies was that, three weeks earlier, I'd undergone a procedure at the James Cook Hospital in Middlesbrough – about which the company had, of course, been told – to have fitted those two coronary stents to which a previous chapter alluded. Angina had unexpectedly and inexplicably manifested itself in early summer. Though mobility had been severely restricted, I carried on working. After the angioplasty, the surgeon signed me off for a month, but the columns continued in the belief that my stuff was at least different – distinctive even – and that the struggling paper still benefitted from it. It also meant that I hadn't had a day off sick for 20 years. If the man on the tractor were indeed the grim reaper, his timing could have been a little more sensitive.

It also didn't help that at the time of the phone call Sharon was in Singapore visiting the younger bairn and his family, he on a lengthy attachment with the BBC. It wasn't a great night to be home alone.

To the company it appeared not to have mattered that, way beyond my brief, I passed on or wrote numerous news stories. Just a couple of weekends before the harvest was gathered I heard, soon after the event, of a football referee in Stockton who'd collapsed and died during a Sunday league game. He was 87. A call to the newsdesk's direct line produced a voice-mail message advising to ring the main switchboard number; a call to that number gave the number for the newsdesk. This was the communications industry.

In some desperation, I emailed everyone I could think of. The story never appeared.

The subsequent formal redundancy letter, basically a very slightly amended version of that sent to others nationwide in the same sinking boat, added something about "refocusing feature content", a tawdry nonsense which meant replacing my stuff with monochrome, pot-boiling pap.

Money was probably the root of it. I hadn't had a pay rise for ten years – like others with far greater need of one – originated all my own stuff, wrote all my own headlines, took almost all my own photographs, never once missed a deadline, claimed nothing (though still a staff member) for office allowance, telephone bill or computer repair and maintenance and very happily worked an average 30 hours a week for the 12.5 hours pay set eight years earlier. The bean counters had concluded that it wasn't enough. To this day I have no inkling of the real reason for my sudden departure. But the nominal hourly rate probably had something to do with it.

In recent years I'd also been expected to buy my own newspapers, including the one for which I'd worked for more than half a century, though some might have supposed them essential tools of the trade. Nineteenth century coal miners were expected to take their pick, of course, but those were the bad old days.

Probably it didn't help that I'd always been allowed to claim a few bob for buying beer for those on the journalistic round, without the need for receipts – an old school exemption approved in writing by the regional managing director – though it should be confessed that the claims were rarely genuine. They almost always understated the expenditure.

Since it would have been difficult for me to find the motivation, the heart and – most of all – the stomach to continue self-starting through a three-month notice period, the company agreed to waive both that and the formal, formulaic, consultation. A week later my final column appeared, abruptly ending almost 55 years as an inky tradesman and service for more than a third of its existence to the *Echo*. In all that time I never once took foot off the pedal.

The columns had almost been collegiate, a journalistic comrades' club. Writing them became more difficult because the interaction with readers, in full surge 20 years earlier, had evaporated as the readers themselves had faded away. Sometimes it almost seemed like writing into a vacuum: my personal, football-related, blog attracted far more feedback from a vastly smaller number of readers. It didn't help that for years the paper seemed curiously and habitually reluctant to promote my stuff. Still those expansive columns had to be filled, though always I held to the belief that something would turn up. Whether that would have been Micawber or Messiah I never could decide.

The condemned man made two final written requests, the first seeking permission to use company photographs in the book – granted, and I'm very grateful – the second that I be allowed to retain remote access to the *Echo*'s electronic archive, where almost everything I'd written since 1988 was stored.

Partly it was for research purposes in writing the book, the source already having proved invaluable, but mainly because half a lifetime's memories were there enshrined, word for whimsical word. Access was made possible through an elderly, company-owned PC which we kept upstairs at home and which was used only for that purpose.

The second request was never answered, either verbally or in writing. On the second morning of the rest of my life, however, one of the technical guys emailed to say he'd been instructed to come and take away the computer. It prompted an immediate check upstairs: the remote access plug had already been pulled.

Kind folk suppose me a wordsmith, but there were no words to illustrate my contempt for the people – no doubt many a mile from Darlington – who made that decision, and for the way it was transmitted. The industry had inevitably diminished, but that seemed small indeed – miserable and mean-spirited, a valedictory V-sign which spoke louder, much louder, than words.

Upon sudden departure there was no company presentation and – save for the statutory minimum redundancy money – no handshake, golden or blood red, physical or financial. That lunchtime telephone call was the last time I ever spoke to anyone in a senior position on the paper or with the company. The last day came and went without even a bit of string in the cabbage.

There were no personal letters from management, no well done thou good and faithful servant, no pie, no pint, no offer of occasional freelance work, no nod or wink to a half-blind cuddy and no suggestion of how in the future the paper might bridge the ever-growing chasm between the average age and interests of its journalists and those of its remaining readers.

Where else might they keep abreast of the Demon Donkey Dropper of Eryholme, Bulldog Billy Teesdale, the One Armed Bandit or the Queen of Green?

There was no explanation, honest or otherwise, for what was happening. After more than half a century, I just dropped through time's trap-door – and even that was remotely accessed. The grave is doubtless unmarked.

There was, however, another standard letter stating that if provisionally successful in gaining another job with the company – there was a vacancy in Alloa, after all – I'd need to complete a four-week trial. After serving sentences for 55 years, another trial seemed a bit recidivistic.

Another standard letter sought the return of the swipe pass for the office, presumably lest I half-inch a couple of pencils from the stationery cupboard – or, more heinous yet, seek in-house to access the archive.

Worst of all, my final column – December 7 2019 – was amended for probably the first time in 30 years. They removed the phrase "I am redundant", fostering the mistaken – some might say mendacious – belief that I'd simply and suddenly retired. Two others, including the sports editor, were made redundant at the same time one said to be happy to go and the other later given a different post.

The 150th anniversary supplement acknowledged my service in a kind enough paragraph, but again without any explanation for the columns' sudden disappearance. After all those years, they had neither the honesty nor the respect for readers properly to explain my demise.

A few days before that lunchtime phone call, however, five paragraphs on page two had announced yet another cover price rise. They appeared beneath the headline 'Supporting investment in quality journalism.' What was that about irony?

PETE Barron, as kind and supportive in his own new life as he'd been as editor, wrote in his freelance *Echo* column in December 2019 precisely what he'd said in October 2011 on my retirement from full-time journalism – that in his view I'd had more impact and influence on the *Echo* than any of its great editors, including Sir Harold Evans. It was a huge compliment; clearly not everyone agreed.

It had been a marvellous run and I'm truly grateful to the company for making so rich and rewarding a working life possible. They had been golden years. Hundreds of messages from readers were overwhelming and comforting. Several emails began "They must be mad", others simply said that their subscription, on-line or through the letter box, would be cancelled. One town mayor not only cancelled his paper but told the company in terms neither civic nor civil where they might relocate it.

Circumstances notwithstanding, I urged them all to reconsider. We, at least, still buy the *Echo* daily.

The employment rope had for many years been very loosely and liberally held; that in time it became an ever-tightening noose was simply a reflection of straitened circumstances in the newspaper industry. Already there's a lengthy casualty list – it's impossible to suppose that many more provincial titles, and some of the nationals, won't soon be added to it.

These days most provincial newspapers don't even publish circulation figures for the paper itself, just 'readership' stats which include on-line visits and goodness knows what else. A few weeks before I left, however, a note from the editor announced that hard copy sales had fallen by a "slightly disappointing" 12 per cent year-on-year but that we'd also overtaken the *Yorkshire Post* and the *Chronicle* in Newcastle again to become the region's best-selling daily paper.

To have made that claim fifty years earlier, it would have been necessary to have sold more than 120,000 copies each morning to outstrip the *YP* and substantially more to do better than what was then the *Evening Chronicle*. I believe the *Echo*'s circulation at its anniversary to be considerably under 20,000, without sign or hope of revival and clearly not helped by the subsequent coronavirus crisis. It's very sad.

Remember the stats when I became news editor in 1978? Sixteen offices, 35 reporters, 11 photographers and a sizeable army of freelance correspondents contributing to six distinct editions embracing the North-East and North Yorkshire? By 2020 there were three offices – Darlington, Durham, Bishop Auckland – with one staff photographer, one edition and a greatly reduced reporting team, some part-funded by external agencies like Facebook. To some surprise, the *Echo* launched a new Teesside edition early in the new year.

Probably I hadn't myself realised the speed of the industry's decline until 1996 when my elder son so badly injured his shoulder playing rugby that, allegedly, he was unable to carry a newspaper bag. For a few days I took over his round, genuinely astonished that in our middle class village not ten miles from Darlington only about a quarter of homes took any paper at all – and not many of those the *Echo*. The decline accelerated thereafter.

These days those multi-tasking reporters who remain must not just fill the paper but supply a rolling news service to the website and other outlets. No wonder that many young journalists have little time to leave the office or to develop what the trade calls contacts. Little wonder that so much of the paper – all provincial papers – is filled by a monstrous regiment of public relations people, corporate and institutional, not so much pushing at an open door as driving a coach and eight unchecked through the portals.

It's hard also not to wonder how much lower yet the sale might be but for the classified deaths column to which so many first turn – and with the usual joke about making sure they're not in it.

The *Northern Echo* is now contract printed elsewhere, the four-storey building which once throbbed and hummed – sometimes almost shook – for 18 hours a day now empty and silent by 7pm. Sister weekly papers like the *Darlington & Stockton Times*, once with their own substantial editorial staff, now also fall to the lot of the core team producing the *Echo*. It seems to me a very melancholy place, attempts at selling that great mausoleum so far unsuccessful. Debenham's were said once to be interested but felt icy blasts of their own. Conversion into apartments has been mooted but seems to have stalled; as coronavirus peaked it was temporarily abandoned.

It's not a blame game. Save for the dismal manner of my departure I don't want to bite the hand which so agreeably fed me for so long. Almost everyone's in that same leaking vessel and with no sign of a journalistic lifeboat bobbing over the horizon. Economies accrue; I have no resentment and no regrets, save that they might have been a bit more honest at the end.

In semi-retirement I was crafting two multi-faceted and

fairly idiosyncratic columns each week, both of them about people and events, not opinions. In total they were around 3,200 self-originated words, not a syllable influenced by the public relations industry and nothing whatever that might be supposed other journalists' cast-offs.

It's not the journalists' fault, least of all the countless youngsters with meretricious media degrees queuing to get a start in newspapers, that they may never know the joy, the challenge, the fun, the camaraderie and even the lunchtime pint that their predecessors shared for all those years. Now those who remain seem mostly to shovel stuff onto an inexorable and a ceaseless conveyor belt – a journalistic mail order warehouse – before themselves leaving to add to the ranks of the public relations people. Though the old guard grieves, there seems little alternative.

These days hardly a soul under 50 buys a hard copy newspaper, happy to rely on instant information from hand-held\ sources. Attempts to diversify into websites and other electronic media have often been less successful than hoped, particularly in attracting advertising. For decades I'd tell any who'd listen that the cost of the *Northern Echo* for a week was still not much more than the price of a pint, considerably less than 20 fags, and that the *Echo* wasn't likely to give them cancer.

For those final eight years I'd worked from home, an agreement probably beneficial to both sides, only surfacing to puff to the top floor of head office to ferret yellowed information from the cuttings library, abandoned and unloved.

It meant that young journalists, mostly graduates, came and went without my ever having met them. What did they make of the grey-haired grammar school boy occasionally haunting the building like the Ghost of Christmas Past? Did they, like youngsters in general, find it hard to make a connection with that old school? Was I seen as an anachronism? Was the paper itself thought anachronistic, a temporal means to a more ethereal end?

Most of them are no doubt able; every one of them is to be wished great good fortune. All that disappoints me, save for the absence of checking – whatever happened to proof readers, or for that matter sub-editors? – is the apparent ignorance of basic English language and grammar, even the ability to match a singular verb to a singular noun. It seemed timely that, on the day of my "risk of redundancy" notice, the 96-year-old who for 17 years had run the Apostrophe Protection Society should announce that he was giving up the struggle.

There are journalists, some in high places, who don't know the difference between 'principal' and 'principle', who (all the time) have folk sat awkwardly when they should be sitting comfortably, who genuinely believe that 'infamous' is a synonym for 'famous' and who commit myriad other treasons against the Queen's English, who can't spell for toffee and who probably believe a subjunctive to be a member of the peasant class in one of those former Yugoslavian states which now issues postage stamps of their own.

There've even been reporters who appeared not to know the difference between 'formally' and 'formerly' and who've written 'would of' when, presumably, they meant 'would have'. Ah me, Geoff Hill would soon have sorted them out.

STILL the most egregious examples, particularly the first of the dozen which follow, reduce me to propelling the paper across the sitting room, sometimes displacing a full coffee cup – an intemperance to which the carpet bears witness. Here's an old hack's blacklist:

✗ *Pre-planned:* You cannot plan retrospectively, any more than you can plan ahead. You plan or you don't. Nor can you pre-book and you sure as apples can't pre-record.

✗ *Exclusive:* probably the most misused term in provincial journalism. Usually means "It was our turn on the PR department's rota for a stereotyped interview with a stereotypical sportsman."

✗ *Nestled:* Housing estates, factories and the like do not nestle anywhere, especially within 50 yards of the A19, not unless they're made of milk chocolate.

✗ *Are celebrating:* overused in many a first paragraph, meaning "have had some mildly good news, quite often a not-quite-as-bad-as-was-feared Ofsted report".

✗ *So-and-so might have....but:* usually the intro in sports reports. Clapped out and cliched.

✗ *Descend upon:* also greatly familiar in opening paragraphs: possibly means "visit". If it's the constabulary doing the descending, it's probably because "mystery surrounds" the occasion.

✗ *Set to:* as in "Thousands are set to descend upon a car boot sale". Probably means "could". In Scotland, a set-to is a stooshie.

✗ *Told the Northern Echo (or whoever):* probably means "We actually spoke to someone instead of just putting a new intro on top of the press release."

✗ *Glittering:* any occasion at which prestigious awards are presented. "Prestigious" means "comes with a certificate." A glittering occasion should not be confused with a gala dinner, however. A gala dinner is a prestigious occasion with balloons.

✗ *Revealed* – worse, *sensationally revealed*: usually on the sports pages, means that the manager's pre-match press conference was even more stultifying than usual, but there were still 25 column inches to fill.

✗ *Little did he know when...* Something has happened that nobody could possibly foretell, but the reporter can't think of a better intro. As in "Little did Fred Arkwright know when he left home yesterday morning that he would end up dead in a corporation cess pit".

✗ *Refuted:* Mis-used to mean denied or rejected allegations of something. It doesn't. It means proved beyond all reasonable doubt and the speaker has undeniable evidence that will stand up in court if he and/or the paper (more likely) is sued for saying someone else is telling porkies.

ON a bright and blustery May day in 2019, Sharon and I hoofed up an old drove road to the top of Harkerside Fell in Swaledale, North Yorkshire, about 2,000ft above the sea. I was 72, she 70, and it was great to be alive and fairly effortlessly to be capable of such exertions. A few weeks later I couldn't walk more than a couple of hundred yards without, breathless, having to pull up.

The GP sent me immediately to A&E, the hospital finally diagnosed stable angina and after an angiogram – referred to earlier – those coronary stents were inserted on November 4: no anaesthetic, a very nice bowl of sticky toffee pudding and custard thereafter (just the stuff to aerate the arteries) and home the same night but a bit too late for the dominoes. It appears to have been the proverbial magic bullet, leaps and bounds again.

Medically and empathically it seemed to me that the NHS was first rate. Administratively and in the way they communicated, I was much less impressed. Three weeks later the company rang to say that, journalistically at any rate, I'd had it. I live, but no longer to tell the tale.

Save for that self-inflicted business with the lawn mower, that and the pesky pulmonary embolism, I'd almost always enjoyed – that's the word – good health. Both professionally and physically, however, I'd never been great with heights, able to get by but better with feet firmly on the ground. Twenty-odd years ago, on the bridge over the Tyne between Prudhoe and Ovingham in Northumberland, everything changed for the worse.

After a couple of pints in Ovingham, the need was to get back across to Prudhoe railway station. The bridge was quite high, the torrential river both visible and audible below. Panicked, utterly unable to proceed, I'd hazardously to flag down a car in order to catch the train. The car driver may with justification have thought he'd picked up an escaped madman.

The subsequent fear of bridges, formally gephyrophobia, became a fear of all heights. All but the lowest and most familiar bridges were out of bounds, escalators escalated, ships' rails were suddenly a suicide risk, the upper tiers of theatres and sports grounds impossible, anything above first floor level towered titanically. It became a constant and a confounded nuisance.

Flying, oddly, had never been a worry – save for the gangway to the plane – but was in any case ruled out after the DVT and PE (as we victims call it) of May 2000.

These days it's a little bit better. Sharon, as always, has worked wonders in trying to help. It was the company for which I'd faithfully grafted for more than half a century which permanently brought me down to earth. What's to be kept in the back trouser pocket now that – downward spiral – there's no need for a notebook?

The strangest thing is no longer having constantly to be on the prowl for column material, mentally sifting every encounter for the possibility of a paragraph, expectantly scanning emails, mordantly reading the deaths and all manner of other publications, picking up leaflets, peering at village noticeboards – still, after all those years – in search of the improbable, the inconsequential with consequences.

Like a dog at a lamp post, a walk through any town or village would constantly be interrupted by the need to stop at the notice board, in search of pearls, however small, amid the parochial oyster. That all changed. They quickened my pace but killed my curiosity.

I'd also become an assiduous, possibly obsessive, observer of personalised vehicle registration plates. The most memorable may have been 32 CUP, cherished for more than 60 years by Dorothy Morton, who lived near Bishop Auckland. "I get honked at everywhere I go, especially by lorry drivers on motorways," she said.

The parping, Dorothy added, became rather less stentorian when they overtook and realised that the driver in the slow lane was 90. The registration plate, she added, was worth a lot more than the car was. None of it resolved the ambiguity of The Little Bra Shop, formerly in Yarm on Teesside. Perhaps that was 32 CUP, too.

There's precious little hope of further paid employment, even occasional work, and still less chance of being offered something I'd ever want to do. Other columnists, usually freelance and on the *Echo* as elsewhere, have been finished but told that they can continue if prepared to do it for nothing.

Though continuing after 65 was never principally about the money – it was about the daft joy of writing, of working with words, of bi-weekly pressing "send" – it was perhaps fortunate that that option was never put to me. The answer might not have befitted someone who'd spent so long campaigning against offensive language.

So finally I may have to become the retiring type, which by way of last word explains why the title of the book was changed from *Is There Much More of This?* to *Unconsidered Trifles*.

Had it remained the former, the sad but thankful answer would have been "No, I'm afraid there's not."

INDEX LINK

A T LEAST two people in *Unconsidered Trifles*, Peter Freitag and the late Harry Whitton, are gently teased for being incorrigible name droppers. As my old mum would have said – and she had some memorable phrases – it's like kettle calling the pan grimy arse.

She was also much given to the observation that folk talked like a ha'penny book, though these days even ha'penny books cost about ten quid.

It was hypocritical, at any rate, because if you don't have to be a peer, a bishop or at the very least a knight of the realm to make it into this index, it certainly helps. Mad Frankie Fraser's inclusion is perhaps a bit more surprising: those who habitually read the index first will just have to look up the appropriate pages.

The Royal Family, indeed, has a place of honour right at the start. The inclusion of Princess Michael of Kent was the subject of much debate between me and the indexer-in-chief; by that token, the omission of Mary Queen of Scots seems unfair.

When last counted – by someone who four times failed O-level maths – the index embraced eight lords (one of whom was also a field marshal), two baronesses, a dame, a countess, a Lady, 17 knights, Pope John Paul II, two archbishops, eight bishops, sundry mother senior churchmen, two presidents – of America and Malaysia – two judges and plain Mr Tony Blair, who seems adroitly to be avoiding the honours committee. There's even a saint in there and he, it's said, the patron of lost causes.

If not random, the index is undoubtedly idiosyncratic. Why else would it include Sisyphus and Sooty in close proximity? Why else list Orville the Duck, Meatloaf and Willie Worktop? One of those, apparently, is real.

Lest the index prove longer than the book itself, many who are mentioned in passing have invidiously failed to make the cut. One or two have simply been mislaid: I could have sworn Lord Kinnock was in there somewhere. Him, come to think, and Karl Marx.

In the interests of gender equality, I've also excluded both Miss Whiplash and Mr Whippy, though both get a mention.

My parents, bless them, are also not included – for the simple reason that they're never mentioned by name – and neither am I. There are other Amoses, however, ranging from a cat to an ostrich and from a rusting tug on the Tees to a ventriloquist's blackbird, banned for life from Southport Floral Hall amid simultaneous claims of racism, sexism, anti-Semitism and probably one or two other things, as well.

There's also another Michael Amos – one of the better stories for which those who begin at the end must backtrack to page 360.

It's also for reasons best described as voluminous that there's no index of places, not even Shildon, but chiefly for fear of forgetfulness that suffixes like MBE are omitted.

That's enough, anyway. Apologies to all those who first peruse the index to see if they're in it and who discover that they're not – and to everyone else, thanks a million.

INDEX

NUMBERS underlined indicate a photograph, though usually there's further reference on that page.

387